RIVER BOATS OF AMERICA

RIVER BOATS

FRANK DONOVAN

OF AMERICA

THOMAS Y. CROWELL COMPANY

NEW YORK   ESTABLISHED 1834

For Kathy, Chris, and Suzy

Other Books by Frank Donovan

THE MEDAL: THE STORY OF THE MEDAL OF HONOR
THE EARLY EAGLES
WHEELS FOR A NATION

Contents

The Running Roads

The smell of cordite pervaded Battery Park on Wednesday as the weapons of a French fleet banged in New York City's upper bay. Thursday morning eighty-four guns on four German warships slammed, and in the afternoon as many British vessels repeated the salute. Smaller contingents of warships had already arrived from Italy, Mexico, Holland, and Argentina and all were greeted by nineteen American dreadnaughts anchored in the Hudson River, plus cruisers, torpedo boats, submarines, tenders, and cutters without number. It was rather quiet on Friday, but on Saturday, September 25, 1909, bedlam reigned in New York waters as bands played in several tongues, guns boomed, whistles tooted, bells rang, and crowds cheered. It was the start of the most dramatic and memorable pageant that New York and the Hudson Valley have ever witnessed.

The occasion was the opening of the Hudson-Fulton Celebration. Henry Hudson had sailed up the majestic river that bears his name three centuries before. Robert Fulton had followed him 198 years later. So far as the latter was concerned it was not exactly a centennial, but it was near enough, and the two events were combined in a fortnight of parades, pageants, banquets, art exhibits, aquatic sports, and fireworks that left the citizens of the valley from Albany to New York limp with fatigue and excitement.

The *pièces de résistance* of the affair were replicas of the *Half Moon* and the *Clermont*. Henry Hudson, with what was described as the "largest display of unharvested whiskers recently seen in these parts," trod the quarterdeck of the former. A top-hatted Robert Fulton stood majestically on the stern of the latter, accompanied by his costumed fiancée, Harriet Livingston, and his partner, Robert Livingston.

The first act of the celebration was a marine parade of the ancient ships, with 500 escort vessels, from the bay past the warships anchored in the river. The parade was somewhat confused at the start because the eighteen sailors from the Dutch navy who manned the *Half Moon* took their roles too seriously. The square-rigged replica of the Dutch vessel

[1]

was supposed to be towed. The *Clermont*, which the *Half Moon* was to follow, had a functioning reproduction of her original engine and moved under her own power. As the festivities were about to begin, the *Half Moon*'s crew decided that they would not be hauled ignominiously behind a cutter. They cast off the towline, clumsily set canvas, and started to sail gaily up the river. It would have been a fine sight except that the young argonauts from the Netherlands had no idea how to handle a square-rigger in the brisk breeze that was blowing. The *Clermont*'s wheezy engine moved her at only four miles an hour—not fast enough to get out of the way of the onrushing *Half Moon*. The Dutch ship, perhaps jealous of sharing the honors of the day with a vessel that she considered an interloper, crashed into the little steamship and tore away twenty feet of rail abaft the starboard paddle wheel. The international fleet and the New York crowd waited while landlubber carpenters repaired the damage.

But the sight was worth waiting for. A reporter of the day described it by writing, "Motionless lay the fleet—as motionless as the *Half Moon* at anchor three hundred years ago. Then suddenly, at the discharge of a gun signal, it thrilled with life. Like a Titanic sea serpent, clad in scales of steel, belching smoke and hissing steam, it unwound its folds of half a thousand ships, headed for the Hudson, and proceeded up the river, until abreast of the chain of warships, effulgent with armor, bristling with guns. . . . As the reproductions passed in review, battleship after battleship, cruiser after cruiser, gunboat after gunboat, thundered out its tribute to these symbols of peaceful conquest."

Two days later the *Half Moon* again threw the celebration into confusion. This was another *Half Moon*, mounted on a float for a parade down Fifth Avenue. At the start she crashed into a lamp post, which tore away a section of her canvas ocean. This casualty disrupted the order of the floats and escorting organizations in the parade. Thus the St. Nicholas float was accompanied by members of a Syrian organization in red fezzes, and the escort of the old Dutchmen playing the first game of bowls on Bowling Green was a French Society enthusiastically shouting the "Marseillaise." The procession was supposed to depict the history of the United States in chronological sequence, but in the resulting confusion Washington was taking the oath of office as the first

Full-scale replicas of the Clermont *and the* Half Moon *seem dwarfed by the ships from Europe and Latin America that gathered in New York Harbor for the Hudson-Fulton celebration in 1909. The occasion had a two-fold purpose, to mark the tercentenary of Henry Hudson's discovery of the Hudson River and the 98th year since the launching of Robert Fulton's* Clermont.

President seven blocks ahead of Henry Hudson discovering the Hudson River. But it was all taken in good part by the public, if not by the parade committee.

During the ensuing two weeks the pageant, spearheaded by the re-created vessels, moved up the Hudson to set off festivities in riverside cities and towns. Yonkers, Kingston, Newburgh, Hudson, Pough-keepsie, Catskill, Albany, and Troy all had their days of parading school children and speech-making politicians. On the face of it they were honoring an English explorer and an American inventor, but the real hero of the celebration was neither of these. It was the lordly, the majestic, the beautiful Hudson River—the Rhine of the New World and the gateway to the West.

It was appropriate that the Hudson was acclaimed as a symbol of the watercourses along which America unfolded and by which its commerce and culture grew. The rivers were the trails of most of the early explorers. They were the roads on which the first colonists moved inland. They were the routes along which the settlers migrated to the great midwestern valley. They determined the location of cities and connected communities with each other and with the hinterlands. White men have been on the North American continent for some four and a half centuries. For more than three and a half of these centuries rivers were their principal means of getting from place to place, finding new land, marketing their produce, and meeting their fellow man.

Before the white man came, the running roads had been the migratory routes of the Indians. Long centuries ago the red man realized that it was far easier to float than to walk. He knew the principle of the wheel, but he did not bother to use it. This would have involved building roads, an obvious waste of time when nature's watery ways went every place he wanted to go. Most of the red man's overland trails, which the early white man's roads followed, led from the headwaters of one water-course to the upper reaches of another. The forebears of Lo, who sold Manhattan Island to the Dutch, may have reached that valuable piece of real estate by floating down the western tributaries of the Missouri, from somewhere in Wyoming, to the Mississippi; paddling up the Ohio to the Allegheny; up that stream and French Creek to Lake Ontario; along the lake shore to the Niagara; up the Niagara to Lake Erie (after walking around Niagara Falls); along Lake Erie to the mouth of the Oswego; up the Oswego to Lake Oneida; across that lake to the Mohawk; down the Mohawk to the Hudson; and down the Hudson to the Atlantic coast.

The earliest conflict between the white man and the red was not over acreage *per se*. There was plenty of land, but the Indians, good economic strategists, occupied the best real estate on the Delaware, Chesapeake, and Massachusetts bays and on the Connecticut, Hudson, Delaware, Potomac, James, and other eastern rivers. The white man bought some of these choice locations—those of New York City, Philadelphia, and Providence, for instance—and pre-empted others. Later he would cheat or fight his predecessors for the best sites on the western rivers and the Great Lakes; Chicago was named for the Indians who founded the midwestern metropolis long before the white man came.

The original white colonists established almost all their settlements at the mouths of rivers and expanded upstream or moved from river to river. An exception were the Pilgrims, who were too impatient to get off the crowded and smelly *Mayflower* to wait to find a good location for their settlement. But Boston, at the mouth of the Charles River, soon became the most important city in the New World. The sons of the original settlers, and newcomers, spread up the Merrimack and Kennebec to establish settlements that would become the cities of New Hampshire and Maine, and up and down the Connecticut to settle the communities of that colony, while Roger Williams moved from the Bay Colony to the mouth of the Providence River to found Rhode Island.

By the time the colonists were ready to consider independence, representatives came to the first Continental Congress from Concord on the Merrimack; Boston on the Charles; Providence on the Providence; Hartford on the Connecticut; New Haven on the Housatonic; New York and Albany on the Hudson; Newark on the Passaic; Trenton, Philadelphia and Wilmington, Delaware, on the Delaware; Baltimore on the Patapsco; Williamsburg on the James; Wilmington, North Carolina, on the Cape Fear; Charleston on the Ashley; and Savannah on the river of the same name.

The growth of the coastal cities was largely controlled by their river traffic. At the dawn of the eighteenth century, Boston was in first place with 7,000 inhabitants, Philadelphia second with 4,000, and New York third with 3,900. But, though Harvard men may demur, Boston's Charles River is an insignificant waterway compared to the Delaware and the Hudson. By the eve of the Revolution, Philadelphia had forged to first place with 40,000 people, New York was second with between 25,000 and 30,000, and Boston had but 20,000. When the Erie Canal opened in 1826 and made New York the water gateway to the Great Lakes and the Northwest, that city became and remained the principal metropolis of the New World. Two years after the canal opened, the receipts of the New York City Custom House were sufficient to pay the entire cost of the Federal Government, except for the interest on the national debt.

Meanwhile, as the eastern river-bank cities were growing, traders from the coastal plains probed inland to set up posts on western streams. In 1753, more than twenty years before the initial Continental Congress, youthful George Washington located the site for the first major city beyond the mountains while carrying a message to the French on the Ohio. After floating down the Monongahela in an Indian canoe, he wrote, "As I got down before [from] the canoe I spent some time in viewing the rivers, and the land in the fork; which I think extremely well situated for a fort, as it has the absolute command of both rivers." The land that he described, at the junction of the Monongahela and the Allegheny, is now the Golden Triangle of downtown Pittsburgh.

The French had already come down the streams from the Great Lakes area and up the Ohio to establish military and trading posts. After the French lost their grip on the Northwest in 1763, at the end of the French and Indian War, British colonists started to trickle across the mountains. Leading the parade was Daniel Boone, who pioneered the overland Wilderness Trail through the Cumberland Gap. But most of those who followed spread their settlements on the river banks. Many of the northern emigrants reached Pittsburgh, the principal take-off point, by backtracking on the water trails of Lo's ancestors. From there they floated down the Ohio to establish Cincinnati, Louisville, Evansville, and points west. They expanded the French river settlement of St. Louis and were ready to fight the Spanish for the river-mouth port of New Orleans.

The trickle of westward emigration swelled to a stream after the Northwest Ordinance was passed in 1792. Within five years a virtual parade of boats were floating noisily down the Ohio carrying neighing horses, grunting pigs, lowing cattle, bleating sheep, clucking chickens, and 20,000 people. The movement was again accelerated in 1803, when the purchase of the Louisiana Territory gave western settlers undisputed access to the markets of the world through New Orleans. By 1810 there were a million settlers along the rivers, whose livelihood depended on the streams that bore their produce to the coast. A contemporary writer described this scene at the way stop of New Madrid, Missouri, with its teeming transient population:

One hundred boats have landed here in a day . . . . In one place there are boats loaded with pine plank, from the pine forests of the southwest of New York. In another quarter there are numerous boats with the "Yankee notions" of Ohio. In another quarter are landed together the boats of "old Kentucky", with their whiskey, hemp, tobacco, bagging and bale rope; with all the articles of the produce of their soil. From Tennessee there are the same articles, together with boats loaded with bales of cotton from Illinois and Missouri, cattle, horses, and the general produce of the western country, together with peltry and lead from Missouri. Some boats are loaded with corn in bulk and in the ear. Others with barrels of apples and potatoes, and great quantities of dried apples and peaches. Others have loads of cider, that has been strengthened by boiling, or freezing. Other boats are loaded with furniture, tools, domestic and agricultural implements; in short the numerous products of the ingenuity, speculation, manufacture and agriculture of the whole upper country of the West . . . . The surface of the boats cover some acres . . . . The boatmen travel about from boat to boat, make inquiries and acquaintances, agree to 'lash boats', as it is called, and form alliances to yield mutual assistance to each other on the way to New Orleans. . . . With the first dawn all is bustle and motion; and amidst shouts, and trampling of cattle, and barking of dogs, and crowing of the dunghill fowls, the fleet is in a half hour all under way; and when the sun rises, nothing is seen, but the broad stream rolling on as before . . . . Although they live on the same river, it is improbable that they will ever meet again on the earth.

The watercraft that carried this produce were as heterogeneous as their cargo. Rafts, canoes, pirogues, arks, barges, batteaux, skiffs, broadhorns, flatboats, and keelboats floated down the watery roads and were laboriously pulled, pushed, poled, rowed, and sailed upstream. One observer commented that "you can scarcely imagine an abstract form in which a boat can be built that in some part of the Ohio or Mississippi you will not actually see in motion." Senator Benton of Missouri once figured that there were 50,000 miles of water in the Mississippi system that were navigable by some kind of boat. His estimate may have been high, but in later days there were 16,000 miles of steamboat routes.

Not content with the running roads as nature had made them, the American colonists sought to improve or connect them. Projects for canals to circumvent falls and rapids, to lead from mines, mills, and factories to river banks, and to unite the headwaters of streams started in the mid-eighteenth century. When the colonies became a nation, canal fever became acute. At the Constitutional Convention Benjamin Franklin proposed to include a specific provision in the U.S. Constitution that the Federal Government be empowered to build canals. It was defeated on the grounds that this might be a precedent for the government to engage in commercial enterprises—the framers of the Constitution had a much different concept of the government they created than the political economists of the twentieth century.

The most prominent of the early canal builders was George Washington, who, when he was not fathering his country, was a very shrewd real-estate operator. After the French and Indian War, Washington pressured Virginia's royal governor to make good on a promise of bonuses of western lands for veterans. His own share, plus claims that he bought from less far-sighted colleagues, totaled 20,174 acres beyond the mountains. After the deeds were in order he set out for the Ohio to, as he told his diary, "obtain information of the nearest and best communication between eastern and western waters and to facilitate, as much as in me lay, the inland navigation of the Potomac." Upon his return he became the principal organizer of the Potomac Canal Company for a project to connect that stream with the Ohio River. He planned an all-water route from his eastern to his western domains along which the commerce of the to-be-settled Northwest would flow past Mount Vernon.

The proposed Potomac Canal was a factor in the location of the nation's capital and in the first political "deal" in United States history. The powerful Virginians in Congress wanted the capital located on the bank of their stream, which, they planned, would become the water route to the West. Standing in the street in front of the executive mansion on New York's Broadway, Secretary of State Thomas Jefferson promised Secretary of the Treasury Alexander Hamilton that the Virginians would back his refunding scheme if Hamilton would swing the vote of New York's congressmen to the Potomac River site for the capital.

The Potomac Canal, as planned, was never finished because a group of enterprising New Yorkers moved faster than the Virginians to provide an all-water route to the West by utilizing long stretches of the Mohawk River to connect the Hudson with the Great Lakes by the Erie Canal and to provide a route from New York City to Canada via a cutoff that connected Lake Champlain with the Hudson.

The Erie was the most significant but by no means the only important canal of the early nineteenth century. The frustrated Virginians turned from the Potomac Canal to join Chesapeake Bay and its many rivers with Delaware Bay and its rivers by cutting a canal across the narrow neck of the peninsula that forms Maryland's eastern shore. The Middlesex Canal connected the Merrimack and Charles rivers in New Hampshire and Massachusetts. The Delaware and Raritan Canal crossed New Jersey to connect those two rivers and provide an all-water route between New York and Philadelphia. In the west the Illinois and Michigan Canal connected Chicago to the Mississippi River system at La Salle, Illinois. Two canals in Ohio connected Portsmouth and Cincinnati on the Ohio and Cleveland and Toledo on Lake Erie. These, in conjunction with the Erie Canal, completed an all-water route—albeit a round-about one—from New Orleans to New York.

Like New York and Virginia, Pennsylvania sought to make its principal city, Philadelphia, the gateway to the West with a canal that would connect the state's western and eastern rivers, but the Allegheny Mountains were in the way. This obstacle was overcome with an ingenious series of inclined planes on which canal boats were lifted over the mountains. A traveler left Philadelphia on a horse-drawn railroad that took him to the bank of the Susquehanna River. Here he transferred to a packet to cross most of the state by river and the Pennsylvania Canal. At the little town of Hollidaysburg the canal boats were taken apart in sections and, still carrying their passengers, lifted 1,400 feet along inclined planes by hawsers powered by stationary engines. After sliding down the other side of the mountain to Johnstown the boats were reassembled and floated down the canal to the Ohio at Pittsburgh. In his *American Notes* Charles Dickens described this by writing, "Occasionally the rails are laid upon the extreme verge of a giddy precipice; and looking from the carriage window the traveler gazed sheer down without a stone or scrap of fence between, into the mountain depths below."

With the dawn of the nineteenth century, steam replaced brawn and breeze to rapidly accelerate the growth of inland America. Upriver trips that had taken four months were made in four weeks, later in four days. When steam power, rated in hundreds of horses, replaced the muscles of straining men, produce by the millions of tons and people

Settlers migrated down the rivers on anything that would float. Typical of these early river boats were rafts made of logs from trees that grew along the bank. Further downstream, the rafts were dismantled and the logs used for building houses.

Before Pittsburgh was founded at the junction of the Allegheny and Monongahela, George Washington had described its site as "extremely well situated for a fort, as it has the absolute command of both rivers."

A strategic departure point for travelers to the West, Pittsburgh became the first major city beyond the mountains.

by the hundreds of thousands created a virtual traffic jam on every navigable stream. The paddle wheels of the noisy, vibrating, smoke-belching steamboats churned America out of a more leisurely way of life as the blunt noses of the river craft spread the industrial revolution across the land.

The river steamboat is now regarded nostalgically as a thing of glamour and romance, excitement and drama. Such titillating aspects were part of the steamboat era, perhaps the most interesting part—but not the important part. The steamboat was the first American invention of world significance. It was the first scientific accomplish-

PENNSYLVANIA HISTORICAL AND MUSEUM COMMISSION

Wanting to make Philadelphia a gateway to the West, Pennsylvanians supplemented their natural waterways with a canal, but they still had to find a way to get travelers and their boats over the Allegheny Mountains. To do this they constructed a series of inclined planes powered by stationary engines. Boats were taken apart in sections, lifted—with passengers still aboard—over the mountains, and reassembled on the other side.

ment that gave man motion beyond the scope of the beast of burden or willful winds. In half a century it moved the boundary of American commerce westward some 2,000 miles, from the Appalachians to the Rockies.

It might be said that the steamboat age lasted a century—fifty years on the way up and a like period on the way down. Paradoxically, the most glamorous and dramatic part of the era were the years of its decline. These were the days of the floating palaces with their gourmet menus and paintings and mirrors hung above acres of specially woven Brussels carpet in luxurious main cabins. This was the period of the most spectacular disasters and the most exciting races, the era immortalized in Edna Ferber's *Show Boat* and countless other almost legendary tales of the river boats.

The nemesis of the steamboat was hatched at about the same time as the craft that it would later, in large part, make obsolete. Seven years after Robert Fulton built the first practical steamboat, an Englishman, George Stephenson, built the first practical locomotive. The next year John Stevens, a brother-in-law of Fulton's partner Robert Livingston, secured the first railroad charter in America. But if the original railroad entrepreneurs envisioned that their iron horses would quickly replace the steamboat as America's primary carrier, they were alone in their dreams.

The principal purpose of the early railroads was usually to feed or connect steamboat lines. The two most important passenger routes in the country in the 1830s were New York to Boston and New York to Philadelphia. An all-water journey to the former involved going to sea to round Cape Cod, so the preferred route was by steamboat to Providence and stagecoach to Boston. To Philadelphia the route was by boat to New Brunswick on the Raritan, by stagecoach to the Delaware, and down that stream by boat. On the Boston route steamboat operators financed the railroad that replaced the stagecoach to feed their watercraft, and the operators of the Philadelphia boats were overjoyed when, in 1828, the Delaware and Hudson Canal Company started to lay track across New Jersey. Even after the railroads started to parallel the steamboat routes, the river men did not see the handwriting on the wall for several decades. Early railroads offered passengers none of the amenities of steamboat travel: no berths, no diners, and, particularly, no bars. The railroads' only point of superiority was speed until the locomotive caught up with and surpassed the steamboat in power to pull greater loads at lower cost.

Steamboat men should have formed a lobby to oppose the passage of the Land Grant Act by Congress in 1850, but they still saw no real threat from a mode of transportation that required a costly roadbed rather than a free river. The first grant of alternate six-square-mile sections of land along the right-of-way led to the construction of the Illinois Central and Mobile and Ohio railroads that connected the Great Lakes to the Gulf of Mexico from Chicago to Mobile. The Father of Waters was no longer the only road that led from the Mississippi Valley to the markets of the world.

Still, the river boats churned up and down nature's roads in greater magnificence, if lesser numbers, well into the twentieth century. Ironically, they had come full circle as a means of travel. They had accelerated the pace of life when they took over from their manually propelled or wind-driven predecessors. Now they became the leisurely, lazy way to travel. Unfortunately, there were not enough leisurely, lazy travelers in time-conscious America. In 1870 the race up the Mississippi between the *Robert E. Lee* and the *Natchez*—at 15 miles an hour—made international headlines. At the time nobody commented on the newspaper reporter who left the *Lee* at Memphis, walked to the railroad station, waited for the train, rode it to Cairo, and joined the throng on the waterfront that was waiting for the *Robert E. Lee*.

Today the river steamboat, with its distinctive whistle or silver-toned bells is an anachronism of a bygone virile and exciting century. A few—a very few—remain, used mostly for nostalgic excursions, as are the steam trains whose rails replaced the rivers as the principal trade routes. Ironically, the same villain who gave the *coup de grâce* to the steamboat also rendered the death blow to the steam locomotive—Rudolph Diesel. With the same type of assist from General Motors' Charles Franklin Kettering that the steam-engine pioneers received from James Watt, the German inventor developed the engine that bears his name as a better source of power for both the boats on the rivers and the trains on their banks.

On the face of it there is little glamour in the diesel tugs that now, like the keelboat men of yore, push and pull hundreds of millions of tons of freight up and down the rivers. Radar has replaced the colorful pilot, to whom the channel was a living antagonist. A fathometer finds the bottom more effectively, if less dramatically, than the leadsman on the guards with his chanting cry of "mark twain!" Low-grade fuel oil has superseded bright-burning pine or glowing anthracite, valve-twisting engineers have replaced sweat-glistened stokers, and electronic gadgets of great complexity function as the eyes and the brains of today's river pilot.

The rivers are still important roads for produce, if not for people, and they are making a comeback as playgrounds, if not as paths. While millions of travelers pass unseeing along their banks at a mad, mad pace on rails of steel and roads of concrete, and others fly far above the calm waterways viewing nought but sky, increasing numbers are returning to the more leisurely streams in a variety of personal pleasure craft. In fact, more boats are churning inland waters in the mid-twentieth century than traversed these placid roads in the mid-nineteenth.

Before the Fire Canoe

> Thus the Birch Canoe was builded
> In the valley, by the river,
> In the bosom of the forest; . . .
> And it floated on the river
> Like a yellow leaf in Autumn,
> Like a yellow water lily.

So Longfellow's *Hiawatha* described the American Indian's picturesque contribution to marine architecture, a type of watercraft still beloved, though seldom used, by Boy Scouts. But the birch canoe was not the first river boat. Trees grew beside rivers. Their trunks would float. The first red-skinned inland argonaut undoubtedly took to the water astride a tree trunk, but this was damp, uncomfortable, and impractical for transporting papooses and possessions. Some pragmatic savage, with fire and primitive tools, hollowed out a log canoe. Tree trunks were a lot bigger in the primeval forest than they are today, and log canoes might be four or five feet wide and forty or more feet long.

Log canoes were heavy craft that rode low in the water, took mighty muscles to paddle, and many men to portage. A more advanced redskin figured out how to build a frame of saplings and cover it with birch bark sewn with roots and calked with pitch. In those days birch trees, too, were bigger than the slim, graceful white saplings that today brighten New England's woods. In the West, where there were no birch trees, Indians stretched the hides of male buffalo over frames to make round bull boats—the same type of craft in which the legendary Irish monk St. Brendan is said to have come to the New World long before the Vikings.

Tree trunks lashed together in rafts formed the white man's first river boats. They transported families and their effects downstream, and they were valuable products in themselves. When the trees along the coast had been exhausted to build shelter, the river raft became the basis of a lumber industry that provided material to expand the early communities and became a principal export to wood-hungry England. Rafts of tall trees from northern forests floated to coastal sawmills on the currents of scores of rivers, or settlers built sawmills at the head of navigation and delivered rafts of the finished product. At sawmills above Albany in the early eighteenth century "whole neighborhoods assembled and made their joint stock into a large raft which was floated down the river with a man or two on it, who, with long poles, were always ready to steer it clear of those islands or shallows which might impede its course . . . . Sometimes one sees a whole family transported on this single conveyance; the mother calmly spinning, the children sporting about her, and the father fishing on one end."

One of the giants of colonial rafting days was Admiral Dan Skinner— "admiral" only of a fleet of log rafts. Skinner had been a sailor. He left the sea and trekked from Connecticut across New York to the headwaters of the Delaware. He realized that the tall pines on the foothills of the Catskill Mountains would make fine masts for the ships of the Royal Navy. The king's agents had never reached these remote

The earliest canoes were probably made from tree trunks hollowed out by means of fire and primitive chisels.

forests to put their broad arrow marks on mast trees, so Dan gathered a group of brawny men and started an industry.

Skinner pioneered in welfare benefits for employees. The members of his picked crews of adventurous roughnecks had to pay an initiation fee to secure their jobs—two large bottles of whiskey for an experienced steersman and one for a deck hand. But the fringe benefits soon returned their initial dues many times over. Dan's method of managing the hairpin turns in the upper river was to stop the rafts above the bend and get the men pleasantly potted on New England rum so that they happily took icy duckings while manhandling the craft around the turn. Below, they finished the rum to take the chill off. The difficult stretch of the Delaware ended at Easton. Here the rafts paused overnight while the crew had a thorough carouse for which Dan provided lodging, food, liquor, and women. Then the hung-over crews floated calmly down to the shipyards at Camden and Philadelphia. From here the men, pockets heavy with their pay, started their walk back to the headwaters of the river, dribbling their earnings at taverns on the way. Most arrived tired and broke—and ready for another voyage.

But rafts were not the answer to two-way river travel, and the square-rigged vessels in which the white men came from the Old World were ill suited to the narrow, often shallow rivers. The colonists

AMERICAN MUSEUM OF NATURAL HISTORY

In the West where there were no birch trees, Indians made "bull boats" by stretching the hides of male buffalo around sapling frames.

soon started to build specialized boats suitable for navigating bays, sounds, and the wider rivers. Some were fore-and-aft-rigged sailboats variously called pinks, sloops, ketches, schooners, lighters, pinnaces, shallops, and pirogues, the difference depending on rigging, hull shape, or local nomenclature.

For narrow or shallow rivers where sails were of little use, they developed the pole boat. The most famous of these were Durham boats, designed in about 1750 by a man named Durham for use on the Delaware. These, the principal type of craft used by Washington to cross that stream, were described as being "60 feet long, 8 feet wide, and 2 feet deep, and when laden with 15 tons drew 20 inches of water. The stern and bow were sharp, on which were erected small decks, while a running board extended the whole length of the boat on each side. They carried a mast with two sails, and were manned by a crew of five men, one steering, and four pushing forward with setting poles, two being on each side." Incidentally, there were few, if any boats on the Delaware of the type shown in the famous picture of Washington crossing that stream, in which the boats are more typical of the water-craft of the Massachusetts coast.

The Dutch on the Hudson developed the most distinctive river sail-boats. In the early 1600s they created a craft called a Hudson River sloop. They patterned these after their buxom wives—well rounded in the bow, broad, and with a high poop. They loved lots of canvas and raised a tremendous mainsail from the ninety-foot booms of their sixty-five- to seventy-five-foot boats. When the English took over from the Dutch they retained both the sloops and the Dutch patois that had become the river language. Many of the river sailors were Negroes, and it was not unusual for a white man from England and six black men from Africa to go skidding up the river chattering in Dutch.

The Hudson lent itself to sail because it is an estuary of the sea as well as a river, and the ocean tide combats the river's flow for most of its navigable length. Voyages were measured by tides—"two ebbs and a flow." But the river did not lend itself to the normal way of changing direction by bringing the head of the vessel through the wind, so the sloop skippers became expert at the frightening process of jibing, in which the heavy boom and bellying sail came flying across the deck at express-train speed, a process which could pull the mast out of the boat if not stopped at an exact instant. On one occasion a loop in the slack of the main sheet dropped around the neck of a skipper while he was jibing and neatly decapitated him. His body dropped on deck while his head flew toward the river bank.

There were market sloops and gaily painted packet sloops. The former took the produce of upriver towns to the metropolis and brought back manufactured and imported goods, the sloop skippers acting as purchasing agents for entire communities. The more elegant packet sloops, their mahogany-paneled cabins hung with mirrors, carried only mail, packages, and passengers. The packets were the United Parcel Service of the day. This letter from a New York City uncle to his upriver niece indicates the type of cargo carried: "I send two baskets of peaches and one of damsons. I have picked them over carefully to try and preserve them. Your corsets were brought home just in time to be put in the box with the shoes." He added, "Mr. Adams is dead and there is a report of the death of Mr. Jefferson this morning." This letter was obviously written a few days after July 4, 1826, nineteen years after Robert Fulton's first voyage up the river in a steamboat.

THE MARINERS MUSEUM, NEWPORT NEWS, VA.

The most distinctive river sailboats used by the early white settlers were those built by the Dutch. Seventy-foot Hudson River sloops appeared in the early 1600s and were retained by the English after they took over the colony. In this painting, a fleet of Hudson River sloops passes West Point.

The sloops successfully competed with the steamers until almost the middle of the nineteenth century. Under some conditions they were faster than the early steamboats, and they were certainly safer, cleaner, and quieter.

James Fenimore Cooper nostalgically described the good old days of leisurely sloop travel:

In that day the passenger did not hurry on board just as a bell was disturbing the neighborhood, bustling his way through a rude throng of porters, cart-men, orangewomen, and newsboys to save the distance by just a minute and a half, but his luggage was often sent to the vessel the day before; he passed the morning in saying adieu, and when he repaired to the vessel, it was with gentlemanlike leisure. . . . There was no jostling of each other, no scrambling for places at the table, no bolting of food, no impertinence manifested, no swearing about missing the Eastern or Southern boats, or the Schenectady, Saratoga, or Boston trains . . . nor any other unseemly manifestation that anybody was in a hurry—on the contrary wine and fruit were provided, as if the travellers intended to enjoy themselves, and a journey in that day was a festa . . . . The vessel usually got aground, once at least, and frequently several times in a trip, and often a day or two were thus delightfully lost giving the stranger an opportunity of visiting the surrounding country.

Some adventurous sloop skippers took their little vessels far from the Hudson. The *Experiment* out of Newburgh made six voyages to China and consorted in Canton harbor with towering clippers. Other Hudson River boats wandered regularly in equally distant seas. For some 60 years a fleet of whalers was based nearly a hundred miles up the river.

In 1783 the Jenkins brothers came from Nantucket seeking land that was less vulnerable than the island on which they had been harassed by the British Navy throughout the Revolution. They found it at Claverack Landing on the Hudson and returned to New England for their families and salt-water friends from Nantucket, Martha's Vineyard, and New Bedford. Next spring the settlers sailed up the river in a fleet of whalers loaded with prefabricated Nantucket-type houses. While stay-at-homes erected houses, a church, a school, and shipyards, the whalers sailed for far-off hunting grounds. Within two years Claverack Landing had become the thriving town of Hudson, with a fleet of twenty-five whalers, a larger fleet than New York City boasted. Behind the town rose factories where whale oil was converted into spermaceti candles.

Jealous of Hudson's prosperity, entrepreneurs started whaling ventures in nearby Newburgh and Poughkeepsie. One of the directors of the latter company was the brewer Matthew Vassar, who used his profits from beer and sperm oil to found a very elite college for young ladies. The archives of the historical societies in upriver towns contain accounts of wide-ranging Hudson sailors who were enslaved by Arabs, eaten by African cannibals, and displayed in a cage by Japanese captors.

The Hudson is the most famed of eastern rivers, in fact and fiction. No other stream had a headless horseman galloping along its banks, a Rip Van Winkle snoozing in its mountains, or a lost Dutchman floating around in its mists. But of greater importance in the building of America was the mighty Mississippi with its fifty-four main tributaries and almost numberless substreams flowing from and through twenty-seven states.

The rivers of the broad inland valley were unsuitable for sailboats. Most were too shallow for a deep keel or centerboard; there was no tide to combat the downstream current; channels were often narrow and sprinkled with snags and bars that a sailboat could not avoid; and in the upper rivers, rapids and falls abounded. Here the canoe was the most common craft, supplemented by bull boats, pirogues, and mackinaw boats.

The canoe of the Missouri and its tributaries was carved from a single cottonwood log and might be thirty-five feet long and four feet wide. It could carry a dozen or more men or a few tons of furs or trade goods and could be hauled through rapids or unloaded and portaged around falls or between waterway and waterway. Less portable was the pirogue which, in Missouri River parlance, was two canoes about 6 feet apart with a platform built between them; in other places pirogues were simply large canoes.

The white man's bull boat was an elliptical enlargement of the Indian craft, with buffalo hides stretched over a sapling frame to make an enormous shallow oval basket about twenty-five feet long and twelve wide. It could carry about three tons of furs on a stream no more than ten inches deep. It was usually poled, and most frequently was used only for downstream travel and abandoned at the end of its journey. This was also true of the mackinaw, which was a larger elliptical craft made of wood.

On the Mississippi and its lower tributaries two types of boats carried most of the more prosaic river traffic—flatboats (also called broadhorns) and keelboats, the largest of which were called barges. Flatboats varied in length from twenty to sixty feet and in width from ten to twenty-five feet. They were essentially rectangular boxes of heavy timber whose sides rose 5 or 6 feet. They drew about two feet of water when loaded. Usually they were decked over and all had living quarters in the stern, complete with hearth and chimney. These unwieldy craft were controlled by three long sweeps, one at the stern and on sticking out on each side like horns—hence the name "broadhorn." Obviously they could not move against the current. When they reached their destination they were broken up for lumber. Most of the early sidewalks of New Orleans were made from flatboat timber, and the town of Algeria across the river was built almost entirely from broken-up flatboats. In the early years of the nineteenth century it was possible to walk on the river for a mile at New Orleans without getting one's feet wet by stepping from flatboat to flatboat moored side by side at the upper levee.

When "Westward Ho" became a byword at the end of the eighteenth century, building flatboats for emigrants became a thriving business at Pittsburgh. It is said that the more responsible builders seasoned the lumber for such boats a whole day. When the settlers arrived at their downstream destination they took the boats apart and used the planks to build houses.

The jerry-built boats offered little protection against the natural

THE MARINERS MUSEUM, NEWPORT NEWS, VA.

Most of the early settlers traveled down the Ohio and the Mississippi on rectangular flatboats from 20 to 60 feet long with living quarters in the stern. In the early nineteenth century so many flatboats crowded into New Orleans that it was possible to walk for a mile on the river by stepping from one boat to another.

hazards of the river, and Indian attacks were still a real threat. The first passenger line from Pittsburgh to Cincinnati advertised, "No danger need be apprehended from the enemy as every person on board will be under cover made proof against rifle or musket balls, and convenient port-holes for firing out of. Each of the boats are armed with six pieces carrying a pound ball; also a number of good muskets, and amply supplied with plenty of ammunition; strongly manned with choice hands, and the masters of approved knowledge. Conveniences are constructed on board each boat, so as to render landing unnecessary, as it might, at times, be attended with danger."

And there were river pirates. The most famous of these on the Ohio in emigrant days was a certain Colonel Plug. His *modus operandi* was to go upstream from his riverside headquarters and pretend to be a traveler marooned on the river bank. When kindhearted settlers took him aboard he surreptitiously picked the calking from the seams of their boat, nicely timing the operation so that the craft would sink in front of his establishment. Then his helpers rowed out to salvage the cargo and save the Colonel—but not the emigrants. Colonel Plug had a wife, Pluggy. He also had a lieutenant known only as Nine Eyes. Pluggy shared her favors with the lieutenant, or at least the Colonel thought she did. When he was in his cups he challenged Nine Eyes to a duel, which resulted in minor flesh wounds. They celebrated the vindication of Pluggy's virtue by finishing a demijohn of whiskey. Plug met his end when he miscalculated the sinking time of a flatboat and drowned with his victims before his henchmen arrived.

The most famed pirate lair was Cave-in-Rock, a few miles from the site of the present town of that name in Missouri at the point where the Ohio joins the Mississippi. This is a 160-foot cave with an arched entrance 55 feet wide about 40 feet above low water. Above it an island deflects the channel to pass under the cave, and below it a series of hazards made a local pilot necessary. Several successive bands of outlaws made their headquarters here, and if a boat was known to contain a particularly valuable cargo they sometimes attacked it in skiffs. A more favored method of pillage was to send the most presentable members of the gang upstream to offer their services as pilots. They would drive the boats aground where their henchmen could replace the crew and sail on to market the cargo. Natural hazards of the rivers were so great and communications in the West so primitive that this went on for years before shippers in Pittsburgh finally realized that their lost boats were never heard of below Cave-in-Rock, investigated, and launched an expedition to wipe out the pirates. In an upper room of the cave were found 60 human skeletons.

Some immigrants came to trade rather than settle; they set up shop on flatboats flying calico flags to denote their nature and fitted with shelves and counters to display a wide variety of manufactured goods for which the settlers had crying need. After collecting all the hoarded cash of goods-starved housewives in a settlement, the merchant-admiral floated on to the next. When his goods were gone he sold his boat and walked upstream to start again or established a permanent store in a community that struck his fancy. Service industries also operated from flatboats. Millers, toolmakers, and blacksmiths stopped to serve the settlers along the river while they were traveling to their new homes. Flatboats carried museum exhibits, raree shows, and theatrical troupes as well as barrooms and brothels. A frontier minister demanded that something be done in order to restrict "the inmates and practices of these floating mansions of iniquity."

Keelboats were for two-way travel. Their ends were pointed and their bottoms slightly rounded and based on a keel that was merely a heavy timber that would absorb the shock of running aground. The larger ones were sixty to seventy feet long and fifteen to eighteen feet wide. Their sides were slightly lower than those of a flatboat, but a long shed covered most of the hull amidship to provide a commodious cargo hold and cabin.

Keelboats were propelled upstream by several methods, although they are almost invariably pictured being poled. A team of boatmen carrying long iron-tipped poles were stationed at equal intervals along cleated walkways on each side of the boat, facing aft. On command, they set their poles against the bottom of the river, placed the upper end against a shoulder pad, and walked toward the stern. As each crewman reached the stern he ran back to take his place at the end of the line in the bow. Each time the men moved from bow to stern they propelled the vessel forward one boat's-length.

Where the water was not suitable for poling, the boat was moved against the current by cordelling, warping, or, in flood waters, bushwhacking. The cordelle was a rope up to 1,000 feet long that was tied to the boat and taken ashore by the crew, who walked along the bank like canal horses or Volga boatmen. Of this practice an Irishman who was working his way up the river as a boatman said, "Faith, if it wasn't for the name of riding I'd as soon walk." When there was no suitable bank the cordelle was sent forward in a skiff tied to a snag or tree, and the boat was warped forward by taking in the line on a capstan or hand over hand. In bushwhacking, the boat was taken out of the flooded stream and pulled forward through the woods by grasping the branches of trees. Some boats had masts, and sail was used when possible. In the deep lower river, where no other manual means of propulsion would serve, they were rowed. Keelboats covered the 1,950 miles from Pittsburgh to

New Orleans in from four to six weeks, depending on the stage of the river. The trip back took four to six months or more.

Navigating a keelboat required skill and experience as well as brawn. At certain places the current flowed upstream where eddies were created by points or bends. The keelboat "patroon" who knew when to hug one shore and went to cross to the other made better time than a less experienced skipper. Luck was a factor. No one knew where a sawyer or a planter—collectively called "snags"—might wait to tear the bottom out of a boat or rise to impale it. A planter was a floating tree whose roots had taken hold on the bottom and whose trunk slanted up toward the surface. A sawyer was a planter whose trunk bobbed up and down periodically with a sawing motion and which might come up under a boat.

Eddies below bends and islands were traps for unwary flatboat and keelboat men, particularly the former, whose unwieldy craft might spin for hours in the swirling waters. One Kentucky keelboat captain, going downstream at night, passed a brightly lighted house where a party was in progress. Half an hour later he passed another, and then several more at like intervals. He wondered what this section of the river was celebrating until dawn disclosed that he had been going around in circles in a vast eddy, passing the same house over and over again.

While flatboats could travel downstream only, keelboats could go upstream as well. This sketch of a gaff-rigged keelboat shows two means of propulsion when the water was too deep for poling: in addition to her sails, she carried eight oarsmen in the bow.

THE

NAVIGATOR:

CONTAINING DIRECTIONS FOR NAVIGATING

THE

| MONONGAHELA, | OHIO, AND |
| ALLEGHANY, | MISSISSIPPI |

RIVERS;

WITH AN AMPLE ACCOUNT

OF THESE MUCH ADMIRED WATERS,

FROM THE

HEAD OF THE FORMER TO THE MOUTH OF THE LATTER;

AND A CONCISE DESCRIPTION

OF THEIR

TOWNS, VILLAGES, HARBOURS, SETTLEMENTS, &c.

———

WITH ACCURATE MAPS OF THE OHIO AND MISSISSIPPI.

———

TO WHICH IS ADDED

An Appendix,

CONTAINING

AN ACCOUNT OF LOUISIANA,

AND OF

THE MISSOURI AND COLUMBIA RIVERS,

AS DISCOVERED BY THE VOYAGE UNDER

CAPTAINS LEWIS AND CLARK.

———

SIXTH EDITION—IMPROVED AND ENLARGED,

———

PITTSBURGH,

PUBLISHED BY ZADOK CRAMER AND SOLD AT HIS

BOOKSTORE, MARKET-STREET.

[PRICE ONE DOLLAR.]

———

FROM THE PRESS OF CRAMER & SPEAR......1808.

e nearest thing to a chart of the Mississippi River system was The
igator, published in 1802 by Zadok Cramer, a consumptive who never
near the water. Its sketchy information on channels was gleaned
keelboat men who traveled the rivers.

Another type of river craft that had a brief career on the Mississippi was the horse boat. This was a small keelboat with paddle wheels that were turned by horses plodding on a treadmill in the hull. It could move upstream at a couple of miles an hour, but it was never practical because the horses tired and the current did not. When relief horses and the hay to feed the horsepower were carried there was not much room for anything else. On remote Lake Winnipesaukee, New Hampshire, where there was no current, the horse boat lasted for the better part of the nineteenth century. One was still in use in the late 1880s transporting fuel for steamboats.

The men who moved the boats on western waters before the coming of steam were a rugged and hardy breed, a race apart whose exploits developed into Mississippi Valley folklore. Mark Twain described them as "hordes of rough and hardy men; rude, uneducated, brave, suffering terrific hardships with sailor-like stoicism; heavy drinkers, coarse frolickers in moral sties like the Natchez-Under-the-Hill of that day, heavy fighters, reckless fellows, every one, elaphantinely jolly, foul-witted, profane, prodigal of their money, bankrupt at the end of the trip, fond of barbaric finery, prodigious braggarts; yet, in the main, honest, trustworthy, faithful to promises and duty, and often picturesquely magnanimous." Actually, Samuel Clemens was himself being magnanimous; most of the rivermen were merely roughnecks, but they were colorful roughnecks.

The majority of the boatmen on the Mississippi proper were Creoles of French extraction with a mixture of Negro or Indian blood. Those from the Ohio country were generally called Kentuckians whether or not they came from that state. Originally they were recruited from the rough est and toughest of the frontiersmen. As a class they were tall, gau big-boned, and more vicious and bellicose than the Creoles, who inclined to be rather lighthearted and good-natured. The nature o labor made the boatmen fine physical specimens who worked ha they worked and played hard when they played. By their own they were genuine ring-tailed snorters from away back, calamity who could lick their weight in wildcats with the and outdrink, outfight, and outcuss anything in this wor

Favorite leisure-time pursuits of the boatmen were b and sex. The order of preference depended on the indi was the favored pastime of most. There were clean fi the latter being more common when keelboat mer their natural enemies. When two boats met in the for them to moor together while picked tean Brannigan on the deck of the flatboat. Such bystanders could not interfere and knive weapons were forbidden. Fists punched, feet kicked, knees bucked at un-protected crotches, fingers clutched at throats, and thumbs gouged at eyes. Teeth bit off ears, noses, and lips. A boatman who had two ears was considered a sissy.

Self-styled champions wore red feathers in their hats, which com-mitted them to accept any challenge. Such stalwarts bragged mightily of their prowess, using language full of colorful simile, although it is doubtful that the best of them ever uttered a challenge with the felicity of that penned by Mark Twain: "Look at me! I'm the man they call Sudden Death and General Desolation! Sired by a hurricane, dam'd by an earthquake, half-brother to the cholera, nearly related to the smallpox on the mother's side! Look at me! I take nineteen alligators and a bar'l of whiskey for breakfast when I'm in robust health, and a bushel of rattlesnakes and a dead body when I'm ailing. I split the everlasting rocks with my glance, and I quench the thunder when I speak! Whoo-oop! Stand back and give me room according to my strength! Blood's my natural drink, and the wails of the dying is music to my ear. Cast your eye on me, gentlemen! and lay low and hold your breath, for I'm about to turn myself loose!"

Ashore, the "half horse, half alligator" men usually kept to themselves in such places as Natchez-Under-the-Hill, the Pinchgut in Memphis, and the Swamp in New Orleans. All river-bank cities had such roisterous sections were boatmen had their own barrooms, gambling halls, and brothels in which to while away the merry hours. Their play was rather rough. If a bartender in a water-front saloon offended it was fun to push the building into the river. If it were not on the river bank they might tear it apart board by board or, if that were too much effort, merely burn it. Shooting at passing boats for the fun of it was another favored sport.

Boatmen did not generally disturb more respectable citizens unless they were provoked. Although there were a few instances of the militia being called out when large, boisterous bands erupted from their own quarters, in most places there was a gentleman's agreement that the minions of law and order would stay out of the river men's section and vice versa. Sometimes high spirits would lead the boatmen to play pranks like stretching a rope across the main street and running down the thoroughfare to topple all peaceful citizens. When a boat moored near an isolated settler's cottage for the night, the owner was well advised to sit up with a gun and keep his women under cover. Although the river men usually preferred the willing females of their own sections, some thought it fine fun to capture a settler's daughter and did not consider rape a very serious offense.

Some boatmen attributed their vigor to drinking the muddy water of the Mississippi, which, they claimed, was far more healthful than the clear water of the Ohio. According to Huckleberry Finn, "The Child of Calamity said that was so; he said there was nutritiousness in the mud, and a man that drunk Mississippi water could grow corn in his stomach if he wanted. He says; 'You look at the graveyards, that tells the tale. Trees won't grow worth shucks in a Cincinnati graveyard, but in a Sent Louis graveyard they grow upwards of eight hundred foot high. It's all on account of the water the people drunk before they laid up. A Cincinnati corpse don't richen the soil any.' "

Favorite playground of the river men was Natchez-Under-the-Hill on the river bank at the foot of a bluff on which stood the upper town of sedate, white-pillared mansions. The lower section contained two mile-long streets in which, but for a few warehouses, every building was a saloon, gambling house, or brothel. When the boatmen reached Natchez on the downriver trip they had accomplished the worst of their journey and could relax. For the flatboat men who were walking upriver this was the last chance for a fling until they reached far-off Nashville at the upper end of the Natchez Trace. Except for New Orleans, where the men were paid off, Natchez provided the best prostitutes and the most accommodating gamblers and bartenders. Natchez-Under-the-Hill has been romanticized in legend, but in the eyes of an early writer it was "a stale, sordid, sodden place" with "broken, half sunken sidewalks" and "tawdrily arrayed, highly rouged females . . . Negroes, mulattoes, pigs, dogs and dirty children." Yet it was not all thus. Madame Aivoges ran a select carpeted and curtained house in which white and octoroon girls played the spinet for carefully screened customers and poured wine as well as Monongahela whiskey. Legend has it that Madame Aivoges was killed by her son, whom she had maintained in an expensive eastern school, when he discovered the nature of her business by coming to the house as a customer with some aristocratic friends from a plantation on the hill. At the other end of the scale from Madame was Anne Christian, who operated a floating brothel and was said to be six feet eight inches tall and able to hold her own with the most bawdy, brawny boatman.

The most famous flatboat man in American history engaged in none of the immoral pursuits of his brethren, but Abraham Lincoln was a young amateur who made only two trips downriver. Abe was 19 when a neighboring farmer named Gentry hired him to build a boat and captain it on a thousand-mile trip to New Orleans with a load of pork, flour, meal, bacon, and potatoes, his first journey away from his natal neighborhood. Most of the voyage was uneventful except for the ordinary vicissitudes of the river, but one night when the craft was moored to the bank seven river pirates boarded it, intent on murdering the crew and stealing the boat and cargo. In the brawl that ensued Lincoln got a gash over his right eye, the scar of which he bore to his grave.

The bumpkin from upriver wandered wide-eyed through New Orleans, jostled by sailors from distant ports, ogled by dusky-eyed, soft-voiced quadroons, probably confused by the swarms of roustabouts, teamsters, river men, poor whites, squatters, and other riffraff of the levee. Here the Great Emancipator first saw gangs of chained slaves destined for the cotton fields and heard talk of the technique of using a mule whip on humans. But of the trip upriver on a steamboat he later remarked that the Negro roustabouts seemed to be the happiest people whom he had ever seen.

Another part-time flatboat man who was better known for other exploits was Davy Crockett. Some time after the frontiersman's death at the Alamo a multivolumed publication appeared entitled *Davy Crockett's Almanack of Wild Sports in the West*, which his heirs solmenly averred had been written by Davy. Although this seem sunlikely, one anecdote describes what seems to have been the normal social relationship of boatmen. Crockett is supposed to have written:

One day as I was sitting in the stern of my broadhorn, the old Free and Easy, on the Mississippi, taking a horn of midshipman's grog, with a tin pot in each

THE SMITHSONIAN INSTITUTION

Abraham Lincoln built a flatboat and captained it down the Mississippi and later invented a device for "combining adjustable buoyant air chambers with a steamboat or other vessel for the purpose of enabling their draft of water to be readily lessened to enable them to pass over bars." His invention was awarded a patent in 1849, and the model shown here is now in the Smithsonian Institution.

hand, first a draught of whiskey, and then one of river water, who should float down past me but Joe Snag; he was in a snooze, as fast as a church, with his mouth wide open; he had been ramsquaddled with whiskey for a fortnight, and as it evaporated from his body it looked like the steam from a vent pipe. Knowing the feller would be darned hard to wake, with all this steam on, as he floated past me I hit him a crack over his knob with my big steering oar. He waked in a thundering rage. Says he, halloe stranger, who axed you to crack my lice? Says I, shut up your mouth, or your teeth will get sunburnt. Upon this he crooked up his neck and neighed like a stallion. I clapped by arms and crowed like a cock. Says he, if you are a game chicken I'll pick all the pin feathers off of you. For some time back I had been so wolfy about the head and shoulders that I was obliged to keep kivered up in a salt crib to keep from spiling, for I had not had a fight for as much as ten days. Says I, give us none of your chin music, but set your kickers on land, and I'll give you a severe licking. The fellow now jumped ashore, and he was so tall he could not tell when his feet were cold. He jumped up a rod. Says he, take care how I lite on you, and he gave me a real sockdologer that made my very liver and lites turn to jelly. But he found me a real scrouger. I brake three of his ribs, and he knocked out five of my teeth and one eye. He was the severest colt that ever I tried to break. I finally got a bite hold that he could not shake off. We were now parted by some boatmen, and were so exhausted that it was more than a month before either could have a fight. It seemed to me like a little eternity. And although I didn't come out second best, I took care not to wake up a ring tailed roarer with an oar again.

The greatest keelboat man of history and legend was Mike Fink, the Paul Bunyan of river lore—except that there really was a Mike Fink. He was born near Pittsburgh around 1780, served as a scout in the Indian wars and then worked up to the ownership of two keelboats. When the glorious days of keelboating passed he went farther west and became a trapper for the Missouri Fur Company.

Although Mike actually lived, most of his exploits were legendary. To him was attributed every heroic quality and accomplishment of the river man in literally hundreds of published stories which became an important part of midwestern folklore. The first printed Mike Fink story appeared in 1829 in a velvet-bound "female gift book." Parents of today's teen-agers will remember his last resurrection by Walt Disney, some ten years ago, as a pal of Davy Crockett's.

All Mike Fink stories deal with his prowess in various directions ashore, not with his skill as a boatman. It was said that he could drink a gallon of liquor a day without showing its effect and that he was never bested in a brawl or a shooting match. His marksmanship was so renowned that he was always given the fifth quarter—the hide and tallow—to stay out of beef-shooting matches. His favorite demonstration was shooting a cup from the head of an associate. Mike was fond of what he called practical jokes. In one such he is supposed to have brought his current paramour ashore, ordered her to lie down, and covered her with dead leaves. He then set fire to the leaves and stood over the girl with a gun. When the scorched female could stand no more she dashed for the river as Mike shouted, "That will larn you not to look at fellows on other boats."

There are a half dozen stories of Mike's death. In the most prevalent one it is attributed to a cup-shooting match with two friends named Carpenter and Talbot. The former served first as the target supporter, but he and Mike had had some difference about a woman. Fink "elevated a little low" and shot Carpenter between the eyes. Knowing that this must have been deliberate, Talbot gunned him down.

Although handwriting on the wall appeared for the manually operated river boats when steam made its bow on the Mississippi in 1811, their most colorful era was during the following thirty years. Flatboats lasted as freight carriers until they became steam-towed barges, and the demise of the keelboats was a lingering one. Like the Hudson River sloops, they were able to compete with the earliest crude steam-powered craft. As late as 1840, keelboats were still arriving at Pittsburgh at the rate of eight a day. As the thrashing stern wheels poked the noses of shallow-draft steamboats farther up the tributaries, the keels were forced farther back. But neither the steamboat nor the railroad completely wiped them out. Until well into the twentieth century the raucous note of the horn of the keelboat man still might be heard far up the shallow headwaters of western streams. They continued to carry the produce of remote settlements until the Model T Ford pioneered a new type of land transportation in the hinterlands.

The Coming
of Walk-in-the-Water

The surest way to achieve fame in American history was to get one's name into the fourth-grade school books during the nineteenth and early twentieth centuries. Here generations of young Americans learned that Henry Hudson discovered the Hudson River and that James Watt invented the steam engine and Robert Fulton the steamboat. Of course, none of this was true. Giovanni da Verazzano found the river more than eighty years before Hudson, and there were steam engines in use long before Watt's time. The schoolbook Robert Fulton built the first steamboat, named it the *Clermont*, and sailed it up the Hudson on its maiden voyage on August 17, 1807. The only thing accurate about this is that Fulton did sail up the Hudson on that date. He did not invent the steamboat; the one on the Hudson was not the first steamboat or even his first steamboat; that trip was not its maiden voyage; and Fulton never called it the *Clermont*.

The idea of steam as a source of power goes back to 150 B.C., when Hero described an aiophile—"a circular vessel from which issued the vapor of steam, causing it to rotate." The idea of a steamboat goes back to at least 1618, when an Englishman named David Ramsey applied for a patent on his plans "to make boats runn upon the waters as swifte in calmes, and more safe in storms, than boats full seyled in greate wyndes." Ramsey did not mention steam, but he did say that his device could also "raise water from lowe pitts by fire." He obviously had in mind some kind of a steam engine. An American gunsmith, William Henry, built a steam-powered craft that sank in the Conestoga River in 1763. In the 1770s several Frenchmen built model or experimental steam-powered vessels, some of which worked, after a fashion, but none well enough to justify the continuance of the project. There were other experiments and designs too numerous to mention—one serious study of American transportation claims that there were forty-eight steamboats before Fulton's. Workable boats started to appear, mostly in America, in the 1780s.

[34]

By the early years of the nineteenth century the question "Who invented the steamboat?" opened a Pandora's box of controversy. Each of half a dozen pioneers had his coterie of faithful supporters who defended their idol with vehemence. The four principal candidates, other than Fulton, were John Fitch, James Rumsey, Oliver Evans, and William Symington. All except the last were Americans, and each had a workable steamboat—not a model—in use before Fulton's. Rumsey's vessel was propelled by a jet of water ejected from the stern. Evans' was an amphibian that waddled out of the water of the Schuylkill River and rolled around Independence Square in Philadelphia, the first self-propelled land vehicle in America. Symington's was a tug boat that pulled barges on the Clyde Canal. All this happened between 1787 and 1805—from two to twenty years before Fulton—and, except for Evans, these were not their first boats.

Fitch, who is usually called "poor John Fitch" because of a lifetime of hard luck, went farther than any of the others. His first boat was propelled by paddles that were lifted up and dipped by the engine. He gave up this principle and went to paddle wheels in a boat that, in 1790, ran up and down the Delaware River from Philadelphia to Trenton carrying paying passengers. On June 14 of that year an advertisement in the *Federal Gazette* proclaimed: "THE STEAMBOAT is now ready to take passengers and is intended to set off from Arch Street Ferry, in Philadelphia, every Monday, Wednesday, and Friday, for Burlington, Bristol, Bordentown and Trenton, to return on Tuesdays, Thursdays, and Saturdays. Price for passengers, 2/6 to Burlington and Bristol, 3/9 to Bordentown, 5s to Trenton." During that summer the boat ran regularly, logging between two and three thousand miles.

There has never been a satisfactory explanation of why, in view of the several previous boats, particularly Fitch's, Fulton has been credited as the inventor. The time and place probably had something to do with it. In 1790 not enough conservative Philadelphians were ready to try Fitch's new, noisy, and perhaps dangerous form of transportation to make it pay. Although Fitch's boat was half again as fast as Fulton's later craft, it was not as fast as the stage that made the same trip along the river bank. The difference in the personalities and sponsorship of the entrepreneurs was also a factor. Fitch was poor, uncouth, eccentric, and uneducated and seemed to compulsively rub people the wrong way. Fulton was personable, convincing, and knew how to "win friends and influence people"—and he was associated with Robert Livingston, dean of a prolific and affluent family of Hudson Valley land owners. Perhaps the best answer to the question of why poor John Fitch was an obscure suicide in Kentucky while Robert Fulton went down in the history books is that Fitch's boat lost money and Fulton's made a profit. In materialistic

America a steamboat that was not profitable was a rather useless invention.

Perhaps James Watt deserves most of the credit for the steamboat. Although he did not at first believe that the engines he built could be used to propel a practical boat or vehicle, his improvements on the steam engine made it efficient enough to move more than its own weight; but the story of the invention of the steam engine does not start with Watt. The Marquis of Worcester built an engine in 1655 that was regarded only as a novelty. Captain Thomas Savary put one to work pumping water in a coal mine in 1695. Thomas Newcomen improved on Savary's, in 1705, to make the "mine engine" a widely accepted apparatus for keeping mine shafts dry. Newcomen employed the same principle to activate a pump that would later be used to turn paddle wheels.

The Newcomen engine consisted of a vertical cylinder open at the top into which a piston was fitted. The piston was connected by a rod to one end of a lever with a support at its center. From the other end of the lever was suspended the plunger of the pump, weighted to exceed the weight of the piston. This lever later became the walking beam of the

Although Robert Fulton is often credited as the inventor of the steamboat, John Fitch built a steam-powered paddle boat that he launched on the Delaware River in 1786, more than 20 years before Fulton's famous Clermont. *In 1790 another of Fitch's steamboats, with paddle wheels, carried passengers between Philadelphia and Trenton.*

steamboat. Steam was injected into the cylinder when the piston was up, followed by a jet of cold water that condensed the steam. This caused a partial vacuum in the cylinder, and the weight of the atmosphere on the piston pushed it down and raised the plunger of the pump—thus its name, "atmospheric engine." When the vacuum was broken by admitting more steam, the counterweight pulled the piston up and the engine was ready for another stroke, which it made at the rate of five or six a minute.

In 1763 Watt, a lecturer at the University of Glasgow, was asked to repair a Newcomen engine. Instead, he improved it to greatly increase its efficiency. His principal change was to add a separate condenser in which the steam was returned to water without cooling the cylinder. Later he converted the atmospheric engine to a double-action reciprocating engine by closing the top of the cylinder and injecting steam into both ends, above and below the piston. It was this engine that made the steamboat, the steam coach, and the locomotive practical; it was the first that was efficient enough to move itself, its fuel, and a payload.

Robert Fulton started as an artist in Lancaster, Pennsylvania, and, in

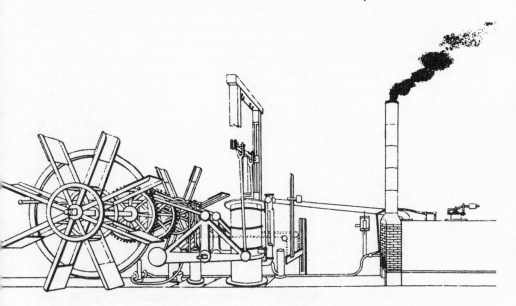

In constructing his steamboat, Fulton preferred success over originality. He saw no reason to build his own steam engine when he could purchase a proven model from James Watt, the English inventor. Watt's engine, for which Fulton designed a hull, had a cylinder 24 inches in diameter and a piston with a 4-foot stroke.

1786, went to Europe with a letter of introduction from Benjamin Franklin to the American artist Benjamin West, who had an atelier in London. Fulton was a fair but not dedicated painter who was more interested in money than the muse; one might say that he was a very good hack. He also had an inborn mechanical ingenuity that would prove to be more profitable than his palette. His great enthusiasm in the 1790s was canal building, on which he wrote a treatise that he sent to George Washington, among others. From canals he turned to submarines and built one that was a great advance over the undersea craft created by David Bushnell during the Revolution. He did not succeed in selling it to either the French or the British but, even after his steamboat was a success, he believed that his submarine and a torpedo he had invented were more important contributions to humanity because, like all new fearsome weapons, they would make war too horrible to contemplate.

While he was working on canals and submarines and supporting himself on the proceeds of a panorama of the burning of Moscow that he painted and exhibited in Paris, Fulton was also tinkering with steamboats. In his first designs he sought to imitate a fish, with a vertical paddle at the stern connected to a large bow that was bent by the power of a steam engine. When the tension was released the bow was supposed to move the paddle like a fish's tail.

In 1801 Robert Livingston came to Paris, where Fulton was then building his undersea *Nautilus*. Livingston was a patrician owner of vast estates, a statesman who had, with James Monroe, engineered the purchase of the Louisiana Territory, and a self-styled philosopher of mechanics. In America he had already financed Nicholas Roosevelt—granduncle of Theodore—in an unsuccessful steamboat venture. He had also secured a twenty-year monopoly from the State of New York for operating steamboats on the Hudson River. Livingston needed somebody to build a boat. Fulton was willing.

Fulton was thoroughly familiar with the work of all the steamboat pioneers on both sides of the Atlantic, particularly that of Fitch and Rumsey, who had both come to Europe and whose plans Fulton had studied. He differed from his predecessors in that he was the first to apply a practical engineering mind to the subject, and his concern was with being successful rather than original. He described his concept of an invention in this way: "For this invention to be rendered useful does not consist in putting oars, paddles, wheels or resisting chains in motion by a steam engine—but it consists in showing in a clear and distinct manner that it is desired to drive a boat precisely any given number of miles an hour—what must be the size of the cylinder and velocity of the piston? What must be the size and velocity of the resisting chains? All these things being governed by the laws of nature, the real Invention is to find them.—Till the artist knows the necessary proportions . . . . he must work in the dark and to great uncertainty, and can not be said to have made any clear and distinct discovery or useful invention."

Fulton first built a clockwork-powered model to experiment with various systems of propulsion. He had already given up his fish's tail and after trying a screw propeller, sculls, and paddle wheels he settled on a series of flat paddles on an endless chain running over pulleys at bow and stern. When he learned that a Frenchman had already patented this device, he switched to paddle wheels. His agreement with Livingston provided that the latter would put up £500 for a full-sized experimental craft. Fulton built this on the Seine at Paris; it was "70 French feet long, 8 French feet wide, 3 French feet deep," and in it "he placed a steam engine of about 8 horses power, which was hired of Mr. Perrier for this experiment." The vessal had side paddle wheels 12 feet in diameter. In 1803 its maiden voyage was thus described in the pages of the *Journal des Debates:*

A trial was made of a new invention, the complete and brilliant success of which should have important consequences for the commerce and internal navigation of France. During the past two or three months there has been seen at the end of the Quai Chaillot a boat of strange appearance, equipped with two large wheels mounted on an axle like a cart, while behind these wheels was a kind of large stove with a pipe as if some sort of a small fire engine was intended to operate the wheels of the boat . . . .

At six o'clock in the evening, helped by only three persons he put the boat in motion . . . . and for an hour and a half he afforded the strange spectacle of a boat moved by wheels like a cart, these wheels being provided with paddles of flat plates, and being moved by a fire engine. As we followed it along the quay, the speed against the current of the Seine seemed to be about that of a rapid pedestrian.

Fulton next bought an engine from Watt for shipment to America. Unlike his predecessors, he saw no reason to build one of his own when the English already were making an engine that would serve the purpose —and Livingston had the money to pay for it. The cylinder of the engine was 24 inches in diameter and the piston had a 4-foot stroke. He designed a hull generally similar to those of sailing ships; it was 130 feet long by 16 feet wide, with a depth of hold of 7 feet, and it had two sail-bearing masts. This was constructed by a shipbuilder named Charles Browne on the East River. He installed Watt's engine and on each side of the hull he hung two unguarded paddle wheels 15 feet in diameter, each with eight boards—called "buckets"—4 feet long that had a dip of 2 feet. The wheels were not quite complete when he took the vessel for a shakedown cruise on the East River a few days before his first trip on the Hudson, at a speed of two miles an hour against the current.

In describing this trip Fulton wrote, "Whatever may be the fate of steamboats on the Hudson, everything is completely proved for the Mississippi, and the object is immense." Why, in view of their monopoly, Fulton was dubious about commercial success on the Hudson is not clear. The recent Louisiana Purchase had excited great interest in the Mississippi, and Fulton may have realized that his crude craft had a long way to go before it would make the Hudson River sloops obsolete. He seems to have underestimated the usefulness of the steamboat, even after he had built one.

During its construction, Fulton called the craft "the steamboat." Later it was advertised as *The North River Steamboat*. After it was remodeled it was registered as *The North River Steamboat of Clermont*. In all correspondence Fulton called it either *The North River Steamboat* or the *North River*. The vessel was apparently first called the *Clermont*— the name of Livingston's upriver estate—in a biography of Fulton written two years after his death by his friend Caldwalder Colden. Since Colden's writing was considered "official," the name was picked up and the vessel has come down in history under that appellation.

– Later accounts of the trip up the Hudson on August 17, 1807, describe the cheering crowds and wild excitement at the beginning of the voyage. Actually, the event seems to have aroused little advance interest. Only one newspaper mentioned it, in a single paragraph: "Mr. Fulton's ingenious steamboat, invented with a view to the navigation of the Mississippi from New Orleans upward, sails today from North River, near State's Prison, to Albany. The velocity of the steamboat is calculated at 4 miles an hour. It is said it will make a progress of 2 against the current of the Mississippi, and if so it will certainly be a very valuable acquisition to the commerce of the western states." The vessel, while under construction, was called Fulton's Folly, and when Livingston sought to borrow money to complete the boat some personal friends put it up only on condition that he did not reveal their names—they did not want to be associated with such a "crackpot" undertaking.

The passengers of the first upstream trip were forty guests, mostly Livingstons and including Fulton's fiancée, Harriet Livingston. Her uncle announced their engagement when the boat stopped at Clermont; this may have been coincidental, or the consent of the family may have depended on the success of the boat.

Fulton described the voyage in a letter as follows:

The moment arrived in which the word was to be given for the boat to move. My friends were in groups on the deck. There was anxiety mixed with fear among them. They were silent, sad and weary. I read in their looks nothing but disaster, and almost repented of my efforts. The signal was given and the boat moved on a short distance and then stopped and became immovable. To the silence of the preceding moment, now succeeded murmurs of discontent, and agitations, and whispers and shrugs. I could hear distinctly repeated—"I told you it was so; it is a foolish scheme; I wish we were well out of it."

I elevated myself upon a platform and addressed the assembly. I stated that I knew not what was the matter, but if they would be quiet and indulge me for half an hour, I would either go on or abandon the voyage for that time. This short respite was conceded without objection. I went below and examined the machinery, and discovered that the cause was a slight maladjustment of some of the work. In a short time it was obviated. The boat was again put in motion. She continued to move on. All were still incredulous. None seemed willing to trust the evidence of their own senses. We left the fair city of New York; we passed through the romantic and ever-varying scenery of the Highlands; we descried the clustering houses of Albany; we reached its shores,—and then, even then, when all seemed achieved, I was the victim of disappointment. Imagination superseded the influence of fact. It was then doubted if it could be done again, or if done, it was doubted if it could be made of any great value.

Despite Fulton's lack of faith, the apprehension of the passengers

THE MARINERS MUSEUM, NEWPORT NEWS, VA.

Except for the smokestack and paddle wheels, Fulton's steamboat, which he called the North River, *looked like a sailing vessel. It was 130 feet long, 16 feet wide, and had two sail-bearing masts. After his death, a biographer referred to the boat as the* Clermont, *a name that stuck. The above model is in the Mariners Museum, at Newport News, Virginia.*

In an idealized painting of Fulton's vessel after it was remodeled, the artist lettered the name "Clermont" on the stern, although it never ap-

peared there. He also has the wind blowing the smoke in one direction, the sail in the other.

seems to have turned to enthusiasm when they realized that the unique craft was not going to blow up and was going to go up the river. They gathered on the stern and coasted under the Palisades singing a favorite song of Fulton's, "Ye Banks and Braes o' Bonny Doon." Ashore and afloat, spectators expressed mixed emotions by cheering or quailing at the sight of a smoke-belching craft that defied the laws of nature and of which one yokel said that he had seen "the devil going up river to Albany in a sawmill." At night, with sparks and flame streaming from the stack and the firebox glowing, this monster marching upstream in defiance of the winds and tide was a fearsome sight to most of the simple people of the valley, but none of them described her with such felicity as the Indians, who called the early vessels "boats that walk in the water." (Incidentally, *Walk-in-the-Water* was the name of the first steamboat to plow Lake Erie between Detroit and Buffalo, in 1813. She lasted only three seasons, perhaps because of the cost of the eight yoke of oxen needed to help her against the current of the Niagara River.)

The *North River* made the 150-mile trip to Albany in thirty-two hours' sailing time, an average of about five miles an hour. Although Fulton had not invented anything, he had clearly demonstrated the practicality of the first American invention of world-shaking importance, and he had done it in such a way that others could follow. Unlike Fitch, Rumsey, and the others, most of whom accomplished something without really knowing what they were doing, Fulton had carefully planned and experimented, and his boat, although crude, was basically sound from an engineering standpoint.

The partners quickly moved to remedy some of the crudeness. The engine was boarded up and decked over, the cabins fore and aft decorated and equipped with twelve berths each, and the paddle wheels provided with guards. Advertisements ran in the New York and Albany papers saying:

THE NORTH RIVER STEAM BOAT

Will leave Pauler's Hook Ferry on Friday the 4th of September, at 6 in the morning, and arrive at Albany on Saturday, at 6 in the afternoon.

Provisions, good berths and accommodations are provided.

The charge to each passenger is as follows:

To Newburgh	$3	time	14	hours
To Poughkeepsie	$4	"	17	"
To Esopus	$4½	"	20	"
To Hudson	$5	"	30	"
To Albany	$7	"	36	"

When the *North River* was laid up for the winter after about six weeks of commercial operation, she had logged 1,600 miles and, according to Fulton, "after all accidents and delays, our boat cleared 5 percent on the capital expended . . . . Another boat which will cost $15,000 will also produce us $10,000 a year . . . . This is the only method which I know of gaining 50 to 75 percent."

Livingston, moving toward what Fulton believed to be their main chance, started to negotiate for a monopoly of steamboating on the Mississippi. He was successful in securing one only for the area at the mouth of the river, in the present state of Louisiana. In 1809 the partners sent Nicholas Roosevelt west to make a survey of the rivers from Pittsburgh to New Orleans. Roosevelt took his bride and made the trip their honeymoon on a specially constructed flatboat with a bridal suite of bedroom, dining room, and kitchen at the stern and a gay awning over the afterdeck to protect the bride from the southern sun. Despite the plush accommodations it was a rather rugged trip, with fears of Indians and pirates, snags and sand bars; but the honeymooners seemed to enjoy themselves and Roosevelt's report led the combine—of which he was now a member—to build a steamboat at Pittsburgh.

In designing the *New Orleans*, the first steamboat on western waters, Fulton made a grievous error. The vessel was similar to the *North River*, with a hull that was generally patterned after a deep-water ship rather than a Mississippi River keelboat. This served well for the deep channel of the Hudson, with its alternating tides, but it was not suitable for the shallow, shifting channel of the Mississippi, with its inexorable current.

The first steamboat voyage on the Mississippi, starting in September 1811, on the Ohio River at Pittsburgh, was perhaps the most exciting ever made. The Roosevelts and a gigantic Newfoundland dog named Tiger were the only passengers. Pittsburghers had great interest in the venture but not to the extent of risking their necks in a floating sawmill. The vessel was well manned with captain, engineer, six deck hands, cook, steward, and two maids. Mrs. Roosevelt was very pregnant at the time, and the women of Pittsburgh considered her husband a monster for taking a woman in her condition on such a dangerous journey.

The first three weeks of the voyage were uneventful. The boat chugged steadily past limitless forests, broken occasionally by clearings where settlers stared or cheered. Those aboard were, said Mrs. Roosevelt, "as jolly a set as ever floated on the Ohio." At Cincinnati a group of dignitaries came aboard, excited but sorrowful. "We see you for the last time," said the mayor. "Your boat may go *down* the river, but as to coming up, the very idea is absurd." The trip continued without incident to Louisville, where most of the town turned out in welcome, although some cowered in their quarters, convinced that the hissing steam and the shower of sparks were from the comet of 1811 that, they believed, had fallen in the Ohio.

Before the *New Orleans* lay the Falls of the Ohio, an old obstacle for keelboat men. Below Louisville the river dropped twenty-four feet in three miles over limestone ledges, forming a swift, tricky channel that the boat could not hope to negotiate except at high water. They waited for several days, during which the number of passengers was increased by 25 per cent when Mrs. Roosevelt quietly had her baby. Finally the water rose to provide an estimated clearance of five inches and, with her safety valve hissing from the pressure needed to provide steerage way in the rushing stream, the boat leaped into the white water. Everybody aboard but the dog and the baby hung on grimly as spray

FREDERICK WAY, JR.

When Fulton designed the New Orleans, *the first steamboat to sail on western waters, he made one serious error—the hull was too deep to navigate the shallow Mississippi safely. But the* New Orleans *set out from Pittsburgh in September 1811, braved earthquakes and sand bars, and finally reached the city for which she was named in January 1812. Above, a replica of the* New Orleans *leaves Pittsburgh during the centennial celebration in 1911.*

drenched the deck and the pilot conned the steersman with hand signals to bring the vessel to a quiet anchorage below the falls.

The relief aboard was short-lived. Something seemed to be the matter with the boat. It quivered and rolled and shook as it tugged at its moorings. But it was not the boat—it was the land and the river; the voyagers had run into the beginning of the earthquakes that wracked the Mississippi Valley in the fall of 1811.

The next day they proceeded down the still-shaking river, tensely silent. Mrs. Roosevelt recorded that "no one seemed disposed to talk, and when there was any conversation, it was carried on in whispers almost. Tiger who appeared, alone, to be aware of the earthquake while the vessel was in motion, prowled about, moaning and growling." At one point a canoeload of Chickasaw Indians came out from the bank, apparently to attack them, but the *New Orleans* easily outdistanced the savages. The red men, who called the steamboat *penelore*, or "fire canoe," connected it with the comet and the earthquakes that were devastating their domain. The night of the Indian approach Roosevelt was awakened by rushing feet on deck and ran out, sword in hand, to repel the savage boarders, only to find the forward cabin ablaze. Most of it was destroyed before the fire was put out.

As they rounded into the Mississippi the earth tremors continued. Wood parties had to wait for the land to stand still before they could cut. The pilot was bewildered, for the quakes had completely changed the channel. Snags that had been loosened from the bottom floated around them. One night they moored to an island that disappeared before they awoke. At New Madrid, where the effects of the earthquake were particularly severe, scores of homeless people pleaded piteously to be taken aboard, a request that Roosevelt refused because they had no food for such a multitude and the crowd would have swamped the boat.

Finally they outran the quake and proceeded downstream with little incident except for the happy termination of a love affair between the vessel's captain and Mrs. Roosevelt's maid. A minister was taken aboard at Natchez and the couple were united before the last short leg of the voyage. The boat laid over for some time at Natchez, and the *New Orleans* finally reached the city for which it was named on January 12, 1812, to complete the first steam voyage on the Mississippi.

While Roosevelt was building the *New Orleans*, Zadoc Cramer, publisher of the *The Navigator*, a pilot's guide to the western rivers, had commented: "There is now on foot a new method of navigating our western waters, particularly the Ohio and Mississippi rivers. This is with boats propelled by the power of steam . . . . It will be a novel sight, and as pleasing as novel, to see a huge boat working her way up the windings of the Ohio, without the appearance of sail, oar, pole, or any manual labor about her—moving within the secrets of her own wonderful mechanism and propelled by power undiscoverable!—This plan, if it succeeds, must open to view flattering prospects to an immense country, an interior of not less than two thousand miles of as fine a soil and climate as the world can produce, and to a people worthy of all the advantages that nature and art can give them . . . . The immensity of country we have yet to settle, the vast riches of the bowels of the earth, the unexampled advantage of our water courses, which wind without interruption for a thousand miles, the numerous sources of trade and wealth opening to the enterprising and industrious citizens, are reflections that must rouse the most dull and stupid."

These were fine and true sentiments—but the *New Orleans,* or any craft like her, would never open the "numerous sources of trade and wealth" of the midwestern valley. The mayor of Cincinnati—and many others—had been right; she could not hope to go upriver with her relatively deep draft and weak power. She was the first steamboat on the Mississippi but she was not a true Mississippi River boat. Nor were two that followed her, the *Vesuvius,* another Fulton-Livingston craft, and the little *Comet.* All three of these operated only on the short, smooth stretch of river between New Orleans and Natchez.

In 1807, while Fulton was building his steamboat in New York, a man named Henry Shreve was building a keelboat at Brownesville, Pennsylvania, on the bank of the Monongahela. This twenty-one-year-old farmer's son preferred adventuring on the river to plowing its bank. With a Creole crew he carried cargo picked up in Pittsburgh down the Ohio and up the Mississippi to St. Louis, to trade for furs he then brought home and shipped by wagon to Philadelphia. Bored with this after a few trips, he pushed his keelboat past St. Louis and headed for the Indian lead mines on the Galena River, far up the Mississippi. This was virtually virgin territory to keelboat men; the lead trade had always been in the hands of the British and French coming downstream from the Great Lakes in pirogues. Shreve's Creoles manhandled the boat through eight miles of the Des Moines rapids and another eighteen miles of white water at Rock Island before reaching a relatively placid stretch of the Mississippi; from there they poled to the Galena.

At first the Sac and the Fox who operated the mines were stand-offish. The downriver men and the boat were strange, and they sought to trade with practical things like nails, rope, pots and pans, spades and hoes—no whiskey; Shreve was a temperance man. He finally won the respect of the red men with his prowess as a runner; they held a feast, he gave them presents, and the savages uncovered their hoard of lead—sixty tons of it. Shreve built a flatboat and bought a pirogue and set out with his heavy cargo for New Orleans. Here he transshipped to a schooner and sailed the lead to Philadelphia for a profit of $11,000.

On Shreve's next trip downriver in a much larger keelboat he passed the *New Orleans* on her first voyage, waiting for the water to rise at Louisville. On a subsequent trip he met the *Vesuvius* stranded high and dry, pointing upstream. He was now convinced that steam and only steam would make the Mississippi Valley bloom with prosperity, but he also knew that the Fulton type of boat was not the answer. Yet when a man named Daniel French built a boat of this type on the Monongahela, Shreve jumped at the chance to command it. When he brought the *Enterprise* into New Orleans in December 1814 loaded with ordnance and ammunition, the city was seething with preparation for the last battle of the War of 1812. Andrew Jackson promptly commandeered both captain and vessel to run errands for the army. Shreve evacuated women and children upstream, ran supplies down to Fort St. Philip past British batteries, went back upstream to find several boatloads of delinquent Kentucky riflemen, and towed them to the battlefield.

After Jackson released him Shreve picked up freight and passengers and started upstream, very dubious as to whether he could reach Pittsburgh with the rather rickety deep-draft *Enterprise*. Luck was with him; the river was rising. By the time he passed Natchez it was out of its banks and flooding the lowlands. For much of the voyage Shreve left the river and steamed over fields, on which the water was calm. He reached Louisville and, finally, Pittsburgh and Brownesville, but the vessel was limping so badly that it could hardly make the last miles.

There was great excitement about the first upriver trip of a steamboat. In far-off Baltimore *Nile's Weekly Register* reported: "The Steamboat *Enterprise*, worked up from New Orleans to Bardstown, nearly 1,500 miles in 25 days . . . How do the rivers and canals of the old world dwindle into insignificance compared with this, and what a prospect of commerce is held out to the immense regions of the West by means of these boats! It is thought that the freight from New Orleans to Louisville . . . will soon be reduced to $3.50 per c." This was a 50 per cent reduction, and steam would make it possible—but not the *Enterprise* or any vessel that had yet been built. Shreve told Daniel French, the boat's builder, that only the flood had made the upriver trip possible. He proposed that French build another boat of a very different type, but the builder was proud of his first-born and paid no attention to Shreve's ideas. The latter realized that if the Mississippi River steamboat was to be born, he would have to father it.

The vessel that Shreve built at Wheeling and called the *Washington* bore little resemblance to the Fulton boats. It was, in fact, an overgrown keelboat with a low, almost flat-bottomed hull 136 feet long and 28 feet wide. There was no room in the hold of this shallow hull for machinery, so Shreve decked it over and put the engines and boilers on deck. Then he built a second deck above this to create the first two-decker and topped all with a pilothouse, above which rose two side-by-side smokestacks, inordinately high to provide a draft. It was an esthetic atrocity compared with the beautifully proportioned deep-water craft, but its perfect functionalism gave it a strange appeal. Of far more importance than its appearance was the fact that it rode *on* the water rather than *in* the water.

Daniel French had designed a high-pressure engine quite different from those used by Fulton; it was much lighter and had no condenser. Shreve improved on this by creating a flue-type boiler, and installed both the pistons and the boilers horizontally. He used two engines, one for each wheel, so that the vessel could turn around in its own length. Both engines weighed but a fraction of a single Watt-type power plant and consumed much less fuel.

A prototype of the Mississippi River steamboat, Henry Shreve's Washington was the first to be built with two decks and a broad, flat hull for shallow waters. She was also on her maiden voyage the first victim of a steamboat boiler explosion. But repairs were made and she completed the upriver trip to Louisville, a distance of 1,500 miles, in a record 24 days. The same voyage had usually taken keelboats four to six months.

The ladies of Wheeling embroidered a banner for the *Washington* with the legend "Our friends shall not take from us what we have wrested from our enemies." This referred to the freedom of the river, which was challenged by the Fulton-Livingston monopoly at New Orleans. With his banner proudly flying, Shreve left Wheeling on June 4, 1816, and headed for disaster. Below Marietta the *Washington* ran aground. While the crew was trying to haul her off with a kedge anchor, a boiler blew up, enveloping crew and passengers with clouds of scalding steam and hurling many of them, including Shreve, into the river. A contemporary account of America's first steamboat explosion said, "It was terrible beyond conception. Death and the most excruciating pain was spread around. . . . Six or eight were nearly skinned from head to feet, and others slightly scalded to the number of 17. In stripping off their clothes the skin peeled with them."

Leaving the freshly mounded graves on the bank of the Ohio, Shreve resumed his trip in a repaired boat. The *Washington* glided easily over the Falls of the Ohio and reached New Orleans without further incident. This, of course, was no great feat; flatboats and keelboats had been doing it for years. But the *Washington* promptly turned around and

Walk-in-the-Water, *the first steamboat on the Great Lakes, carried immigrants from Buffalo to Detroit.*

steamed *upriver* to Louisville, a distance of 1,500 miles, in twenty-four days, a voyage that took keelboats four to six months—and she did it without strain. On her second trip upriver, combating spring freshets, her time was 21 days.

Steam had arrived on the western rivers. The *Washington* was the prototype for all future Mississippi River steamboats. At a victory dinner after his first trip Shreve said, "The upstream trip from New Orleans will some time be made in as short a time as ten days. We have only just begun." He did not live to see the day when the voyage was made in little more than four days by boats of the type he had devised and which, by the 1850s, outweighed in tonnage all the vessels of the Atlantic seaboard and the Great Lakes combined.

Steamboats in the East

At one time or another, particularly when they were seeking monopolies from legislatures, all the steamboat pioneers discoursed on the service that they would render mankind. They projected themselves as noble, unselfish servants of humanity whose shining goal was the betterment of man's lot by moving him more rapidly from place to place. This made for fine, high-sounding speeches and eulogies but, sadly, most of the entrepreneurs really had a more crass objective: *money*. Steamboating became a most vicious dog-eat-dog competition in which some of the top dogs amassed fabulous fortunes.

Robert Fulton liked to say that "the freedom of the seas would be the happiness of the world," but together with global happiness he sought a 50- to 75-per cent profit. After the *North River*'s first successful season she was virtually rebuilt with a longer, wider hull and three cabins with fifty-six berths. She became "a floating palace, gay with ornamental paintings, gilding and polished wood." Fulton quickly built more boats, the *Car of Neptune* and the *Paragon* for the Hudson and the *Raritan* that steamed between Manhattan and New Brunswick, New Jersey.

These early river craft were profitable even though they carried so much machinery and wood to fuel it that there was little or no room for freight. But they had their problems. Sloop captains considered them unfair competition and skillfully caused their vessels to "accidentally" crash into paddle wheels. Breakdowns were frequent, and the steamboats had to resort to their clumsy sails. Passengers were alternately soaked with spray from the paddles and scorched by sparks from the stack, and there was much talk that noxious fumes would leak into the "birth" rooms (as it was then invariably spelled) as well as wither crops on the river banks. Many were uneasy about going "agin' nature" in one of these infernal machines. One Quaker matron asked her nephew, "John, will thee risk thy life in such a concern? I tell thee she is the most fearful wild fowl living, and thy father ought to restrain thee."

At first, as with the early automobiles, the *North River* and her sisters seemed to have been pets of the "in" people. On her early trips the passenger list of the first vessel contained—in addition to scads of Livingstons—the names of many of the valley's upper crust. "Mr. Jay" (presumably John) patronized the *North River*, as did "Mr. P. V. Rens-salaer & Lady, Mr. Peter Schuyler, General Gansevoort & Daughter & Lady & Servant, Mr. Morris, Mr. T. P. Grosvenor, Mr. [Aaron] Burr, Mr. G. E. Verplanck, Matthew Vassar, Mr. Brevoort & Lady." Other elite passengers represented a directory of Manhattan's downtown streets: Miss Duane, Mrs. Varick, Mr. Bleecker, Mr. Beekman and Mr. Pell all were of families whose names are still on New York lamp posts. Incidentally, one crosstown street in lower Manhattan is very appropriately named; early in his career Fulton developed the double-ended, steam-powered, paddle-wheel ferry boat and ran one line from New Jersey across the Hudson and another from Long Island across the East River to opposite ends of the same street. Obviously it was called Fulton Street.

The first non-Fulton steamboat, the *Phoenix*, was built in 1808 by John Stevens, Livingston's brother-in-law, at his estate in Hoboken, New Jersey. He planned to run from there to New Brunswick, but Livingston claimed that his monopoly extended to the high-water mark on the New Jersey bank of the Hudson; Stevens could not even legally use his own dock. The brothers-in-law argued the monopoly question on the same premise, though with less eloquence and erudition, that Daniel Webster would later use in the Supreme Court. Stevens claimed that a state could not restrict the use of a new invention beyond the protection given by a U.S. patent. Livingston replied, "Suppose a man to patent a new musical instrument. Would this give him the right to play in your garden and set your children a-dancing when you wished them to study? No, your garden is your own." Stevens thereupon wrote, "very sprightly and ingenious but by no means analogous. My garden is my exclusive property . . . . I can prevent any other man from entering it . . . . This is by no means the case with the states." Fulton had two patents, one on mechanical details that other boats did not infringe, the other on the use of paddle wheels. Since this principle went back to antiquity, the protection offered by the infant patent office was so shaky that the combine's lawyers never based a case on it.

Stevens did not push his claim. The *Phoenix* was taken around to Delaware Bay—the first steam voyage in the open ocean—and operated from Philadelphia to Trenton. With Fulton's *Raritan* running from New York to New Brunswick, and an assist from a stagecoach in the middle, this provided the first steamboat service on the country's most heavily traveled passenger route.

The merchants of upriver Albany were naturally unhappy about the new form of transportation being controlled at the other end of the river. They defied the monopoly, pooled their resources, and built two boats, the *Hope* and the *Perseverance*. The former inaugurated the dangerous but dramatic practice of steamboat racing by challenging the *North River*. The two speed demons churned up the river neck and neck at almost six miles per hour until they crashed into each other with much noise and little damage.

The Livingston-Fulton combine promptly sought an injunction against the upriver boats, the first of many that the New York courts would issue for them. Fulton indignantly wrote that he was engaged in

THE MARINERS MUSEUM, NEWPORT NEWS, VA.

The first steamboat to go to sea was the Phoenix, *built by John Stevens, a brother-in-law of Fulton's partner. When the Fulton-Livingston monopoly prevented the* Phoenix' *owners from using her on the Hudson, they sailed her down the New Jersey coast to the Delaware River.*

"an interesting lawsuit to crush 22 pirates who have clubbed their purses and copied my boats and have actually started my own Invention in opposition to me . . . . A more infamous and outrageous attack upon mental property has not disgraced America." The court ruled against the Albany merchants, and their boats were broken up.

The Livingston monopoly seems like a most odious example of vested interest grinding the public interest under an unfeeling heel. In fact, it was—but there was nothing unusual about it in those days. All state legislatures believed that they had not only the right but the responsibility to so encourage pioneers in science and new industry. Livingston's was neither the first nor the last such monopoly. Rumsey had secured the rights for the exclusive operation of steamboats in the states of Virginia, Maryland, and South Carolina. Fitch had a later monopoly in Virginia and others in New Jersey and New York. With his great political influence in his home state, Livingston had no difficulty in upsetting Fitch's grasp and securing a twenty-year monopoly nine years before he had a steamboat, which was subsequently extended. His was the most memorable because it led to the first Supreme Court clarification of Federal versus State law and later to the Interstate Commerce Commission and the Federal Communications Commission.

The case that finally came to the highest court in 1824 was between two contentious individuals named Thomas Gibbons and Aaron Ogden. By this time Robert Livingston and Robert Fulton were long dead, the former since 1813, the latter since 1815. Gibbons and Ogden started as partners, the latter running his *Atlanta* from New York to Elizabethtown Point, New Jersey, where passengers were transshipped to Gibbons' *Bellona* for New Brunswick. John Livingston, Robert's younger brother, had bought the rights to the New York end of this route under the monopoly and started suit. Ogden gave in, bought a license, and broke with Gibbons.

Gibbons was the more irascible and headstrong of the pair. He bought another little boat, the *Stoudinger*—affectionately called the *Mouse*—to run in opposition to Ogden's *Atlanta* on the New York end of the run, and hired Cornelius Vanderbilt to run it. Ogden promptly brought suit.

Vanderbilt, or "the Commodore" as he was later called, might be called a genius—any man who parlays a borrowed $100 into $100,000,000 might be called a genius. He borrowed the $100 from his mother, at the age of sixteen, to buy a sailboat that he operated by day as a ferry in New York bay and in which, at night, he ran supplies to New York's harbor defenses during the War of 1812. By the time Gibbons hired him he had a fleet of small sailboats. Convinced that steam was the coming thing, he sold them and went to work as a captain for a relative pittance. He claimed to be opposed to the monopolists in principle and, in fact, Vanderbilt always opposed monopolies, except those that he owned.

For six years Cornelius had fine fun playing cat and mouse with the monopolists, first on the *Mouse* and then with Gibbons' *Bellona*. At first he transshipped passengers in midstream to a licensed vessel, a sometimes dangerous but exciting operation. Then he became more bold and developed numerous tricks to thwart process servers while landing his passengers in Manhattan. The traveling public and friendly boatmen on the New York water front gleefully aided him in his war against the interests. He had a secret compartment constructed on the *Bellona* where he hid when constables came aboard. The monopoly swore out writs against the vessel's entire crew and boarded the vessel in the river. Water-front friends had warned Cornele and thus the deputies found neither captain nor crew aboard, merely a pretty girl passenger whom the skipper had taught to hold the wheel. When the law-men left, Cornele and the engineer crawled from their hiding place and the vessel resumed its journey.

Vanderbilt was finally caught, one Sunday morning, standing brazenly on the pier in New York. The sheriff hustled him to Albany and haled him before a judge to whom the Commodore blandly explained that the *Bellona* was, for that day only, rented to a licensee and was operating legally. When he was released he presented a bill for his time and expenses. As a final effort to rid himself of the pesky captain, Livingston offered him a job at a 250 per cent increase in salary. Cornele stuck to Gibbons.

The New York courts decided *Ogden v. Gibbons* in the former's favor. Gibbons retained Daniel Webster as head counsel to handle his appeal to the Supreme Court, of which John Marshall was Chief Justice. The case was far more significant than a dispute about ferry boats. It involved a basic interpretation of the U.S. Constitution. This controversial document rather vaguely gave Congress the right to "regulate commerce . . . among the several states," but it did not define commerce. Was transportation commerce? Webster argued that it was and that the New York legislative acts covering the monopoly were unconstitutional, for if a state could restrict the navigation of its waterways, all interstate commerce would return to the chaos that had reigned before the Constitution.

Ogden's lawyers learnedly defined commerce as "buying and selling" in opposition to the concept of "intercourse" propounded by Gibbons' counsel, an interpretation that obviously must include transportation by any means. Staunch Federalist Marshall agreed with Webster and handed down a decision that "so much of the several laws of the State of New York, as prohibits vessels licensed according to the laws of the

United States from navigating the waters of the State of New York by means of fire or steam, is repugnant to the said constitution, and void."

The decision in *Ogden v. Gibbons* has been called the "emancipation proclamation of American commerce." It led to later Federal regulation of railroads, the telegraph, the telephone, oil and gas pipelines, interstate trucks and busses, radio, television, and airplanes. As to Ogden and Gibbons, the former died bankrupt and the latter a millionaire.

Monopolies had retarded steamboat progress for seventeen years. The Supreme Court decision inspired a rush to the water by more and better boats from many builders. The *Albany*, launched in 1826, was typical of the new boats—212 feet long with a 65-inch cylinder with a 10-foot stroke to turn 24-foot paddle wheels which were 14 feet wide. Its speed was triple that of the *North River*, fifteen miles an hour.

The bigger boats were now triple-deckers. The English actress Fanny Kemble described the one on which she rode as having "three stories; the upper one is, as it were, a roofing or terrace on the head of the second, a very desirable station when the weather is neither too foul, nor too fair . . . . The second floor or deck, has the advantage of the ceiling above, and yet, the sides being completely open, it is airy and allows free sight of the shores on either hand. Chairs, stools, and benches, are the furniture of these two decks. The one below, or third floor downwards, in fact the ground floor being the one near the water, is a spacious room completely roofed and walled in where the passengers take their meals, and resort if the weather is unfavorable."

Night boats had private staterooms and separate general cabins for ladies and gentlemen with three tiers of curtained bunks ranging along their sides. Unless they could afford a stateroom, husbands and wives did not travel together. The larger men's cabin was also used as a dining saloon. After the novelty of the steamboats wore off they were patronized by more of the four million and fewer of the four hundred. Fulton found it necessary to post regulations for passengers whose manners and conduct did not befit his floating palaces. After telling prospective travelers at way stops to be at the dock two hours before the announced time of the boat's arrival because "the time at which the boat may arrive at the different places may vary a few hours" and that they could not bring their horses aboard because "if they were to move about too much, there is difficulty in steering the boat," the rules continued:

According to the order in which passengers pay their fare, they will be entitled to entry into the wash-room . . . . Cleanliness, neatness and order are necessary; it is therefore not permitted that any person shall smoke in the ladies cabin, or in the great cabin, under the penalty, first, of one dollar and a half, and a half a dollar for each half hour they offend against the rule; the money to be spent in wine for the company. It is not permitted for any person to lie down in a berth with their boots or shoes on, under penalty of one dollar and a half, and a half a dollar for every half hour they may offend against this rule . . . . Hitherto the cabin table has been much encumbered from gentlemen throwing their small garments upon it. This will not be permitted for the future . . . . In the ladies cabin, and in the great cabin, cards and all other games are to cease at 10 o'clock at night, that those persons who wish to sleep may not be disturbed.

In those more gracious days even a gentleman who wore his boots to bed and threw his small clothes on the table had respect amounting to reverence for the weaker sex. Of the treatment of women on the boats a British traveler wrote, "All must give way to them. No man is admitted into the dining saloon until all the ladies are seated at the table, when they rush in pellmell. After that should a lady require either, the chair is, without ceremony, taken from under you and the plate from before you. No male epicure will here be able to gratify his appetite with tid bits. Should he make an attempt to do so it will be futile. A lady, sir! is considered sufficient . . . . The Americans pride themselves on their courtesy to women and consider it a sign of high civilization; and they are no doubt right, but it seemed to me to be carried to

After the Supreme Court broke the power of the Fulton-Livingston monopoly, other builders rushed their boats to the water. The Long Island Sound steamboat Chancellor Livingston, launched in 1827, was typical of the new breed.

an extreme; that women were treated like petted children and that they must often feel rather annoyed than pleased by the excessive politeness and consideration shown them. At the same time it is an honor of this country that an unprotected woman of any age may travel through its length and breadth . . . without insult or the slightest attempt to take advantage of her youth or inexperience."

From the earliest days of the night boats there were some females who sought a different kind of consideration. As one traveler noted: "A man was always sure to find a pleasant lady companion aboard who was not loath to share his food, drink and bed, if he so desired it; and while the officers were given orders to keep a weather eye out for these women, who made it a business to travel nightly on these boats, making themselves a very substantial amount of money on some trips, they considered it unwise and in some cases a poor policy to interfere or make a scene if the lady's companion happened to be of a well known family, or a regular well tipping passenger of the line. After all, these women were high class madames, not to be had for the asking, catering to those who were good spenders or known to be wealthy and so in most cases were considered to be a necessary evil which had to be endured."

One concession to women, and timid souls, was the safety barge. Boilers exploded with sufficient frequency, roasting passengers with scalding steam, to keep alive the feeling that steamboats were not entirely safe. The safety, or ladies', barges were engineless craft towed behind steamers, whose owners advertised as follows: "Why sleep on the edge of a volcano? Passengers on board the Safety Barges will not be in the least exposed to any accident by reason of the fire or steam on board the steamboats. The noise of the machinery, the trembling of the boat, the heat from the furnace, boilers, and kitchen, and everything which may be considered unpleasant on board a steamboat are entirely avoided."

The first such barges, the *Lady Clinton* and the *Lady Van Rensselaer*, were ornate affairs as elegant as the steamboats, with private rooms, a luxuriously furnished cabin and dining saloon, promenades, and a gold-braided captain to sit at the head of the table. As boilers became more rugged and speed more important the barges' prestige dropped. Instead of carrying crinolined females they bore horses for New York's streetcar lines and calves and lambs to the slaughterhouses, and their bleating and baaing disturbed the repose of the few passengers who were left in the once-handsome saloons. Some barges ended up as hay or ice boats, while others had a happier fate as the carriers of Sunday School picnics. Many a curvesome Hawaiian pagan was covered by a muu-muu with funds raised by a jolly trip on a safety barge to the picnic grounds at Mount Beacon.

At least one safety barge was still in use in the early years of the twentieth century, a so-called floating hospital that, in the summer months, was used to take mothers and babies from New York's tenements for rides on the cool waters of the rivers and bay, an early welfare measure that brightened the lives of slum dwellers.

The new steamers that hit the Hudson after the monopoly was broken arrived just in time to participate in the great event that would make that stream by far the most import in the East—the opening of the Erie Canal. At 10 A.M. on October 26, 1825, a battery of cannon five hundred miles long began to thunder as the barge *Seneca Chief* moved from Lake Erie into the western end of the "Hellespont of the West." Gunners in Rochester, Syracuse, Oneida, Utica, Schenectady, Troy, and other canal-side towns that would soon become impressive manufacturing cities pulled their lanyards when they heard a boom from the west

THE MARINERS MUSEUM, NEWPORT NEWS, VA.

Advertised as free from vibration, noise, smells, and boiler explosions, the safety barge Lady Clinton had all the luxuries of the steamboat but none of the dangers. Barges of this type, which were towed behind steamboats, enjoyed a brief popularity, but as boilers became more rugged, they fell from favor, and in later years were relegated to carrying animals to slaughterhouses.

to pass the word to cannoneers in the Hudson Valley towns. In eighty-one minutes New York City had the news that the first canal boats were coming.

Past cheering crowds and thundering cannon four gaily painted, pennant-bedecked canal boats floated slowly along the man-made water route toward Albany bearing, in addition to more distinguished passengers, two Seneca Indian boys, a black bear, two eagles, two wolves, four raccoons, a fawn, and a fox. Their trip was uneventful except for the two amateur gunners at Weedsport who excitedly rammed a second charge into their gun and were blown to bits as the flotilla passed.

Next morning the barges were lowered by the lock to the surface of the Hudson and each was taken in tow by a steamboat. The *Chancellor Livingston*, on which Fulton had been working when he died, led the parade towing the *Seneca Chief*. The little *Porpoise*, "spouting like a dolphin," raced sportively back and forth along the colorful column. As night fell the passengers feasted on "sumptuous fare" and imported wines, and the *Chancellor Livingston* hurled colorful rockets aloft to proclaim the coming of the vessels from the west. At midnight the marine parade paused at West Point to receive a twenty-four-gun salute

In 1825 steamboats towed canal boats down the Hudson to New York to celebrate the opening of the Erie Canal.

and take the cadet band aboard the *Chancellor Livingston*, then steamed toward the dawn and the ringing bells, tooting whistles, and booming cannon of New York City. One passenger wrote that "after Alexander of Macedon had carried his arms into India he did not descend the Indus with greater triumph or make a prouder display."

The steamer *Washington*, carrying the New York City dignitaries, met the cavalcade off present-day Greenwich Village, turned and escorted it toward the lower bay. By now there were fourteen steamers in the procession that plowed to Sandy Hook, where the escort vessels formed a three-mile circle around the barges as New York's Governor De Witt Clinton poured Lake Erie water from bright-green kegs with gilded hoops into the ocean brine, saving enough to send to the Marquis de Lafayette in an American-made bottle encased in a box constructed by Duncan Phyfe. Dr. Samuel Mitchell, the speaker of the day, diluted the lower bay with the contents of vials of water from the rivers of the world—the Elbe, the Nile, the Ganges, the Amazon, the Orinoco, the Neva, the Seine, and the Thames were represented as "a symbol of our commercial intercourse with all ports of the world."

Then everybody went back to the Battery for a parade up Broadway, the theme of which was the union of the waters. The needleworkers cleverly combined their trade with the theme of a banner displaying Adam and Eve with twin slogans—"United We Are" and "I was naked and ye clothed me." On a horse-drawn float the printers' guild operated a gilded press that produced broadsides which were tossed to the crowd by a resurrected Benjamin Franklin seated in the seer's old armchair. After a glance at these, many mothers snatched them from the hands of teen-aged daughters. There was a little too much nakedness and sex in this celebration of the union of the waters to please the straight-laced. The broadsides proclaimed:

> 'Tis done! the monarch of the briny tide
> Whose giant arm encircles earth
> To virgin Erie is allied
> A bright-eyed nymph of mountain birth
>
> Today the *Sire of Ocean* takes
> A sylvan maiden to his arms
> The Goddess of the crystal lakes
> In all her native charms
>
> She comes attended by a sparkling train;
> The Naiads of the West her nuptials grace
> She meets the sceptred father of the main
> And in his heaving bosom hides her virgin face.

Although the Hudson was the cradle of steamboating, the smoking "fire sloops" were not long confined to that stream. In fact, a slim volume has been written to prove that the Connecticut River was the *real* birthplace of the steamboat because of a Yankee named Samuel Morey who defied the wrath of the Puritan Lord and chugged down that stream in a home-made steamboat on a Sunday morning in 1790; but Morey's boat was little more than a model, with no room for anything but him and the engine. The first practical steamboats started to appear on most of the other eastern rivers in the teen years of the nineteenth century. Most were locally and crudely built, and some had to be adapted to special conditions. On Florida's rivers, for instance, side-wheelers would not do; only stern-wheelers could hope to push their way through the masses of floating water hyacinths that clogged the streams. Here the crew had to be alert to slay snakes that slithered from the Spanish moss on the overhanging trees to the deck of the boat and to shoot alligators before they tangled with the paddle wheel. When this happened usually neither the saurian nor the wheel survived the encounter, although until quite recently a mammoth blind alligator, Oscar, who had been chopped from the paddle wheel of the little *William Howard*, was on display in a pen as a tourist attraction at Silver Springs.

Not only were boats adapted to rivers, but rivers were adapted to boats, usually by means of short canals with locks to lift or lower vessels around falls or rapids. There was great interest in opening the Connecticut River all the way to Barnet, Vermont. When a canal was built at Bellows Falls, an enterprising Connecticut Yankee, Blanchard by name, built a little stern-wheeler, the *Barnet*, at Hartford which would draw but two feet fully loaded. She proudly sailed up to Bellows Falls, there was a big banquet and then everybody turned out to watch the *Barnet* come through the canal. Then there was a great argument. Some said the boat was too wide for the canal, others that the canal was too narrow for the boat. Blanchard had, in effect, built his boat in the cellar—it could not get through the canal. He sailed back down to Hartford; apparently nobody thought of hauling it through the streets of the town with oxen as was done with a later craft.

Protected bodies of salt water that were calm enough for river boats were part of the river-road system of the east coast. Georgia's rivers empty into the sea behind a chain of protective islands, those of North Carolina into Pamlico and Albemarle sounds. Robert Fulton had plans for a north-south chain of steamboat routes from New England to Georgia, with stagecoach hops where there were no protected waterways. The two most important bodies of salt water that united the river systems were Chesapeake Bay, which receives the rivers of Maryland and Virginia, and Long Island Sound, into which empty those of Rhode Island and Connecticut.

Steam appeared on the Chesapeake in 1813 when the little Baltimore-built *Chesapeake* huffed and puffed from her home port down the Patapsco, across the head of the bay, and up the Elk to Frenchtown, whence a short stagecoach hop brought the traveler to the head of Delaware Bay and another steamboat trip to Philadelphia. Soon the *Chesapeake* was joined by the little *Eagle*. Only 110 feet long, the *Eagle* boasted a "great" cabin, but no pilothouse. She was steered by a stern tiller and her captain in his stove-pipe hat stood atop one of the paddle boxes and bellowed orders to the quartermaster or jumped down to stamp on the deck to signal the engineer. Still, the tiny craft did not hesitate to go down the bay and up the James to Richmond or all the way to Norfolk at the bay's mouth.

Between intercity trips the bay boats ran excursions. One poetic copywriter described the delights of steaming to Havre de Grace and Port Deposit on the *Susquehanna* as follows: "This trip is offered to

In Florida only stern-wheelers could push through the massive debris that clogged the streams. Crews had to be alert for such hazards as snakes dropping from overhanging trees and alligators that attacked the paddle wheels.

the public for recreation, pleasure and convenience. In passing up the river the novelist will be delighted with the various scenes of nature and art: the ingenious limner will find employment for his pencil, the historian for his pen, and the philosopher subjects for contemplation."

Steam came to Long Island Sound in 1815 when Robert Fulton's *Fulton* wheezed to New Haven in eleven hours—poor time, for which the *Fulton*'s engineer apologized by explaining that New York City's wood did not make good steam. Also, the first vessel probably waited for the tides before traversing the tricky strip of water between Ward's Island and Manhattan that the Dutch had named Hell Gate and which Washington Irving described as "being at the best of times a very violent and impetuous current . . . boiling in whirlpools; brawling and fretting in ripples; raging and roaring in rapids and breakers; and, in short, indulging in all kinds of wrong-headed paroxysms. . . . It may be compared to a quarrelsome toper, who is a peaceful fellow enough when he has no liquor at all [i.e., at low tide] or when he has a skinful [at high tide], but who, when half seas over, plays the very devil."

The New York steamboats were soon denied entry into Connecticut ports in retaliation to the monopoly under which Connecticut vessels were restricted in New York waters. The skipper of the Fulton-Livingston-owned *Firefly* then gathered his courage and braved the briny deep beyond the eastern end of protective Long Island, rounded Cape Judith at the foot of Narragansett Bay and steamed up to Providence, Rhode Island. "P'int Judy," frequently fog-bound, has as bad a reputation as any cape on the coast, with tides pouring in from three directions to make a "mad nautical merry-go-round." Block Island, off the point, was long called Graveyard Island for good reason. Even after the giants of the sound made their appearance, the dining saloons of boats out of Narragansett Bay were sparsely patronized as passengers groaned in their berths with *mal de mer*.

Sailing-packet owners sought protection for their New England-New York trade from the Rhode Island legislature in the form of a toll on steamship passengers. They did not succeed in this, but they carried the fight to the newcomers by ramming their bowsprits into paddle wheels whenever the occasion presented itself. By the 1820s larger boats were making the New York-Providence run from dawn to dusk or vice versa. A short stagecoach ride placed the traveler in Boston in a little over 20 hours at a cost of about $15, a trip that might have consumed a week and cost close to $100 before the steamboat.

Many of the contemporary descriptions of early steamboat travel were written by wide-eyed foreigners, for there was nothing like the American river boats in their native lands. We owe much of our detailed knowledge of early steamboats to the meticulous descriptions and sketches of a visiting French engineer who wrote a *Memoire sur les Bateaux à Vapour des Etats-Unis*. Most of the European visitors were properly, if sometimes reluctantly, impressed with this new Yankee way to travel. An exception was Charles Dickens, who found nothing good on his visit to his country's rebellious offspring. However, even the sarcasm of England's great novelist is worth quoting. He first journeyed down the Connecticut from Hartford on a small craft that he described in this way:

It certainly was not called a steamboat without reason: I omitted to ask the question, but I should think it must have been half a pony power. Mr. Paap, the celebrated dwarf, might have lived and died happily in the cabin, which was fitted with common sash windows, like an ordinary dwelling house. The win-

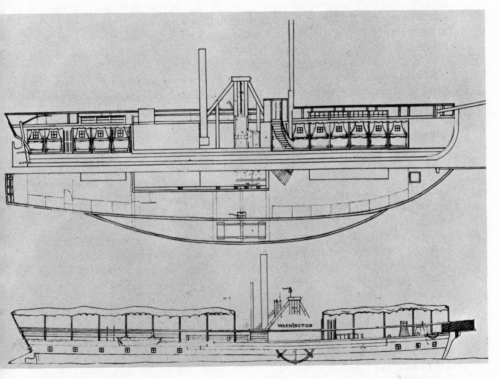

Europeans, who had no steamboats of their own, learned of the new Yankee ways of traveling from people who visited the United States. These sketches, made by French engineer Jean Baptiste Marestier in 1818-19, were published by the Royal Press in Paris. The upper sketch is the Robert Fulton. *The lower, labeled "Washington," is probably Shreve's first vessel of that name.*

dows had bright red curtains, too, hung on slack strings across the lower panes; so that it looked like the parlor of a Lilliputian public-house, which had got afloat in a flood or some other water accident and was drifting nobody knew where. But even in this chamber there was a rocking chair.

I am afraid to tell how many feet short this vessel was, or how many feet narrow; to apply the words length and width to such measurements would be a contradiction in terms. But I may state we all kept the middle of the deck, lest the boat should unexpectedly tip over, and that the machinery, by some surprising process of condensation worked between it and the keel; the whole forming a warm sandwich, about three feet thick.

Dickens then took a larger vessel down Long Island Sound to New York, and his narrative continues:

To an English eye it was infinitely less like a steamboat than a huge floating bath. I could hardly persuade myself, indeed, but that the bathing establishment off Westminster Bridge, which I had left a baby, had not suddenly grown up to enormous size; run away from home; and set up in foreign parts as a steamer. Being in America, too, which our vagabonds do so particularly favor, it seemed the more probable.

The great difference in appearance between these packets and ours is that there is so much of them out of water, the maindeck being enclosed on all sides, and filled with casks and goods, like any second or third floor in a stack of warehouses, and the promenade or hurricane deck being a-top of that again. A part of the machinery is always above this deck; where the connecting-rod, in a strong and lofty frame, is seen working away like an iron top-sawyer.

There is seldom any mast or tackle; nothing aloft but two black chimneys. The man at the helm is shut up in a little house in the fore part of the boat (the wheel being connected with the rudder by iron chains, working the whole length of the deck); and the passengers, unless the weather be very fine indeed, usually congregate below. Directly you have left the wharf, all the life, and stir, and bustle of the packet ceases. You wonder for a long time how she goes on, for there seems nobody in charge of her; and when another of these dull machines comes splashing by, you feel quite indignant with it, as a sullen, cumbrous, ungraceful, unshiplike leviathan; quite forgetting that the vessel you are aboard of is its very counterpart.

There is a clerk's office on the lower deck, where you pay your fare; a ladies' cabin; baggage and storage rooms; engineer's room; and in short a variety of perplexities which render the discovery of the gentlemen's cabin a matter of some difficulty. It often occupies the whole length of the boat (as it did in this case) and has three or four tiers of berths on each side. When I first descended into the cabin of *Newyork* it looked, in my unaccustomed eyes, about as long as the Burlington Arcade.

Dickens finally found a steamboat of which he fully approved: a Canadian-owned vessel on the Great Lakes that flew the flag of the Empire.

By 1830 there were five steamboat lines on the Hudson and the cutthroat competition that would last for more than 20 years had started. During the monopoly days the *North River*'s original fare of $7.00 to Albany had come down only to $5.00. It soon tumbled to $1.50, then, during rate wars, to $1.00, 50¢, and 25¢, and finally, nothing. The free ride did not, of course, include meals and, particularly, drinks. Early accounts of the steamboats give the impression that the passengers were largely lushes—the bar was the most popular place on the ship. As the fare went down, the price of whiskey went up, in some cases to as much as an unheard-of 20¢ a drink.

A steamboat operator could almost break even on the proceeds of the bar and dining saloon, even at 50¢ for a five-course dinner. The direct cost of labor and wood for a trip between New York and Albany was about $200. Boats that carried two to three hundred passengers could make 100 per cent profit at the normal fare of $1.50. Annual profits of 70 per cent were not unusual, and one line paid a dividend of 6 per cent a *month*.

After the first flurry of rate cutting most of the well-established lines formed an association, led by the Stevens family, who had bought out the Livingston interests; old John Stevens, now playing with trains in Hoboken, must have seen ironic justice in his house flag replacing that which had forced his *Phoenix* off the river. The association stabilized fares until Cornelius Vanderbilt appeared on the river and developed a scheme for gouging the interests that would become standard practice.

Cornele had bought out Gibbons and made himself so obnoxious to John Livingston by rate cutting on the New Brunswick run that the latter bribed him to go away from the Raritan. Vanderbilt shifted to the New York-Albany route and started the People's Line. The name indicated that he was the champion of the common man against the ubiquitous "interests" which demanded the exorbitant amount of $1.50 to take him to Albany; Vanderbilt asked only 50¢. The association had eliminated some rivals by "purchase, or threats, or running into them," but the Commodore was made of sterner stuff. They finally paid him $100,000 plus $5,000 a year to get off the river. Cornele went around to Long Island Sound.

The association soon learned the axiom that blackmail once paid never ceases as others stepped into Vanderbilt's shoes. In 1839 the New York *Herald* ran an exposé in which they interviewed several ex-steamboat owners "who walk about the streets with their hands in their breeches pockets, and who are each receiving from $5,000 to $10,000 annually for staying in the city doing nothing; and yet they make more money being idle than they could by laboring hard all year round."

Vanderbilt's tactics were, by the standards of the day, fair competition. One who went farther in bilking the established operators was "Deacon" Daniel Drew, a rather slimy, very wily operator who later gained an unsavory reputation as the rigger of the Erie Railroad stock fraud and the perpetrator of the gold panic. Drew had started as a cattle drover and is said to have originated the practice of "watering" stock—originally this meant cattle, not securities. Drew used to give his herds all the salt they wanted to lick and deprive them of water until just before sale time. Then he let them drink to the bursting point and quickly sold them by weight.

Drew went into steamboating with one vessel, took over the name People's Line, and joined the association. Soon he put another boat on the river under an assumed name, started a new rate war, and told his associates that he "might" be able to buy out the annoying independent, but it would cost a substantial sum. When the association agreed he left the directors' meeting, walked around the block, and returned to announce that he had made a deal. He then pocketed the bribe, "bought" the boat from its nonexistent owner, and ran it as an association boat.

The independents usually posed as the unselfish friends of the public, whose support they sought in combating villainous "big business," as represented by the association. They made righteous and piteous pleas in the press such as this:

MONOPOLIES AND PERSECUTION

Are the people aware of the disgraceful manner in which the Hudson River monopoly . . . persecutes the steamboat "*Napoleon*" and her owners especially, by hiring the most abandoned and profligate wretches to run against her for passengers, and making use of the most disgraceful language to prevent passengers from going on board of her? They are guilty of the foulest lies and assertions, for they . . . asserted that the Old Line . . . had bought the *Napoleon;* that is to say she had become a Judas and betrayed the people.

We solemnly declare that it is false, and that no such crusaders can ever by their power, threats or money induce us to abandon our honest and honorable pursuits in which we are engaged. We had been bred, we thought, on the free waters of the United States, but if this is the manner in which the people are to be driven from their lawful and honorable pursuits, away then with our boasted freedom and let us sink back into monarchy.

The owners of the *Napoleon* may have been justified in their contention that their vessel was a special target of the association boats. One morning as she was passing the slip at which the *De Witt Clinton* was waiting, that vessel's mooring lines were suddenly let go and, under a full head of steam, she shot into the river and crashed into the *Napoleon,* whose captain expressed his displeasure with several pistol shots aimed, ineffectually, at the captain of the *Clinton.*

The "profligate wretches" mentioned in the advertisement for the *Napoleon* were runners whom all lines employed to lure passengers to their respective boats. These worthies roamed the water front crying the merits of their respective employer's craft. Each proclaimed that his boat was the fastest, the safest, the most luxurious, and the most prompt. The rival boat captain was a racing fiend who cared nought for the safety of his passengers; his boat had a high-pressure engine, and all knew how dangerous they were. The competitor also had iron boilers, whereas the runner's had safe boilers of copper. (If it did not, the iron boilers were probably copper-painted.) Little old ladies were sometimes assured that the runner's boat had *no* boilers. Any luggage-laden traveler who approached the water front found his carpetbag snatched from his hand as he was hustled aboard his captor's boat, hypnotized by the runner's panegyric. The carpetbag did not always get aboard, but it mattered not so long as the passenger did.

Steamboat passengers who were carried free or for a pittance were not treated like VIPs. As many as could be carried were jammed aboard to gasp and swelter in fetid cabins and scramble and jostle for food. A mayor of New York, after a political trip to the state's capital, reported that "our boat had three or four hundred passengers and such a ragtag and

LIGHTHOUSE GALLERY, SHELBURNE MUSEUM, SHELBURNE, VT.

For more than 60 years the twin brothers James and John Bard painted the steamboats on the Hudson River and Long Island Sound. The pictures were prized for their accuracy and detail, but their most striking characteristic was the people, who always looked the same.

bobtail I never saw on board a North River steamboat." Another conservative condemned transportation progress by writing, "The rich and the poor, the educated and the ignorant, the polite and the vulgar, all herd together in this modern improvement in travelling . . . . Steam so useful in many respects, interferes with the comfort of travelling, destroys every salutary distinction in society, and overturns with its whirligig power the once rational, gentlemanly and safe mode of getting along on a journey." The only thing about which there were no complaints was the food, at least the quantity thereof. A typical steamboat breakfast included beefsteak, chicken fricassee, all the pancakes one could eat, and, for finicky feeders, something called "Baptized Toast," which, at home, was milk toast.

Passengers for way points that were advertised as stops could not expect the vessel actually to halt to discharge them. With their luggage they were placed in a small boat towed beside the steamer. The large vessel then swerved toward shore and slackened the towline, and the impetus sent the small boat toward the landing place. In a matter of seconds debarking passengers jumped ashore as embarking passengers took their place while more and more towline was paid out from the moving steamer. When all the line was out, ready or not, the small boat was yanked away from the pier and bounced through the steamer's wake as deck hands reeled their load of human fish in with a windlass.

Things were very different when steamboats honored a distinguished visitor to the valley. All important foreigners were taken for a ride on a steamboat as soon as they reached New York, and a steamboat escort was the equivalent of today's ticker-tape parade. The old Marquis de Lafayette was so honored when the *James Kent* picked him up after a ball at Castle Garden, together with a throng of young female gatecrashers who would not get off the boat until more interesting military men were offered by a stop at West Point. Jenny Lind, the Swedish Nightingale, was taken from that same Castle Garden on the *Reindeer* to warble in Albany. A more solemn, ceremonious use of the steamboat was the transportation of General Richard Montgomery's body from Quebec forty-three years after he had died attacking that stronghold during the Revolution. With the casket, "canopied with crepe and crowned with plumes," on her foredeck the *Richmond* stopped her engines to float past "Montgomery Palace" on the Hudson's bank where the general's aged widow watched with outward calm until the paddle wheels started to revolve again. Then she fainted.

A distinct class of boatmen on the Hudson were the inhabitants of the floating towns of canal barges that were towed up and down the river, moving almost imperceptibly in groups of up to 60. These were the floating homes of their owners, who were derisively called "shanty-boaters." The derision was probably based on the envy of many who led better-ordered but more humdrum lives ashore. These river men were a different breed than their brethren on western flatboats and keelboats. Almost all were family men and the barges housed innumerable children and were overrun with pets.

The shanty boat was so named because its living quarters consisted of a little bungalow erected on the stern deck. Few of these were shanties. They glistened with spotless paint set off with bright shutters and were trimmed with perky flowers, usually geraniums, in boxes at their windows. Awnings on the roof or deck shaded hammocks and swings for the children, who romped about the barges and jumped from deck to deck with an abandon that landlubbers viewed aghast. Almost all boats had a musical instrument aboard and someone who could play it. They floated down the stream to lively strains from concertinas, fiddles, guitars, banjos, and mandolins. Except for loading at one end and unloading at the other there was little work on a barge. It was a lazy life with much time for contemplation of nature and man's mad race to subdue it. When the ice started to form upriver the barges moored somewhere along the bank for the winter and the kids went reluctantly to school.

The shanty boats lasted well into the twentieth century. This writer remembers delivering grocery orders, as a fourteen-year-old in 1920, to three shanty boats moored to the bank of the Hudson at New York on Christmas Eve. I rode the load down to the river bank on a sleigh and carried the boxes across the slippery, swaying, cleated plank that gave the barge families access to the metropolis. Each tiny bungalow had a candle-lit Christmas tree making a gay show behind lamp-lit windows. I also recall that the shanty-boaters tipped better than most of the dwellers in the expensive apartments that reared above the stream on swank Riverside Drive. If the male shanty-boater was about he might offer a wee drop of whiskey to a hard-working lad on a cold night, a practice which a parent could not condone; but it was well meant.

Most of the towboats of the early days were steamboats that had been outmoded for passenger carrying. The lives of the first generation of river boats were usually very short, perhaps four or five years; they were not rugged vessels. This completely changed in about the 1840s, and some of the boats built from that time on lasted half a century or more. The *Norwich*, which was built as a towboat, holds the record for longevity. For eighty-seven years it plowed up and down the Hudson—from 1836 until 1923. Nobody knows how long the first steamboat lasted; there is no record of the *North River* after the early teen years. One story has it that she was sent to the Cape Fear River in North Carolina, another that she was broken up and her ribs used to build a wharf in Jersey City, a third that she sank off Poughkeepsie. Since Robert Fulton

Built in 1845 for use on Long Island Sound, the Naushon had a varied
career. After losing money on the Sound she was purchased by the New
York Herald. Renamed the Newsboy, she ferried reporters to meet in-

coming Atlantic steamers at Sandy Hook and rushed back with ships' news. Later she became a Coney Island excursion boat and, finally, a Civil War troop carrier.

was a thrifty soul a likely explanation is that he cannibalized her for material for later vessels.

By 1840, when there were over a hundred steam-powered packets on the Hudson, the new vessels had advanced to almost their ultimate in size, power and speed, and anthracite coal had replaced wood for fuel. The *Isaac Newton* was typical of that era; it was 345 feet long and had a cylinder 8½ feet in diameter with a 12-foot stroke that spun paddle wheels that were 39 feet high—taller than a three-story house. They had a 4-foot dip that gave her a speed of about twenty miles per hour. The *Isaac Newton*, by the way, was not named for the natural philosopher who observed the downward tendency of falling apples; that Isaac Newton had a namesake in New York who built nearly a hundred steamboats, steamships and barges and who named one of them after himself.

The boats of the 1840s and 1850s were approaching the "floating palaces" that would come later. Their runners emphasized elegance, service, sumptuous fare, and special features much as airlines now extol their roomy reclining chairs, attentive stewardesses, champagne dinners, and in-flight movies. The mid-nineteenth-century counterpart of the latter was the steam calliope that some boats sported to waft the strains of "The Belle of the Mohawk Vale" and "Way Down Upon the Swanee

THE MARINERS MUSEUM, NEWPORT NEWS, VA.

In the 1840s the steamboat Isaac Newton *was advertised as "the largest in the new or old world." She was 345 feet long and had paddle wheels 39 feet high—taller than a three-story house.*

River" through the Hudson hills—and deafen the passengers. These did not last long because they used too much steam, and the boat had to slow down when the calliope player sat down at the steam Steinway, which recalls the story that Abraham Lincoln used to tell about a little steamboat with a whistle so big that when she blew it the boat stopped.

Steam could not be wasted for entertainment—speed was of the essence. In the days when there was no telegraph or telephone and before the through railroad, a steamboat that was even a few minutes faster than its competition could command the patronage of time-conscious business travelers, and even passengers who had no reason to be in a hurry preferred to ride on a "queen of the river." Steamboat racing, which had started 'way back with the *Hope* and the *North River*, became more intense, and more dangerous, with the passing years. When a new boat met a former champion on the river, or left at the same time, a scratch speed trial was likely during which an engineer might seek to augment his vessel's pace by hanging a flatiron on the safety valve and plugging up the steam gauge after the pressure blew the mercury through the top.

One famous staged speed contest was between Cornele's new *Commodore Vanderbilt* and the speed queen *Oregon*, owned by the colorful "Liveoak" George Law. Vanderbilt proclaimed, "Now, I say, I will run the *C. Vanderbilt*, untried as she is, against any boat afloat to any place they name where there is sufficient water to float her, for any sum from $1,000 to $100,000. This challenge is open until Saturday next, when I propose trying my boat." Liveoak accepted the challenge for a $1,000 bet, and a race was arranged from Manhattan's Battery upriver to Sing Sing and return. On the day before the race all unnecessary bric-a-brac was removed from both vessels to cut weight, the hulls were cleaned to reduce friction, and the bilges were pumped and, on the *Oregon*, sponged to remove the last drop of water.

The boats swept upstream for thirty miles bow to bow past Yonkers, Dobbs Ferry, and Tarrytown as though they were bolted together. Then the Vanderbilt's engineer, probably with a weighted safety valve, increased the speed of her paddle wheels to 20 revolutions a minute, and she nosed ahead until the *Oregon* put out $21\frac{1}{2}$ turns and closed the gap. As they jockeyed for the turn at Sing Sing, the *Vanderbilt* crashed into the *Oregon*'s side, crumpling her starboard wheel housing without retarding her speed. At the turn the excited Commodore started to give orders in conflict with those of his pilot. Confused by wildly ringing bells in the engine room, the engineer stopped the engines and the *Oregon* swept by before her rival could regain momentum.

In his concern for weight, Liveoak had limited the *Oregon*'s coal supply, and he had miscalculated; the coal ran out at Yonkers. To maintain his vessel's lead, Law ordered that first the furniture and then the wainscoating be fed to the flames under the boilers. The *Vanderbilt* slowly started to close the gap but the *Oregon* reached the finish line in front before she ran out of woodwork. It cost Liveoak a great deal more than $1,000 to put his boat back in shape—but he beat Vanderbilt. "It was a great race," wrote New York's mayor, "seventy-five miles in three hours and fifteen minutes—a rate of speed which would carry a vessel to Liverpool in five or six days." The victory made Liveoak so cocky that he challenged the *Hendrick Hudson* to the same race for the same stake "with only one wheel." This race was never run.

Another Vanderbilt boat, the *Lexington*, was beaten by the *Richmond* in a race that became part of the steamboating lore of Long Island Sound, principally because of the disastrous end of the *Lexington* a short time later. The contest started at Stonington, Connecticut, with Cornele's brother Jake—"whose reputation for daring deeds with a steamboat has been equalled by few"—in command of the *Lexington*. The *Richmond* got the jump on her rival in pulling away from the pier and took a short lead. The rest of the contest was thus described by a reporter aboard the *Richmond*:

THE MARINERS MUSEUM, NEWPORT NEWS, VA.

The New York water front, 1848. In that year United States steam tonnage was 427,891, compared with Great Britain's 168,078. Most of the American tonnage was in "enrolled" vessels that traveled the home and inland waters.

For ten or a dozen miles down the Sound there was no perceptible change in the relative position of the boats. Then dense clouds of smoke poured from the *Lexington,* a sheet of flame shot up from her stack, her wheels turned swifter, and a cheer burst from the passengers as they realized the gap between them and the *Richmond* was closing. It was an anxious moment on board the *Richmond* for the *Lexington* was gaining fast. Where was Captain Townsend? There was no reply. He was not to be found. But the movements on board *Lexington* had not escaped his eye. The moment that the boat left Stonington men had been set picking out the most resinous wood and piling it for immediate use. The engineer had been tightening bolts and screws, and *Richmond* was ready for the race.

At the first puffs of black smoke from *Lexington,* Captain Townsend had rushed to the engine room and was consulting the engineer. "Oh, she can stand considerably more," said that functionary; and the Captain answered, "Well, put in the fat wood and let her go." She did go. Volumes of smoke poured from her funnel, and the roar of her fires could be heard all over the boat. A column of flame stood like a pillar of fire above her. She trembled at every revolution of her wheels. The water seethed and boiled beneath her, fire and smoke were round about her overhead. She advanced like the rush of an avalanche—she was a moving volcano. Slowly, steadily, she moved away from the *Lexington;* wider and wider grew the interval between them until at last *Richmond* dashed between the rocks at Hell Gate and *Lexington* was seen no more until she came by an hour after the *Richmond* had made fast at her pier.

Two years later the *Lexington* was bound for Stonington with a cargo of cotton piled amidships on the lower deck, close to the stack. Late at night the hot stack ignited the cotton and within minutes a pillar of flame mounted amidships, forcing the passengers to bow and stern and the black gang from the engine room. The captain sought to beach the vessel, but the tiller ropes had burned away and the boat plunged on at top speed through the dark as passengers were forced by the flames to jump into the icy water. Steamboats carried few, if any, lifeboats; in this case none was launched. At least 119 passengers and crewmen were burned, drowned or frozen to death in the dark water as they clung to timbers and cotton bales. Only three survived, one after floating two days and two nights on a bale of cotton.

The last steamboat race on the Hudson started at 7 A.M. on July 28, 1852. Runners at Albany cried, "Hurrah for Harry of the West! Take the *Henry Clay!*" Other runners answered, "Be in New York first! Take the *Armenia!*" A rate war was in progress and fares dropped from 50¢ to 25¢ as the last of *Clay's* 300 passengers were hastened up the gangplank. The *Clay* backed into the river first, closely followed by the *Armenia,* and the boats started down the river in that order. The owners of both boats piously advertised that their vessels did not engage in the dangerous practice of racing, but it was quickly apparent from the shaking of the boats, the high hum of the blowers, and the density of the smoke that this was a race.

The *Clay* had increased her lead by the time she swung into the bank for the stop at Hudson, but her crew's satisfaction changed to consternation when the *Armenia* swept down the river without stopping. At this the fare was raised to a dollar for passengers embarking at Hudson and the *Clay* hastened after her rival, which was now a mile ahead. At Catskill, where both vessels stopped, the lead had been cut to a quarter mile. A little above Kingston the bow of the *Clay* crept past that of the *Armenia*; then the former's pilot swung the wheel hard over, shouted, "All passengers to larboard" and locked prows with the *Armenia*. With her guard resting on that of the rival boat the *Clay* forced her opponent toward the west bank of the river, giving the *Armenia*'s captain a choice of stopping or being run aground. The *Armenia* blew off steam and the *Clay* forged triumphantly ahead.

Apparently intent on beating their rival by the greatest possible margin,

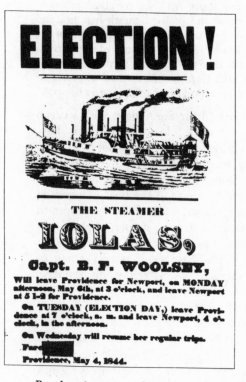

By the 1840s steamboat excursions were the rage for many purposes. The poster on the left advertises an election-day outing between Providence and Newport; the one on the right is a temperance outing on the Connecticut River.

the *Clay*'s officers pressed on at top speed. A delegation of passengers waited for the chief engineer (the captain was ill) to demand that he slow the boat down because the ladies were frightened. When their plea was ignored a timid but wise passenger took a station in the bow with his baggage stacked as a bulwark betwen him and the boiler.

The boat was opposite Riverdale, the last community before Manhattan, by 3 P.M. and the passengers relaxed as the end of the journey neared. Then a stoker spied a whiff of smoke curling from a canvas cover near one overheated boiler. While he sought a pail of water it burst into flames that rapidly engulfed the vessel amidships. The pilot headed for the shore as the passengers raced for the bow until the bartender constituted himself a ship's officer and ordered them to the stern. Many signed their death certificates by obeying. When the vessel struck the east bank of the river at terrific speed the passengers in the bow—including the fore-

THE MARINERS MUSEUM, NEWPORT NEWS, VA.

Fires and explosions were common occurrences in the early days of steam power. In this N. Currier lithograph, the Lexington *is shown in flames on Long Island Sound on January 13, 1840. A hundred people were killed in this fire.*

sighted gentleman and his barricade of luggage—were thrown ashore with nought but broken bones. Those on the stern were over deep water and faced with a wall of flame. As the wind swept the fire aft they had a choice of roasting or, if they were nonswimmers, drowning.

There were instances of heroism in the next 20 minutes that were reported by the press in the florid manner of the day. One gallant gentleman was quoted as asking a panic-stricken young lady, "Will you go with me into the water and run the risk of being drowned or will you be burned to death?" The report concluded, "The female accepted the noble offer and both were saved." Other level-headed passengers threw floatable furniture over the side to those struggling in the water, and, according to the New York *Herald*, "A noble Newfoundland dog named Neptune rushed into the water and seized a young child that was drowning by the dress near the shoulders and bore it safely to shore. He re-

THE MARINERS MUSEUM, NEWPORT NEWS, VA.

Travelers in 1850 could take advantage of an early version of a "package deal" between Lake Champlain and New York City. The package included boat passage from any point on the lake to Whitehall at the southern end, the train trip to Troy, the night boat to New York, and a ticket to Jenny Lind's concert the following night. The ticket holder had the option of staying up to three days in New York before using his return boat and train tickets.

turned and approached a woman to assist in the same way, but she was so frightened that the dog had to be called off and he was thus deprived of the opportunity of extending that relief to the sufferers to which his noble nature prompted him."

It was all over in twenty minutes. When the *Armenia* arrived her two small boats found no sign of life on the Hudson's waters. At nightfall the *Clay*'s bow, high on the bank, continued to burn, and the Westchester County coroner described the scene by writing, "The last scenes of the day were singularly impressive and solemn. The night was remarkably clear, the full moon dimly lighting up the river and the hills; at one side of a gloomy arch over the railroad was the wreck, the bow still slowly burning; half revealed in its lurid light lay the bodies of two men; above the arch a group of some twenty persons were busy with newly discovered corpses, trying to identify them . . . . The surface of the stream, placid and silent as the grave, was broken only by the oars of a few men who were still dredging for bodies." Throughout the night cannon boomed on the bank of the stream in the belief that this would dislodge sunken bodies and bring them to the surface.

The captain of the *Clay*, who had left his sickbed to jump ashore, assured survivors that "there were only ten or fifteen persons drowned and they were common people." The actual loss was reported as eighty, and the tragedy prompted James Gordon Bennett to wage an editorial war in the *Herald* against steamboat racing. He thundered, "How long are human hetacombs [sic] to be thus offered upon the altar of an avaricious speculation which sacrifices all things to itself?" The result was the passage in 1852 of the Steamboat Inspection Act, which ended racing on the Hudson.

By that time Cornelius Vanderbilt's original $100 investment in a sailboat had grown to $11,000,000 on which the paddle wheels of his steamboats and the propellers of his steamships were churning out a 25 per cent annual return—but the end of such lush returns from steamboating were in the offing. In 1851 the Hudson River Railroad (which Vanderbilt later incorporated into the New York Central) had been completed from New York to Albany. The Long Island Railroad stretched the length of that island, whence a short ferry hop connected with the trains to Boston. The Elizabeth and Somerville Railroad (later the Jersey Central) stretched across New Jersey, and the Erie Railroad had come to the bank of the Hudson from the west.

The trains were as crude and uncomfortable in every way as the first steamboats, but some went where steamboats could not go, and travel on the iron roads was much faster than on nature's running roads. It would take more than a half century, but ultimately the lust for speed would prevail.

Steamboats in the West

Old Al usually rose from the river to survey his domain late in the day when the sun was low and a mist hugged the water. He clutched his pipe in his scaly claw and his shiny gold crown towered as high as the soaring smokestacks of a river boat. When Old Al appeared, roustabouts touched their lucky charms or, if the preacher had done his work well, breathed a prayer, followed by a thankful sigh when the giant river king flipped his tail and sank back beneath the surface.

Sophisticated travelers laughed at this fantasy of a great alligator whose kingdom was below the waters of the Mississippi and whose good will was necessary for a successful trip. Only the ignorant on the lower deck believed Old Al could, if he was perturbed, move snags and bars into the channel where none had before existed, obscure the banks with a mist, or do any one of a number of things to bring catastrophe to river travelers. But some of the more civilized cabin passengers who scoffed at the superstitions of the roustabouts blanched if a white cat came aboard or, worse still, a white horse or a white mule. Many would not take passage on a boat with six letters in its name or on one whose name began with the letter M. Black cats were moderately lucky, but not so lucky as rats—this latter was apparently a version of the salt-water legend that rats know in advance when there is going to be a disaster and desert the fateful ship. Strangely, corpses in coffins played no part in the many river superstitions; they brought neither good nor bad luck, but the caskets made good tables for a card game on the lower deck.

Old Al could, if he wished, help the workers of his river kingdom. In the cotton season roustabouts who had labored long toting the bales from the bank at frequent plantation stops would surreptitiously drop pinches of their small stores of tobacco into the river to induce Old Al to smoke his pipe and thus create a fog as the fumes rose from the water. This would stop the boat and give rest to the weary workers.

Although the alligator river king was a figment of fantasy, there was a real ruler of the lower western rivers—King Cotton. Telescoped within less than thirty years several things happened to bring the fluffy white fiber to the throne in the river valleys. In 1793 Eli Whitney's cotton gin made short-staple cotton practical. When coastal planters wore out their lands with this demanding crop Thomas Jefferson added millions of acres of better cotton land by means of the Louisiana Purchase. Then as the white bolls started to burst in the western valleys, the steamboat came into existence to carry the cotton to market. There are historians who say that Eli Whitney's invention caused the Civil War by creating a cotton economy in which slave labor was an essential part. By this reasoning the steamboat is equally guilty, for the development of the great cotton belt through Mississippi, Alabama, Louisiana, Arkansas, and parts of Texas would have been impossible without it.

When the *New Orleans* left Natchez on the last lap of the first steam voyage on the Mississippi she carried, in addition to the Roosevelts, the baby, and the dog, a small amount of cargo—the first shipment of cotton to move by steamboat. At the time the midwestern valley produced about 5,000,000 pounds a year. Within 20 years this had increased to 200,000,000 pounds, virtually all of it carried to market by the steamboats. Little boats nosed to the bank far up the Red River, the Arkansas, the White, the Yazoo, the Tallahatchie, the Tennessee, the Cumberland, and scores of other shallow streams. Loaded beyond their small capacity, they paddled the white gold down to the mighty Mississippi. At Memphis and other upriver cities much cotton was transshipped to big Mississippi boats to go on to New Orleans. By 1840 cotton and steamboats had changed this sleepy French town into the fourth largest and busiest port in the world.

Through the years records for a single cotton cargo were broken and rebroken until, in the 1870s, the *Henry Frank* carried the world's record cotton cargo—9,226 bales piled up to the pilothouse on the guards around a full load of cabin passengers who sat in the dark.

But before this could happen, something had to be done about Livingston's monopoly on steamboat operation at New Orleans, and it was done by Henry Shreve with much less fuss than in the East. True, there was almost a riot when Edward Livingston, Robert's brother, had Shreve arrested, as his war record had made him a hero in New Orleans, but a rising rumble of public protest induced the Louisiana court to decide that it had no jurisdiction in Livingston's suit to attach the *Washington*. In 1819 the monopolists gave up. Sixty boats were built to run on the Mississippi during the next two years.

These were all bigger and better versions of the *Washington*—essentially flatboats that could go upstream. Most were side-wheelers whose main deck, two or three feet above the water, was crowded with engines, boilers, fireboxes facing forward to catch the draft, piles of four-foot cordwood to feed them, cargo, roustabouts, engineers, firemen, and impecunious passengers. Next above was the boiler deck, on which there were no boilers; if they were not on the main deck they were on the guards, which was considered safer. The guards were shelves to carry freight that ran from bow to stern outside the hull, usually as wide as the paddle-wheel housing. Forward on the boiler deck was the main saloon, which doubled as the dining room, and the bar—particularly the bar. Amidships the saloon was lined with private cabins. Astern was the ladies' cabin and around all was an open promenade. Third deck up was the hurricane deck, containing a few more cabins in a penthouse called the texas for officers, honeymooners, and VIPs. Topping all was the glass-enclosed pilothouse.

Cotton was king on the lower western waters. In season, ships were loaded to the pilot-house with cotton. Behind the bales, passengers lived by lamplight.

There is a story that Shreve, in one of his early boats, created the name "stateroom" for private cabins. Winston Churchill (the novelist of that name, not *the* Winston Churchill) helped to perpetuate it in his novel *The Crisis* by having one of his characters say, "There was an old fellow named Shreve who ran steamers before Jackson fought the redcoats at New Orleans. In Shreve's time cabins were curtained off. . . . The old man built wooden rooms and named them after the different States . . . and from this river the name spread all over the world—staterooms." The wide acceptance of the word "stateroom" on both boats and trains may have come about in this manner, but private cabins on sailing ships— usually occupied by men of state—had been so called long before the steamboat.

Because of fluctuating water levels there were few wharves on western rivers. In cities, landings were sometimes made by mooring to wharf boats—old hulks that rose and fell with the river.

Because of the shifting channel and fluctuating water level there were few wharves on the western rivers. In larger cities boats might moor to high levees and in some other spots to wharf boats, old hulks that rose and fell with the river. But most landings were made by nosing the vessel toward the bank, holding it there with the engines, and lowering the long gangplank that was hinged to the bow of the boat and held upright by a boom when it was in motion.

A word should be said about the most prideful possessions of the western river boats—their bells and whistles. The bells started as a strictly utilitarian means of signaling to rouse roustabouts at a landing and to warn passengers and guests of a departure. Gradually they grew into bigger, shinier, and more mellow status symbols. Some weighed up to 1,500 pounds and had quarts of silver dollars melted in their metal. A few of the smaller ones are still calling worshipers to churches in midwestern valleys.

River-boat whistles were far different than the hoarse, blaring fog horns of seagoing steamships. They were melodious, several-toned instruments, keyed to distinguish the separate craft that bore them. It would be an exaggeration to say that no two of the many thousands were alike, but most small boys on the river bank could identify the principal packets by the sound of their whistles a half hour before they reached the landing. Some whistles blew a chord, others a succession of notes, still others a combination of both. The *Annie Laurie* had a famous five-tone whistle that started with a single high note followed by a bass blast that was joined successively by three rising notes until all melded in a mighty chord. This set every dog within miles to barking and brought every small boy racing to the river bank.

Like bagpipe music, the melodies of the steamboat whistles were best heard from a distance, but once heard were never forgotten. Forty years after he had heard the river whistles as a boy Will Percy wrote, "There is no sound in the world so filled with mystery and longing and unease as the sound at night of a river boat blowing for the landing—one long, two shorts, one long, two shorts . . . . The sound of the river boat hangs inside your heart like a star."

The principal mechanical difference between western and eastern riverboats was the high-pressure engine, which was common in the former, rare in the latter. The steam engine and the steamboat came to the West almost simultaneously; there probably were not more than a score of stationary engines in the vast territory before the steamboat. Oliver Evans, who built the first amphibian, had pioneered the high-pressure engine; Daniel French adapted it for the *Enterprise*, Shreve improved it, and as it developed further it became a distinctive type of engine that was particularly suited to the western boats—cheap to manufacture, light in weight to permit shallow draft and capable of temporary surges of great power to free grounded vessels. From a fuel standpoint it was a very uneconomical power plant, but wood was so cheap that this mattered little. With steam pressure sometimes as high as 150 pounds per square inch it was also more dangerous than its low-pressure brother, whose pressure was usually between 20 and 40 pounds. But safety was a minor concern in relation to the profits made possible by its light weight, small size, and low cost.

The high-pressure, non-condensing engine had a much smaller cylinder and shorter stroke than the low-pressure giants, and the piston was moved solely by the expansion of steam, without the partial vacuum caused by condensation. Steam, instead of being fed into a condenser, was exhausted into the air, which necessitated a constant supply of water. This was no problem, as there was an inexhaustible supply in the rivers, although at some times and in some places it was a very fluid mud. Daily stops to clean out the boilers were necessary. One engineer on the

BOATMAN'S NATIONAL BANK, ST. LOUIS, MO.

Fueling was usually a twice-daily chore. River-bank farmers, anxious to clear their fields of trees, supplemented their incomes by cutting wood for steamboats.

Missouri estimated that he removed 200 tons of earth from his boilers during a twelve-day trip.

Fuel was almost as plentiful as water in the early days of steamboating when the settlers on the river banks considered trees something to get rid of. The steamboats burned the forests that originally covered entire town sites at the rate of 20 to 40 cords a day for the smallest vessels. Fueling was usually a twice-daily chore. At first all hands turned out to cut timber on the banks. Later, fuel lots became big business; one wood-yard on the Mississippi kept 20,000 cords on hand. At such yards the "ready wood" was stacked on barges that the upriver boats picked up on the fly and lashed alongside, transferring the wood en route and releasing the barge to float back to its owner when it was empty. River-bank farmers supplemented their incomes and extended their fields by cutting wood for steamboats, trusting their customers to pay for what they took from the unattended stacks with signs such as this:

NOTIC

to all persons takin wood from
this landin pleast to leav a ticket
payable to the subscriber, at $1.75
a cord as heretofore

Amos Sikes.

The boats of the western rivers never attained the mechanical and structural perfection of their eastern brethren. Longevity was rare; the average life of a pre-Civil War vessel was only four or five years. Most were made from quick-growth, poorly seasoned timber by semiskilled artisans. They were turned out fast and cheap, without plans or blueprints, in a great swarm—over 6,000 in fifty years after Shreve built the proto-type in 1812.

Another reason for the inferiority of western boats was that they had to be more or less expendable, as the conditions under which they were used were hazardous. A snag could tear the bottom out of any boat; cotton was a highly flammable cargo and a $200,000 wooden vessel would burn as readily as a $20,000 one. Sinkings and burnings were frequent but by far the greatest hazard, in terms of human casualties, were boiler explosions. Although the boilers of low-pressure engines in eastern boats exploded on occasion, such accidents were far more frequent on the western rivers; in the first thirty years of western steamboating there were 185 boiler explosions resulting in fatalities. And boiler explosions were fearsome accidents. When the *Clipper* exploded as she was about to leave a levee a reporter wrote this description of the catastrophe:

All the boilers bursting simultaneously—machinery, vast fragments of the boilers, huge beams of timber, furniture and human beings in every degree of mutilation, were alike shot up perpendicularly many hundred fathoms in the air. On reaching the greatest height, the various bodies diverged like the jets of a fountain, in all directions—falling to the earth, and upon roofs of houses, in some instances as much as two hundred and fifty yards from the scene of destruction. The hapless victims were scalded, crushed, torn, mangled and scattered in every possible direction—many into the river, some in the streets, some on the other side of the Bayou, nearly three hundred yards—some torn asunder by coming in contact with pickets and posts, and others shot like cannon balls through the solid walls of houses at a great distance from the boat . . . . The second engineer was thrown 150 or 200 yards through the roof and gable end of a house, into the back yard against the fence—one arm torn off and fragments of his carcass scattered over the trees. The watchman, a white man, was thrown alive, one hundred yards through the solid wall of Baker's Hotel, into a bed. He retained his senses perfectly for some time after,

Boats of the western rivers never attained the mechanical perfection of their eastern counterparts. Before the Civil War, their average life-span was only four to five years. This drawing from Harper's Weekly *was merely captioned "The Explosion." The event was so common that the magazine did not even mention the name of the boat.*

but the poor fellow expired during the evening. The cabin boy was thrown about two hundred yards through the roof of a shed, and was picked up in a mangled condition.

As a business, steamboating in the West was very different than in the East. No great fortunes were made, there were no Vanderbilts or Drews, and there were few stock companies. Before the war most boats were owned by their captains individually or in partnership with two or three others—petty capitalists who operated miniature private enterprises. A two-year-old boat might be bought for as little as $5,000. It required as much capital to start a drugstore as to go into the steamboat business, and the latter was a lot more exciting. It was also a lot more speculative. Although steamboat owners did not publish balance sheets it is safe to say that most of those when ventured into this chancy game lost their meager capital, and others, with a few exceptions, made nearer to 6 per cent a year than 6 per cent a month.

In the East most of the river boats were mainly passenger carriers; bulk freight was towed in barges or on vessels that carried cargo only. In the West all boats carried both freight and passengers, and cotton was far more important than people. In season, bales were piled ten and twelve tiers deep on the guards, reaching to the hurricane deck and restricting the view of cabin passengers to the back of a bale of cotton. Captains were so keen for business that they would stop anywhere to pick up a couple of bales. Even the so-called packets, which advertised a schedule between points, forgot the timetable if way freight was offered. In the 1,200 miles between St. Louis and New Orleans there were 1,327 landings at which through boats might stop. On the local run of 135 miles between Baton Rouge and New Orleans there were 1,025—only 16 of which had post offices. In general, boats stopped at any farm or plantation that touched the river bank if a waving handkerchief or lantern signaled that there was a dollar to be made.

Captains were primarily businessmen who had little to do with running their vessels, which was the province of the pilot and the engineer. In an emergency the captain took charge, and he had the same authority to maintain law and order aboard as his seagoing counterpart, but his principal duties were acting as gracious host to well-paying cabin passengers—particularly if they were also shippers—and administering his floating business. The second most important officer on the vessel, other than the pilot, was the clerk, who was business manager, accountant, and the equivalent of the seagoing purser and whose assistant had the engaging title of "mud clerk" because it was his duty to check cargo aboard on the muddy river bank.

In the early days, when most banks issued their own notes, the clerk had to be an expert in the current value of various currencies. His bible was Paddick's *Bank Note Detector*, a publication that kept him abreast of the current discounts on the notes of individual banks. One financial institution that was as sound as the Bank of England used to be was the *Banque de Citoyens* of New Orleans. Its notes were worth 100 cents on the dollar everywhere. Steamboats carried these notes upriver, including $10 bills that bore the French word *dix* on the back. Anybody would accept a "dixie" at full value, and that is supposed to be the origin of the name for the area from which they came—"dixieland."

The mate, instead of being second in command as in the merchant marine, was the lowest officer on the boat and, like the captain, had nothing to do with operating it except to supervise the lowering of the gangplank. His province was stowage of cargo and the supervision of roustabouts. His particular skill was in handling a barrel stave to hustle the bale-toting men along and a cordwood billet to maintain order. Many

In the South steamboats picked up freight and passengers at plantations along the water's edge.

mates were ex-keelboat or flatboat men whose ability as bruisers and colorful vocabularies were their principal qualifications.

The lowest order of humans in the crew were the roustabouts. Song, legend, and story say that roustabouts were always Negroes. In fact, they were originally flatboat or keelboat men and, by about 1840, the majority were Irish or German immigrants who, at the peak of the movement, landed in New Orleans at the rate of some 4,000 a week. They were cheaper than slaves—in New Orleans Irishmen pushed wheelbarrows as assistants to slave masons. And they were expendable; when both slaves and Irish were mixed in a deck crew the Negroes were usually kept farthest from the boilers, as they were worth money and more Irishmen were available for nothing. Slaves also presented a problem on boats that went into northern free territory. Many vessels that had slaves in their

Like most pictures of roustabouts, this one depicts them all as Negroes. Actually, a majority of the pre-Civil War rousters were Irish and German.

deck crews parked them in Kentucky on the way up the river and replaced them with white labor.

The roustabouts were the proletariat of the river population, and their living and working conditions ranked with those of Russian serfs. Except for firemen, who worked four-hour shifts, the deck crew was on duty twenty-four hours a day, seven days a week. They had no living quarters; when they were not working they curled up on a cotton bale or sprawled on the soft side of a deck plank with a few gunny sacks or an old overcoat for bedding. They feasted on left-overs from the table of cabin passengers. A contemporary description of the roustabouts' mess says, "For them the broken meat was piled into pans, all sorts in each pan, the broken bread and cake into other pans, and jellies and custards into still others—just three assortments, and this, with plenty of boiled potatoes, constituted the fare of the crew below decks. One minute after the cry 'Grub-pile!' one might witness the spectacle of forty men sitting on the bare deck, clawing into the various pans to get hold of the fragments of meat or cake which each man's taste particularly fancied. It certainly wasn't an appetizing spectacle."

The rousters' work was arduous and dangerous. Twice a day they carried a half dozen four-foot logs down the river bank and across an often slippery, swaying plank. At way stops they wrestled bales, boxes, barrels, and casks across the same precarious path. Throughout the entire steamboat era little freight was handled by machinery; even handtrucks were unusual. In time of shoal water the deck crew was almost continuously on duty transshipping cargo to flatboats to lighten a grounded steamer or heaving on spars to get it afloat. Mates had a particular disdain for Irish immigrants, and broken skulls, jaws, and limbs were commonplace. If an Irishman was rebellious at such treatment, he was promptly thrown overboard, although few could swim.

The illiteracy of the roustabouts created a problem in handling cotton from the many different plantations. By the time a vessel reached New Orleans, it might be carrying shipments of from two to several hundred bales from fifty or more owners, and each shipment had to be piled separately on the levee. The roustabouts who bore the bales ashore could not read the owner's marks, but they did know blue from red and the difference between a square and a circle. As unloading started, the clerk stood at the head of the gangplank and placed a different flag in the first bale of each shipment. As succeeding bales passed him he called out Blue Circle, Black Cross, Red Square, etc., and the rouster rolled it to the proper pile, a remarkable feat of memory when there might be fifty or more flags flying on the levee.

The least appreciated of the steamboat men was the engineer, and in most cases with justice, for the engineers on western boats were a sorry lot. When the demand for hundreds, and then thousands, of engineers arose in an area that was primarily agricultural, any man with enough mechanical knowledge to know that there was no such thing as a left-handed monkey wrench could qualify, and many engineers knew little more than that about the power plants of which they were the masters. It is probable that most of the boiler explosions were due to incompetent engineers rather than the inherent danger of high-pressure engines.

In all the river lore only one engineer has come down in history, thanks to John Hay, Lincoln's secretary in his youth and later McKinley's and Teddy Roosevelt's Secretary of State. When Hay was not negotiating the treaty that created the Panama Canal Zone, he wrote novels and poetry. In his *Pike County Ballads* he tells the story of one Jim Bludso, engineer of the *Prairie Belle,* who loved not only his engines but his fellow men. According to Hay, Jim vowed that if his boat ever caught fire he would not leave his post until he had done his best to save the passengers. And that is what happened one night when the *Prairie Belle* was racing the *Movaster* with her furnaces fed with resin and a rouster on the safety valve. Wrote Hay:

> The fire burst out as she cleared the bar,
> And burned a hole in the night.
> And quick as a flash she turned and made
> For that willer-bank on the right.
> There was running and cursing but Jim yelled out
> Over the infernal roar,
> "I'll hold her nozzle agin the bank
> Till the last galloot's ashore."
>
> . . . . .
>
> And sure's you're born they all got off
> Afore the smokestack fell,
> And Jim Bludso's ghost went up alone
> In the smoke of the *Prairie Belle.*

High above all others on the western boat, literally and figuratively, was the pilot. In his glass-walled house, with its easy chair, stuffed settee, pot-bellied stove, and gleaming brass spittoon, he stood at the giant wheel of his proud eminence, king of the boat if not of the river. None, even the captain, could gainsay the pilot in the routine handling of the vessel except, at times, the engineer. One of the few prerogatives on which engineers insisted was the right to argue with the pilot about the operation—not the navigation—of the boat. To all others the pilot's word was a regal command. At night his vision must not be marred by a glimmer of light. The mate ran to screen the glare of the fireboxes at dusk while stewards covered the cabin skylights, and even the most august passenger who lit a cigar on the hurricane deck might have it unceremoniously plucked from his lips and thrown overboard, as the glowing tip violated the pilot's order for complete blackness.

Mark Twain, himself a pilot in the late 1850s, has made the Mississippi navigator a legend. Of these craftsmen he wrote, "A pilot, in those days, was the only unfettered and entirely independent human being that lived in the earth. Kings are but the hampered servants of parliament and the people . . . . The editor of a newspaper cannot be independent, but must work with one hand tied behind him by party and patrons . . . no clergyman is a free man and may speak the whole truth, regardless of his parish's opinions; writers of all kinds are manacled servants of the public . . . . In truth, every man and woman and child has a master; and worries and frets in servitude; but, in the day I write of, the Mississippi pilot had *none*. The captain could stand upon the hurricane-deck, in the pomp of a very brief authority, and give him five or six orders while the vessel backed into the stream, and then that skipper's reign was over. The moment that the boat was under way in the river she was under the sole and unquestioned control of the pilot . . . . Here was the novelty of a king without a keeper, an absolute monarch who was absolute in sober truth and not by a fiction of the words . . . . I think pilots were about the only

Each owner's cotton was unloaded to a pile marked by a distinctive pennant. Illiterate roustabouts, unable to read the owner's name, recognized the color and design of his flag.

people I ever knew who failed to show, in some degree, embarrassment in the presence of traveling foreign princes. But then, people in one's own grade of life are not usually embarrassing objects."

There has long been a controversy as to Mark Twain's competence as a river pilot. He learned the trade from one Horace Bixby, to whom he paid $500 for his apprenticeship. His mentor later said that Clemens wrote a better job of piloting than he performed and that he lacked the nerve and decision of a good pilot. Bixby's opinion was generally accepted by river men, many of whom resented the Mark Twain legend. One said of Clemens, in the humorist's own manner, "He was a droll fellow and always getting off something—sometimes it was a sandbar."

The pilot had to know every foot of the section of the river on which he navigated—every bend in the channel, the location of every bar and reef, the depth of water at every point in every stage of the stream,

In the river's social scale, stokers were a cut above rousters. Other than feeding the furnaces they did little work except to help with loading fuel.

the surface characteristics that indicated dangerous underwater obstructions. None of this was marked by buoys or signals until 1875. The pilot learned it by years of observation and built his knowledge into a mental map. Mark Twain mentioned some of the indications that were meaningful to pilots in *Life on the Mississippi*:

This sun means that we are going to have wind tomorrow; that floating log means that the river is rising, small thanks to it; that slanting mark on the water refers to a bluff reef which is going to kill somebody's steamboat one of these nights, if it keeps on stretching out like that; those tumbling "boils" show a dissolving bar and a changing channel there; the lines and circles in the slick water over yonder are a warning that that troublesome place is shoaling up dangerously; that silver streak in the shadow of the forest is the "break" from a new snag, and he has located himself in the very best place he could have found to fish for steamboats; that tall dead tree, with a single living branch, is not going to last long, and then how is a body ever going to get through this blind place at night without the friendly old landmark.

The pilot had to know the river so well that he could navigate it when mist or starlight created optical illusions. Clemens described how Bixby impressed this on him when he was a cub:

"My boy, you've got to know the shape of the river perfectly. It is all there is left to steer by on a very dark night. Everything else is blotted out and gone. But mind you, it hasn't the same shape in the night that it has in the day-time. . . . A clear starlight night throws such heavy shadows that, if you didn't know the shape of a shore perfectly, you would claw away from every bunch of timber, because you would take the black shadow of it for a solid cape; and you see you would be getting scared to death every fifteen minutes by the watch. You would be fifty yards from shore all the time when you ought to be within fifty feet of it. You can't see a snag in one of those shadows, but you know exactly where it is, and the shape of the river tells you when you are coming to it.

"Then there's your pitch-dark night; the river is a very different shape on a pitch-dark night from what it is on a starlight night. All shores seem to be straight lines, then, and mighty dim ones, too; and you'd *run* them for straight lines, only you know better. You boldly drive your boat right into what seems to be a solid, straight wall (you knowing very well that in reality there is a curve there), and that wall falls back and makes way for you. Then there's your gray mist. You take a night when there's one of these grisly, drizzly, gray mists, and then there isn't *any* particular shape to a shore. A gray mist would tangle the head of the oldest man that ever lived. Well, then, different kinds of *moonlight* change the shape of the river in different ways. You see . . . you only learn *the* shape of the river; and you learn it with such absolute certainty that you can always steer by the shape that's *in your head*, and never mind the one that's before your eyes."

It is said that the best pilots had an uncanny sixth sense that defied

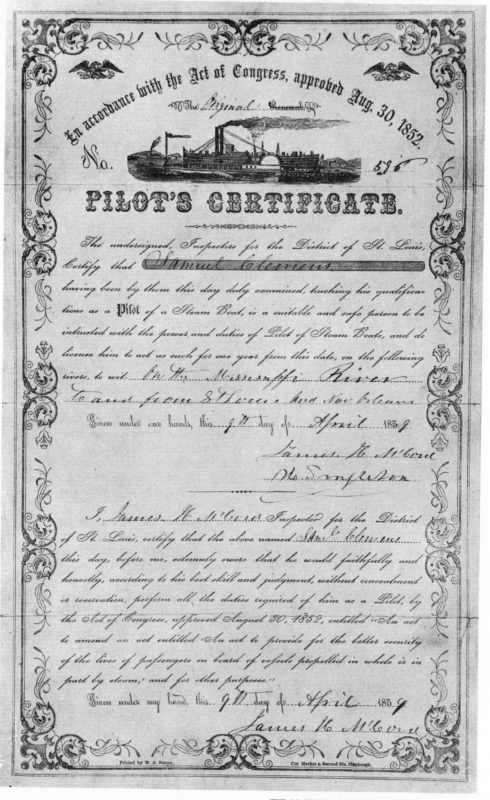

In accordance with the Act of Congress, approved Aug. 30, 1852.

The Original Renewal

No.   596

PILOT'S CERTIFICATE.

The undersigned, Inspectors for the District of St. Louis, certify that _Samuel Clemens_

having been by them this day duly examined, touching his qualifications as a Pilot of a Steam Boat, is a suitable and safe person to be intrusted with the power and duties of Pilot of Steam Boats, and do license him to act as such for one year from this date, on the following rivers, to wit: _On the Mississippi River to and from St. Louis and New Orleans_

Given under our hands, this _9th_ day of _April_ 185_9_

James H. McCord

M. Sampson

I, _James H. McCord_ Inspector for the District of St. Louis, certify that the above named _Saml. Clemens_ this day, before me, solemnly swore that he would faithfully and honestly, according to his best skill and judgment, without concealment or reservation, perform all the duties required of him as a Pilot, by the Act of Congress, approved August 30, 1852, entitled "An act to amend an act entitled 'An act to provide for the better security of the lives of passengers on board of vessels propelled in whole or in part by steam;' and for other purposes."

Given under my hand, this _9th_ day of _April_ 185_9_

James H. McCord

Printed by W. S. Haven,   Cor. Market & Second Sts. Pittsburgh.

description to warn them of shoal water or obstructions and could read signs that were meaningless to the uninitiated. Some steersmen, legend says, could find their way down the mist-shrouded river by blowing the whistle and reading in the echo the location of a bluff, an island, a tree, or a house—and tell whether it was a single house or a double house. One pilot had a personal beacon in the form of a farm dog who barked from a particular place when the whistle sounded. One dark night the bark came from much farther away than the pilot expected. Since his canine friend was infallible the pilot trusted the dog rather than his own judgment—and piled his boat into a bar. *His* dog had died the night before.

The pilot never stopped learning, for the stream that he studied was always changing. The channel was a river within a river which usually crossed from one bank to the other at a bend in the stream, and there were many bends. The Mississippi, with its principal branch, the Missouri, is the longest river in the world. It is also the crookedest. At one point it flows 1,300 miles to cover a distance of 600. In the steamboat era each flood wrought changes in the river's course; cutoffs converted dry land to river bed and vice versa. Virtually all the river that La Salle floated down 300 years ago is now farmland or paved streets; the river is in a different place.

Cutoffs created new channels for pilots to learn, and they also played hob with geography and real-estate values. River-bank towns were changed to rural communities. Where the river was a state boundary, farms were moved from one state to another when a change in its course shifted them to the opposite bank. The town of Delta, originally three miles below Vicksburg, ended up three miles *above* Vicksburg when a cutoff altered the course of the river. A cutoff through the narrow neck of a point of land might quadruple the value of an inland farm by placing it on the new river bank or, equally, decrease the worth of river-bank land by moving the river away from it. There are stories of landowners digging a ditch across a neck on a dark night when high water was impending to encourage the formation of a cutoff that would place their land on the river.

Flood waters eating away the banks constantly changed the channel as earth and trees slid into the river. A government surveyor reported that "the continuous falling of trees on some of the bends makes a noise resembling the distant roar of artillery." Many of these trees became new snags, and snags, old and new, were the principal cause of steamboat

The most famous Mississippi pilot, Samuel Clemens, is better known as Mark Twain. Note that he was licensed only between St. Louis and New Orleans. Most pilots were limited to one or more sections of the river system.

mortality. Nothing was done about them until 1827, by which time the western states were beginning to have some small influence in Congress and that body grudgingly appropriated a pittance to clear obstructions in the river. The War Department appointed Henry Shreve as superintendent of Western River Improvement.

Shreve had, meanwhile, invented another kind of steam-powered craft—a snag boat. This vessel had twin hulls joined amidships by a platform for the engine and at the bow with an M-shaped iron-plated jaw. It bristled with booms powered by strong windlasses and had an ingenious system of rollers to feed timber to steam-powered saws. With his first snag boat, the *Heliopolis*, Shreve started to clear the snags from the river bottom between Louisville and New Orleans.

The snag-boat was basically a battering ram. It crashed against a planter or a sawyer, wedged it into the V in its bow, and ripped it from

Snags, old and new, were the chief cause of steamboat mortality. The above painting is by C. Bodmer.

Twin hulls, strong windlasses, and steam-powered saws were the main features of this government snag boat. Basically a battering ram, it wedged snags into its iron-plated jaws, ripped them from the river bottom, and sawed them into harmless sizes before dropping them back into the river.

the river bed like an extracted tooth, or broke it off at the base. The boat's booms swung the snag inboard, the rollers fed it through the saws, and manageable lengths were rolled through a tunnel at the stern to float harmlessly down river. By 1832 Shreve's craft had done its work so well that not a single vessel was snagged on the river that year. Shreve also developed a harbor-improvement plan for a permanent high-water channel at the levee in St. Louis. In carrying this out he had able assistance from a Lieutenant of Engineers assigned by the War Department —Robert E. Lee.

Shreve's great job was opening the Red River. This stream rose in western Texas, flowed along that territory's northern border, cut across the lower corner of Arkansas, and turned south into Louisiana. In the center of that state it ceased to be a river and spread out to become, at high water, a vast swamp and a series of stagnant bayous covering hundreds of thousands of acres of valley land. Some 200 miles downstream the Red became a river again and flowed for another 175 miles to the Mississippi. The swampland between the lower and upper section was created by the Great Raft of the Red River, a solid platform of tangled trees in the river's channel that had started to form before the white man came. The river flowed under it and around it; brush, willows, and cottonwoods grew on the raft's older section and horsemen could cross it on trails without knowing there was a river beneath. In 1832, when the Choctaws were moved to the Indian Territory above the raft, the army told Shreve to clear the river, with an initial appropriation of $21,000. Shreve gathered 160 men; a new snag boat, the *Archimedes*; three small steamboats; and a dozen flatboats and started up to the head of navigation at Natchitoches.

From dawn to dusk through the high-water period of the spring the *Archimedes* battered at the foot of the Great Raft in the hot, malarial, mosquito-ridden swamp. Men in flatboats and skiffs pulled at the tree trunks loosened by the snag boat like giant jackstraws. The steamboats nudged the timber into the mouths of bayous to form dams to seal them off and re-establish a river bank. By July, when both the water and the money were too low to continue work, sixty miles of navigable length had been added to the river. Shreve returned to the Mississippi to await more water and money. The latter was doled out so sparingly by a niggardly Congress that it took over five years of intermittent work to break through the Great Raft and open the Red for its entire length. The total cost was $300,000 and Shreve estimated that the project added $15,000,000 to the worth of the public domain, a most conservative estimate in view of the fact that he built the only good road to Texas.

Shortly after he finished his work on the Red River, Shreve was fired. Times were hard and Congress would not appropriate more money for the western rivers. New snags took root in the channels that Shreve had cleared. But, in addition to a channel, Shreve left another memento on the Red. While working there his crew camped on a bluff to escape some of the mosquitoes and heat. Two local citizens started a log store to serve the camp. With Shreve they acquired title to the land, laid out a village of eight streets, formed the Shreve Town Company, and offered lots for sale —and so the former camp became Shreveport, Louisiana.

Snags were not the only obstructions in the rivers of the Mississippi system. Wrecks created bars and sometimes islands where none had hitherto existed. Pilots constantly exchanged information on the latest developments in the changing river, and when a pilot was not working he frequently traveled in the glass-walled temple of a fellow expert who was working, to keep abreast of the changing river.

To the pilot the river was a technical textbook to be endlessly studied. To the cabin passengers on the steamboats that slowly moved its length it was, before its banks became industrialized, a flowing ribbon of romance and changing beauty. When he was a columnist on a New Orleans paper Lafcadio Hearn thus described the emotional impact of a steamboat voyage:

There is no perceptible motion of the river vessel; it is like the movement of a balloon, so steady that not we, but the world seems to move. Under the stars the river seems to unroll its endlessness like an immeasurable ribbon of silver purple. There is a noiseless ripple in it as of watered silk. There is a heavy smell of nature, of luxuriant verdure; the feminine outline of the hills, dotted with the chrome yellow of window lights, are blue black; the vast arch of stars blossoms overhead; there is no sound save the colossal breathing of the laboring engines. The stream widens; the banks lessen; the heavens seem to grow deeper, the stars whiter, the blue bluer. Under the night it is all a blue world, as in a planet illuminated by a colored sun.

The calls of the passing boats, sonorous as the music of vast silver trumpets, ring out clear but echoless—there are now no hills to give back a ghostly answer. Days are born in gold and die in rose color; and the stream widens, widens, broadens towards the eternity of the sea under the eternity of the sky.

We sail out of northern frosts into southern lukewarmness, into the luxuriant and somnolent smell of magnolias and lemon blossoms—the sugar coast exhales its incense of welcome. And then, the giant crescent of lights, the steam song of joyous boats, the world of chimneys, the forests of spars, the burst of morning glory over New Orleans.

That was what the pampered cabin passengers saw and felt and smelled. Deck passengers smelled no magnolias over the stench of hot oil, food refuse and each other. The steamboat passenger of picture and story is a lean, elegant gentleman in tight pantaloons strapped under shining boots and a long walking coat over a gaily flowered vest and snowy, beruffled

Two ways of travel sharply marked the inequality between the poor and the well-to-do. Cabin passengers (above) rode in comfort on the boiler deck—where there was no boiler. Deck passengers (below) were crowded into the space below without food, bed, or toilet facilities.

linen who languidly leaned over a southern belle in a full-skirted, tight-bodiced dress, flirtatiously glancing from a frame of ostrich feathers that trimmed her ruching-lined bonnet. There were some of these Rhett Butlers and Scarlett O'Haras on the better boats, but this elite was a very small minority. During most of the pre-Civil War period perhaps four out of five steamboat travelers were deck passengers who knew neither beaver hats nor feathered bonnets. Herman Melville described the typical human cargo of the western river "ship of fools" as follows:

Natives of all sorts, and foreigners; men of business and men of pleasure; parlor men and backwoodsmen; farm-hunters and fame-hunters, heiress-hunters, gold-hunters, buffalo-hunters, bee-hunters, happiness-hunters, truth-hunters, and still keener hunters after all these hunters. Fine ladies in slippers, and moccasined squaws; Northern speculators and Eastern philosophers; English, Irish, German, Scotch, Danes; Santa Fe traders in striped blankets, and Broadway bucks in cravats of cloth of gold; fine-looking Kentucky boat-men, and Japanese-looking Mississippi cotton planters; Quakers in full drab, and United States soldiers in full regimentals; slaves, black, mulatto, quadroon; modish young Spanish Creoles, and old-fashioned French Jews, Mormons and Papists, Dives and Lazaruses; jesters and mourners, teetotallers and con-vivialists, deacons and blacklegs; hard-shell Baptists and clay-eaters; grinning negroes, and Sioux chiefs solemn as high priests. In short, a piebald parliament, an Ararcharsis Gloots congress of all kinds of that multiform pilgrim species, man.

Almost all boats made some effort toward outward elegance for cabin passengers in the main saloon, although the lush packets of legend were few in number and did not have their heyday until after the Civil War. During prewar years the steamboat saloon grew from 40 feet to about 200 in length and became increasingly more ornate in the owner's efforts to dazzle and astonish the traveling public. "Steamboat Gothic," the architectural style, was carried out in intricately carved gingerbread—gleaming white liberally trimmed in gold leaf. Knobs, gilt acorns, and carved flowers surrounded colorful chromos of pastoral and river scenes that adorned stateroom doors. To sophisticated travelers of Europe and the East all this was garish and somewhat vulgar. One described it as "an indefinable sham splendor all around, half disgusting and wholly comical. The paint and gilding, the velvet and Brussels, the plate and the at-tendants show bravely by lamp-light, but the honest indignant sun puts all the dirty magnificence to shame." But to the provincial westerners who were the boats' principal patrons it represented elegance bordering on opulence, just as, in the 1920s, the rococo lobbies of the cinema palaces aroused in most of their patrons a reverent awe. After all, the rivers were the western frontier when the steamboat started and remained a rather raw outback for the first half of the era.

In such a situation a lack of amenities behind the façade was taken for granted. The six-by-six private staterooms contained a narrow shelf for a berth, a tin basin, pitcher, and commode and had no light, no heat, and no screens to protect their occupants from the swarms of mosquitoes. Male and female travelers is the main cabins each had washrooms with rows of tin basins, pitchers of cold river water in which the silt had settled, a comb and brush, and, for those few who were concerned with oral hygiene, a communal toothbrush on a chain. Mark Twain recalled that there was occasionally a pretty good towel in each washroom.

Food was abundant if not, by foreign standards, delectable. Usually the entire menu, consisting of thirty or more dishes, was placed on the table at the same time and diners grabbed what they wanted. Dinner on one of the best boats in the 1840s included one soup, six kinds of boiled meat, five of fish, eleven entrées including such delicacies as fricasseed kidneys and spiced pig's head, nine roasts, five kinds of game, potatoes, rice, corn, etc., fifteen pastries and desserts, fruits, nuts, and decanters of whiskey and rum. Many unsophisticated travelers, unused to a varied menu, merely ate their fill from the dishes nearest to them, which might be rice pudding and fruit tarts, washed down with whiskey and river water. One English traveler who was even more caustic in her criticism of all things American than Dickens was Mrs. Trollope. Of dinner on a western boat she wrote: "The total want of all the usual courtesies of the table; the voracious rapidity with which the viands were seized and devoured; the strange uncouth phrases and pronouncation; the loathsome spitting, from the contamination of which it was absolutely impossible to protect our dresses; the frightful manner of feeding with their knives, till the whole blade seemed to enter into the mouth; and the still more frightful manner of cleaning the teeth afterward with a pocket-knife, soon forced us to feel that we were not surrounded by the generals, colonels, and majors of the Old World, and that the dinner-hour was to be anything rather than an hour of enjoyment."

This description of sham elegance and sumptuous fare applied to the few top boats before the 1850s, which most of the more literate people who wrote about river travel patronized. Perhaps more typical of most western river craft of the first thirty years is the vessel on which John James Audubon traveled from Louisville to St. Louis in 1843 and described as "the very filthiest of all filthy old rat-traps I ever traveled in; and the fare worse, certainly, much worse, and so scanty withal that our worthy commander could not have given us another meal had we been detained a night longer." Inadequate washing facilities, scanty bed sheets, pillows filled with corn husks, and a leaky roof added to Audubon's discomfort. Other travelers characterized the poorer class of boats in similar terms: "A crazy, dirty little craft, which was provided with but twelve berths or sleeping shelves, furnished with scanty and dirty bedding"; "fare coarse and badly cooked and berths intolerable"; "the boat was crowded with passengers and almost sinking with freight, wet, dirty and uncomfortable"; "the food was detestable—salty meats, rancid butter, coffee and tea without milk."

Relaxation on the long river trips consisted of sewing, gossip, snuffing, and watching the bank slide by for the women and, for the men, talk of politics, business, cards, and drinking. An eastern minister expressed his horror of the mores of the western river boats by writing, "I have already spoken of the annoyance . . . from the profanity of those we encountered. And I may now add that gambling is another of the vices that was rife here. On our way from Louisville to St. Louis there has been one incessant scene of gambling night and day. We have evidently had three professed gamblers on board. I am told that there are men who do nothing else but pass up and down these waters, to rob in this way every unsuspecting individual they can induce to play with them of his money . . . . Another crying sin, which abounds on board the western steamboats and is fearfully prevalent through every portion of the western degion, is *the free and unrestrained use of ardent spirits as a drink;* usually on board these western steamboats whiskey is used just as freely as water. All drink. The pilot—the engineer—the firemen—all drink. The whiskey bottle is passed around several times a day, and then the dinner table is loaded with decanters. I am satisfied that more than two-thirds of the disasters that occur on board these steamboats, are attributable to this free use of ardent spirits."

From all reports illicit sex was seldom tolerated on western boats, although one traveler—possibly kin to the minister quoted above—mentioned the "species of wickedness" resulting from allowing "persons of improper character" aboard. "Scenes of shocking depravity" he declared, "have occurred on some boats from this cause . . . . Propriety forbids anything more than a mere allusion to a subject so digusting to every virtuous mind." Opposed to this there are many records of ladies of the evening and unmarried couples being set ashore at a desolate way stop when they were caught. In one case passengers became suspicious of a couple who were traveling as cousins and required the captain to investigate. When the two were found in the same berth a committee of male passengers escorted them ashore at the next town, procured a license and a minister, and supervised their marriage before the trip continued.

In accordance with western custom, law and order were frequently enforced by groups of self-constituted vigilantes among the cabin passengers. Petty theft was common and culprits, when caught, were usually tried by a kangaroo court. Punishment for a thief who was a cabin passenger was to be put ashore far from civilization or, if the offense warranted, on an island, clad only in his drawers. For culprits who were deck passengers or roustabouts this might be preceded by making the victim run the gantlet on the main deck through passengers and crew armed with barrel staves.

Only a thin layer of planking separated the cabin passengers from the deck passengers, but the miserable squalor of the main deck was a world apart from the gilt splendor of the boiler deck. Nowhere was nineteenth-century inequality between the well-to-do and the poor thrown into sharper relief than on the better western river boats on which, during the prewar years, a high percentage of deck passengers were foreign immigrants. To say that deck passengers were treated like cattle would be an overstatement; if there were cattle aboard they were cared for far better than people, which was quite logical as a cow was much more valuable than an immigrant.

Like inanimate cargo, human freight was provided with transportation, nothing more—no bed, no food, no toilet facilities, no shelter except the deck overhead, not even deck space. Boats had no assigned capacity for deck passengers. As many were taken aboard as had money to pay to squat on the freight or seek heat from the boilers by curling up on the fuel piles until chased by the roustabouts. In winter many were frostbitten, and a few froze to death. In the frequent cholera epidemics they died attended only by each other. Some captains with a sense of decency had the corpses buried in unmarked graves on the bank; others merely had them thrown overboard.

A Louisville paper editorialized on health conditions on the main deck as follows: "Boats have passed here within whose narrow decks from three to five hundred human beings have been densely stowed or packed. The filth and stench on such boats are almost insupportable. The food used is of the most unwholesome kind, and the atmosphere which is breathed is impure in the extreme . . . . As well might you expect health in the Black Hole of Calcutta when crammed with human beings, as on the deck of a steamboat, where hundreds are huddled so thick that those who are well in passing to and fro tread on the wretched sick who cannot get out of the way."

The deckers' diet was whatever they could bring aboard, usually sausage, fried herring, cheese and crackers—and, of course, whiskey. Captains frequently understated the length of a voyage to attract passengers, and boats were held up by low water, accidents, and ice. When such delays exhausted the deckers' meager stores they went without for the rest of the trip, unless kind-hearted rousters let them share the grub pile. In sinkings and boiler explosions most of the casualties were deckers and rousters. When the *John Adams* was snagged, all the officers and 84 out of the 100 cabin passengers were saved; only 12 of the 129 deckers and rousters survived. Only when boats burned was their opportunity for escape equal to that of the elite above.

Most officers considered deck passengers as literally worthless, once they had paid their fares. If a decker fell overboard some captains did not stop; a mate might say, "It's only an Irishman." An editorial in the Memphis *Daily Eagle* tells of 100 German immigrants who were put ashore on Island 65 in the Mississippi in freezing weather to lighten the vessel while it crossed a bar. After it crossed, the boat steamed off and left them stranded in midstream without provisions.

The difference between cabin and deck travel was reflected in the fares. The spread was wider than in any other mode of transportation before or since, with perhaps five to one as an average. In the 1820s cabin passengers paid from $100 to $125 for the 1,400-mile three-week trip from New Orleans to Louisville. By midcentury this had dropped to $12 to $15 for a trip that ultimately took little more than four days. In this same period deck fare dropped from $8 or $10 to as little as $3.

Western boat owners, like eastern, used runners to snag customers, although not to the same extent. They had other tricks. A few packet boats advertised regular schedules between certain points and made some effort to keep them, but the great majority of the boats were transients whose captains shifted from route to route—when better business beckoned or the season or stage of the water dictated. Transients proclaimed a departure time, but never left until every stratagem had been exhausted to secure a full load of freight and passengers. As the announced time approached fires would flare in the furnaces, steam would hiss, bells would ring, and passengers would hasten aboard and pay their fares. Then all would quiet down. This process might be repeated a few times for several days before the vessel actually left.

The river boats thus far described operated from the late teen years

The levee at New Orleans shortly before the Civil War.

until the Civil War between New Orleans and Louisville on the Mississippi and Ohio and New Orleans and St. Louis on the Mississippi. Few boats ran the whole distance. Most operated on a certain section of the river, and such routes were called "trades." Even after a canal was built around the Falls of the Ohio, the route from Louisville to Pittsburgh was a separate trade, and the upper Mississippi and the Missouri were separate trades centering on St. Louis. Other steamboats pushed up the many tributaries. From the Ohio they went north up the Allegheny, the Muskingum, and the Wabash and south on the Monongahela, Kanawha, Kentucky, Cumberland, and Tennessee. Lower down on the Mississippi they breasted the Red, the Arkansas, the Ouachita, the Black, the Yazoo, and countless other winding, shallow streams and almost stagnant bayous in the live-oak section of Louisiana. By the early 1820s little boats had pushed up the Cumberland past Nashville carrying sugar, salt, coffee, hardware, and dry goods, and returned with cotton, tobacco, pork, and lard. On the Tennessee, steamboats created a real-estate boom at the foot of Muscle Shoals, where an Italian engineer plotted a pretentious town named for his native Florence, with broad avenues and spreading parks in the wilderness.

From Muscle Shoals, where the river fell 150 feet in 40 rock-strewn miles, it was 300 miles upstream to Knoxville. When the businessmen of this community heard of steamboats on the lower Tennessee they gathered in a tavern and collected a purse as a prize for the first steamer to reach Knoxville and free them from the six-horse wagons that carried their commerce over the Blue Ridge Mountains to eastern markets. It was won by the little *Atlas*, which, in 1828, fought her way up the Shoals to Knoxville with paddle wheel and capstan. Most of the rapids and chutes she traversed are now replaced by the man-made lakes of the TVA.

The river boats that opened the lands on the banks of the southern tributaries sounded the death knell of the southern Indians. During the 1830s Chocktaws, Chickasaws, Creeks, and Cherokees, evicted from their lands by order of Andrew Jackson, drifted down the eastern tributaries to the Mississippi and were hauled up the Arkansas to exile. A doctor who accompanied the first group of 500 Cherokees kept a diary of the miserable story of their exodus to Oklahoma by river boats. They were herded aboard flatboats at Ross's Landing—present day Chattanooga—to drift down to Muscle Shoals. Here they were transshipped to two-story keelboats and towed down the Tennessee, the Ohio and the Mississippi by the *Newark* to the mouth of the Arkansas. Wherever they passed there were those who would trade them whiskey, and the doctor's journal told a sorry story of drunken Indians crammed into low, un-ventilated rooms, fifty by twenty feet, with squaws, children, and their meager possessions, as they succumbed to the white man's diseases. As the medic made the rounds with quinine and camphor the keelboats became floating pest-houses. "At one time I saw stretched around me and within a few feet of each other eight of these afflicted creatures, dead and dying." On the Arkansas the shallow-draft *Revenue* took them in tow and churned up that stream, running aground several times a day, to Forts Smith, Coffee, and Gibson, the end of the line for the Cherokee nation.

For the first half of the nineteenth century, steamboating on the tributaries was a far more primitive and chancy mode of travel than on the main streams. On most of the subsidiary watercourses shoal water, bars, snags, and falls were more frequent, pilots were less knowledgeable, boats less dependable, and owners and captains less reputable. An anecdote about a trip up the Arkansas gives a colorful, albeit undoubtedly distorted, picture of travel toward the far West. After explaining that "the little old *Buzzard*" was a rickety craft whose engines had been salvaged from a wreck, the writer continues:

In face of all these disadvantages, the captain had the audacity to stick handbills on the corners and other conspicuous places, announcing that the new, staunch, fast-sailing *Buzzard*, having splendid accommodations for passengers, etc., would leave for Little Rock, Van Buren and Forth Smith.

The owner of the *Buzzard*, who had no other home, was what might be termed an easy, shiftless, no account sort of chap, fond of sleeping half the time and playing the fiddle the balance of the time. The captain of the *Buzzard* was a different character, a wild, harum-scarum rough species of early riverman. The owner was completely under his thumb, he had beaten him time and again for interfering in the management of the boat. Such was the captain, pilot, engineer; much of the same stripe, ever willing to fight, drink, deal faro, play poker or any other game.

One day the *Buzzard* entered the lower end of a long reach. The engineer now set his engine and proceeded to the cabin, took a smile of whiskey and commenced to deal faro. The pilot lashed his wheel amidships, lit his pipe and proceeded to the cabin to bet against the engineer and captain. The owner of the boat was seated aft in the cabin consoling himself with a plaintive air on the fiddle, he was great on Virginia hoe-downs.

The *Buzzard*, left to her own guidance, was going ahead finely on her own account when she entered a chute, took a sudden plunge into the bank with uncommon velocity, crushed in her bow and knocked a hole in her as large as a hogshead.

"She's sinking," shouted an Arkansas man, "tomahawk me if she aint, sinking sure." The owner heard it but fiddled away with as little concern as Nero did at the burning of Rome.

"Three feet of water in the hold," shouted the captain, "run the d----d old *Buzzard* ashore, if you can."

The owner heard these startling words, but continued to fiddle away. A passenger ran to him and bawled out,—"Did you know the boat was snagged?"

"I suspected something of the kind," cooly answered the owner, and went on playing his fiddle.

"She'll be lost in five minutes," shouted the passenger.

"She's been a losing concern for five years," responded the owner and went on playing his fiddle. "I wish she would settle with me for what I have lost by her before she goes down, and be d----d to her."

"But why don't you speak to the captain, give him some orders what to do in the emergency?" said the passenger.

"Interfering with the officers of this boat is a very delicate matter," meekly remarked the owner. The boat careened, the next moment the cabin was half full of water. The *Buzzard* was a total loss. The owner swam ashore with his fiddle under his arm, his bow in his mouth.

One western river (not part of the Mississippi system) that defied the steamboat for most of its length was the Colorado; in fact, it is still defying all but rubber rafts on its canyon reaches and was not fully explored until 1923. In the early 1850s one George Johnson had a contract to supply forts in Arizona. Johnson had the *General Jessup* built at San Francisco, shipped in parts down the coast and up the Gulf of California to tidewater on the Colorado at Port Isabel, Mexico, and reassembled at the river bank. Two other stern-wheelers, the *Colorado* and *Cocapah*, followed.

The first port of call on the upriver trip was Yuma, 90 miles overland and 175 miles by the twisting, hot, shallow river. From here Johnson's vessel pushed on another 325 miles through the desert to Mojave City. The whole 500-mile trip took about fifteen days, give or take a few, depending on how often and for how long the boats were aground. A pilot was not much good here; the real navigator was an Indian in the bow with a willow pole who felt the way along the bottom. Fuel did not grow along the bank as it did on the Mississippi; woodlots were piles of greasewood in the desert, hauled to the river bank on burros.

Most travelers on the Colorado took the boat to rest their horses. The horse got the shady side of the vessel and its owner supplied Indian boys to keep the flies off. There was but one class of travel and the boats were no packets. When they stopped at night few travelers dared to leave the stifling cabin; the mosquitoes were reputed to be as big as hummingbirds and as voracious as piranhas. It was a leisurely trip, with stops at any remote settler's cabin for gossip and a drink and with daily hunting parties to provide something other than the interminable salt beef to which the Chinese cook was partial.

In 1857 the War Department, with no concept of what the Colorado was really like, built an iron-hulled vessel, the *Explorer*, by means of which it hoped to supply the forts, explore the big canyon, and impress the Hopi Indians in their pueblos. To say that the *Explorer* was not suitable for the job is a classic understatement. Lieutenant Ives, its commander, reported, "We were three days accomplishing a distance of nine miles. A boat drawing six inches less water, could probably have made the same distance in three hours." On its first trip the vessel fetched up against a rock at the foot of Black Canyon, an incident of which Ives wrote: "For a second the impression was that the canyon had fallen in. The concussion was so violent that the men near the bow were thrown overboard; the doctor, Mr. Mollhausen and myself . . . were precipitated head foremost into the bottom of the boat; the fireman, who was pitching a log into the fire, went half-way with it; the boiler was thrown out of place; the steampipe doubled up; the wheelhouse torn away; and it was expected that the boat would fill and sink instantly by all but Mr. Carroll, who was looking for an explosion from the injured steampipes."

When the *Explorer* finished exploring nobody wanted her. She was literally left tied to a tree in 1858. More than seventy years later, in 1930, a survey party, working about thirty miles southwest of Yuma, Arizona, came upon a pattern of rusty iron plates on the floor of the desert in the shape of a boat's hull. This had once been the bed of the Colorado, and the rusted iron was the remains of the *Explorer*.

Steamboats were not alone on the western rivers. As late as 1842 there were still probably ten times as many flatboats as steamers making one-way trips down stream, but now they were towed back instead of broken up. Later they would become barges that were towed both ways. And there were shanty boats that were far different from their eastern counterparts.

The western shanty-boater was America's equivalent of a gypsy, following the seasons downstream on a barge with an unpainted hut of boards, tarpaper, and tin on its stern. He was usually accompanied by dog, a couple of pigs, a work-worn wife, and a brood of children—and they were probably important to him in that order. He did a lot of fishing, some trapping, a little stealing when opportunity offered, and reluctantly worked when necessity demanded. Some of the more enterprising made a practice of acquiring enough corn to distill a little whiskey en route.

There were some more responsible shanty-boaters who painted their floating homes in odd fantasy—peppermint stripes of red and white and checkerboard squares of black and white were favored motifs. These craft, like their eastern brethren, might have flowers at the windows and sometimes towed a raft on which an industrious wife tended a rooster and his harem or even a cow. This class of shanty-boater was usually a migrant laborer who, seeking a less confining life than his land-based fellows, labored in the North from planting to harvest, building a boat in his spare time, and then followed the sun to softer climes, living on his boat and doing odd jobs until he deserted his craft and took deck passage back North in the spring.

There were still store boats and other floating businesses as in flat-boat and keelboat days—blacksmiths, tinkers, tinners, cobblers, mill operators, even tailors. In later years photographers mounted their unwieldy cameras on shanty boats and visited river towns. More exciting were the medicine boats that peddled old Indian remedies made from secret infusions of muddy river water with barks, roots, and herbs, which were sold—with extravagant and compelling patter—as cures for any ill known to man. There were also floating grogshops, some with peep shows and two or three compliant women, that moored above or below a town and sent an advance man into the community to whisper of the delights to be found aboard. Opposed to these were meeting boats in which itinerant preachers floated down the streams and exhorted the dwellers on the banks to repentance and temperance. Un-

THE MARINERS MUSEUM, NEWPORT NEWS, VA.

For most of its length, the Colorado River defied steamboat travel. The War Department tried, unsuccessfully, to navigate the Colorado with the iron-hulled Explorer *in 1857. On her first voyage the* Explorer *dashed up against the rocks and was left to rust on the river bottom.*

fortunately, many of these self-styled saviors, after they had taken the collection and departed, did their part to eradicate the demon rum by downing it copiously from the mouth of the jug. Mark Twain's inimitable characters the Late Dauphin and the Duke of Bilgewater had their real-life counterparts in the wanderers of the rivers.

From the first trip of the *Washington* in 1812 until the Civil War interrupted normal steamboating on the Mississippi, few vessels were of the great, glamorous "floating palace" type famed in song and legend. River boats gradually got bigger and faster, although they never attained the size and speed of the leading eastern boats. Fifteen miles an hour against the current was good speed for a Mississippi boat, and during prewar years the big news in steamboating was of wrecks rather than records, although burnings, sinkings, and explosions were so frequent that only the unusual ones made headlines, such as the explosion of the *Moselle* at the Cincinnati levee that blew the pilot from Ohio across the river into Kentucky. With him, said the Cincinnati *Post*, "150 souls were ushered into eternity." Another accident that made headlines was the snagging of the *Mechanic*, because that indefatigable old steamboat traveler, the Marquis de Lafayette, was aboard.

In April 1825 the old general boarded the *Natchez* at the city of the same name for a thousand-mile trip up the virgin valley to St. Louis— there were at that time but few settlements of consequence between the two points. On the voyage Lafayette passed 11,520 acres of his own land that Congress had voted him out of the public domain, although he surely could not identify it. After banquets, parades, collations, interminable speeches, and all the trimmings that went with being given the freedom of the city, the French hero was taken down to the mouth of the Ohio and transferred to the smaller *Mechanic* to go up the Cumberland to Nashville, where he was met by General Andrew Jackson for another fete.

Although the sixty-eight-year-old marquis seemed to thrive on such adulation, he must surely have been weary when he reboarded the *Mechanic* to go back down the river. He was asleep with his dog in the ladies' cabin when, at midnight, the vessel shuddered to an abrupt halt and the captain burst in to shout that they had been snagged and were sinking. With the help of his valet and secretary the old man was quickly dressed, hustled into a yawl, and landed on the river bank. Bonfires were built in the rain and when a mattress floated ashore that was almost dry on one side the general reclined on it under an umbrella and watched the *Mechanic* carry his dog, his carriage, his papers, and a gift collection of fossils to the bottom of the Cumberland.

In the morning another vessel, the *Paragon*, was flagged down and took the visitor aboard, for the first time without ceremony. At Louisville he was transshipped to the *Herald*, which carried him to triumphant stops at Lexington, Marietta, Cincinnati, and Wheeling. He may have had his fill of steamboating by the time he climbed aboard a stage-coach to travel east to lay the cornerstone of the Washington monument.

One news story that made few headlines but amused river men was the kidnapping of the President of the United States by the steamboat *Saladin*. When word of Zachary Taylor's election reached New Orleans late in January 1849 the elegant, banner-draped *Tennessee*, with a load of dignitaries aboard, set out to pick up the President-elect at his plantation above Baton Rouge and carry him on the first stage of his journey to Washington. Nobody noticed that the *Saladin* slipped her mooring shortly before the *Tennessee* and steamed upriver.

With much ringing of bell and blowing of whistle the *Saladin* nosed in to Taylor's plantation shortly after dawn and took the still-sleepy President and his party aboard. The steamer was flying toward Vicksburg with General Taylor asleep in the cabin before a member of his escort realized they were on the wrong boat. There was much loud argument when young Captain Coleman refused to stop, saying that the President "came on here of his own free will and accord, and I certainly am not going to put the President of the United States off my boat unless he asks to be put off." Awakened to make his first executive decision, Taylor thought for a minute and then said, "Gentlemen, I reckon about all we can do now is to have a drink."

The *Tennessee* finally caught the *Saladin* below Memphis and captured her precious passenger. Then she broke her rudder and was ignominiously towed into Memphis by the *Mohican*. After the usual festivities the *Tennessee* took the President to Nashville for another party, and the *Daniel Boone* started to bear him to Louisville for more of the same until she was stopped in the river by Louisville's *Courtland* bearing that city's bigwigs, who insisted that Taylor change boats in midstream. From Louisville he caught the *Ben Franklin* to Cincinnati and from there set out on the *Telegraph 11* for Wheeling. When that vessel was stranded by low water and ice the President walked through the snow to Moundsville, West Virginia, and proceeded by sleigh over the National Pike to his inauguration. He, like Lafayette, may have been happy to see his last steamboat.

At the midpoint of the eighteenth century, western steamboat owners had only each other to compete with for the ever-increasing commerce of the broad valley. During the past decade they had welcomed a few short railroad lines that brought more cotton from interior plantations to Natchez, Vicksburg, and Memphis. It was not until 1854 that rails reached the east bank of the Mississippi far up at Rock Island, Illinois, to link the West with the east coast. Two years later the Baltimore & Ohio reached St. Louis and the first railroad bridge was thrown across the river from Rock Island to Davenport, Iowa. Few if any steamboat men realized that much of the commerce of the upper valleys would soon be diverted to the ports of the Atlantic coast via the iron rails instead of taking the round-about trip through New Orleans on the running roads.

Steamboat men did not take so kindly to the railroad bridge. When the *Effie Afton* crashed into it two weeks after it was opened, burning itself and part of the bridge, her owners brought suit against the railroad for obstructing the river. Convinced by the railroad's able attorney, Abraham Lincoln, the court ruled that a railroad bridge was not a river obstruction; steamboats would have to contend as best they could with this new menace to navigation. They no longer ruled the river.

Steamboats in the North

A watchman huddled against the glowing stove in the pilot-house of the *A. B. Chalmers,* moored at the St. Louis levee, watched a small group walking across the Mississippi River, a rare sight because the stream seldom froze solid at this point. But the winter of 1856 was a harsh one and, by January first, the rolling river moved under a sheet of firm ice and steamboats stood side by side at the levee, locked rigidly in a frigid foundation for a distance of twenty blocks.

The ice was three or four feet thick by the end of February, when an early, sharp thaw upstream sent a rush of rising water surging down under the solid covering. At first the ice moved slowly, without a perceptible shock. The boats at the end of the line at the levee were raised and shoved gently on the shore, but held upright in their icy bases. Then the *Federal Arch* broke her moorings and was pushed against the *Australia,* whose cables parted in turn as the irresistible ice pushed her against the *Adriatic.* In all, ten boats broke loose in a group and started to move slowly downstream, ice-locked and grinding together until they swept through a fleet of fifty or more barges and wood boats. These frailer craft were splintered into wreckage and the larger boats were crushed. Other steamboats swept down on the group, singly and in pairs, to pile up on the original ten where they had lodged a mile below the city. All of this took little more than an hour. Then the ice broke and piled around the stranded craft, covering them like so many prehistoric mammals caught by a glacier. Some thirty steamboats were sunk, capsized, crushed, or severely damaged by the Great Ice Gorge of '56.

It was the largest steamboat catastrophe that St. Louis had witnessed since the French trader Pierre Laclede Liguest picked this site for a settlement ninety-two years before and named it for his king, Louis XV. He selected the spot on the west bank of the Mississippi sixteen miles below the juncture with the Missouri because the east bank had already been ceded to England at the end of the French and Indian War. He did not know that his new-found village was in the Louisiana Territory, which France was about to cede to Spain, and he was long gone before Captain Amos Stoddard appeared in 1804 to take possession for the United States when his country bought the territory from Napoleon. Stoddard's chore was somewhat complicated by the fact that upper Louisiana had not formally been returned to France by Spain when Napoleon sold it. Acting as a French agent, the resourceful captain first accepted the village in the name of that country. In deference to the majority of French citizens the Tricolor flew over St. Louis for a day before French agent Stoddard lowered it and Captain Stoddard of the United States Army raised the Stars and Stripes.

During the first fifty-three years of its existence the village was the collection point for the furs of the North and West and the supply depot for the traders, but its growth was slow. Then, in 1817, several things happened. A courthouse was built, the First Presbyterian Church was started, the Bank of Missouri was organized, a public-school system was inaugurated, and—more important than any of these to the future of the community and the West—Captain James Read docked the *Zebulon M. Pike* at the foot of Market Street. The first steamboat had reached St. Louis to create a new gateway to the West. During the next forty years steamboats would make it the leading inland city.

When Liguest founded his village he saw it as a site to which furs might be brought down the rivers in canoes and pirogues. He could not know that it would become the hub of all inland river transportation. A few miles to the south, the Ohio brought the commerce of the East into the Mississippi and deposited that destined for the North and West at St. Louis. Twelve hundred miles to the south was the deep-water port of New Orleans. Half the length of the Mississippi was above St. Louis, navigable as far as present-day St. Paul, below the Falls of St. Anthony. The Missouri brought its muddy waters to St. Louis from two thousand miles to the west in Montana. The upper Mississippi and the Missouri, with their many tributaries, were the roads that served over one quarter of the area of the United States, from Illinois to Colorado, from Wisconsin to Montana.

At the time the *Pike* arrived, St. Louis had a population of about 4,000. Little more than one generation later a visitor would write of the new metropolis: "Here is concentrated all the trade of the Upper Mississippi, the Missouri and the Illinois rivers, and a large portion of the Ohio and the Lower Mississippi. Hence is exhibited as busy and crowded a wharf as can anywhere be seen upon which are commingled people of many nations, and products of every clime, and every species of industry . . . . From the condition of a fur-trader's post, it has grown to the quality of a city . . . . From a mere boat load of sailors, its population has gone on multiplying, until it has reached the number of 50,000. From a trade of a few thousand dollars in furs and peltries, a commerce has arisen which counts its millions. It has grown to be the greatest steamboat port, next to New Orleans, in the world."

When the *Pike* visited St. Louis there was nothing above the village except the lead mines around Galena, Illinois, Indian villages, a few trading posts and forts, and the settlement of Prairie du Chien. None of the cities the steamboats would help populate yet existed. At the site of present-day Hannibal, Missouri, there was only a smithy; one settler was clearing land on the bank where Quincy, Illinois, would stand; Dubuque, Iowa, was but a cluster of deserted huts and the grave of Julien Dubuque, who had come there to mine lead; near the site of the Twin Cities was the most northern American outpost, Fort Snelling. Then, in 1823, the 118-foot *Virginia*, not much larger than a keelboat, steamed upstream from St. Louis toward the distant fort, the first steamboat to breast the upper Mississippi. She carried a deckload of salt, pork, flour, beans, and whiskey as well as an immigrant family from Kentucky with their children, chickens, turkeys, and geese. The tiny cabin was shared by a female missionary journeying to the Indians; a Sauk chief named Great Eagle and his two sons; Major Lawrence Taliaferro, the Indian agent at Fort Snelling; and an Italian ex-army officer named Giacomo Constantine Beltrami, who was on a one-man expedition to find the source of the Mississippi.

Beltrami kept a complete and colorful journal of what he described as "an epoch in the history of transportation . . . an enterprise of the boldest, of the most extraordinary nature. Never before did a steamboat ascend a river twenty-two hundred miles above its mouth." Few on the levee at St. Louis believed that a steamboat could pass the two sets of rapids in the upper river, and the country north of the Missouri line was "distinguished only under the name of Savage Lands." Except for a few scattered huts of half-breed traders there was no white civilization in what is now Iowa and Minnesota.

The Italian was most impressed by the wild and beautiful country, the ever-changing river and its tributaries and the several tribes that lived on the banks. He visited Sauk lodges and those of their allies the Fox, the nearly extinct Iowas and some "gloomy and ferocious" Winnebagos; and he reached the upper domain of the fierce Sioux. The *Virginia*'s Indian passengers did not stay with the vessel long; disgusted because the boat grounded when the captain did not follow his advice about the channel, Great Eagle and his sons swam ashore and walked. When the vessel reached their village they were waiting. Beltrami also had to overtake the craft on foot at one point when he went exploring after a flock of wild turkeys while the crew was wooding. Left behind, he hastened along the bank to catch it at the next point where it grounded.

The Italian became lyrical about the scenery, as would many who followed. "Never had I seen nature more beautiful, more majestic, than in this vast domain of silence and solitude" he wrote. At one point he described wooded islands that, "disposed in beautiful order by the hand of nature, continually varied the picture; the course of the river, which had become calm and smooth, reflected the dazzling rays of the sun like glass; smiling hills formed a delightful contrast with the immense prairies, which are like oceans, and the monotony of which is relieved by isolated clusters of thick and mossy trees." Beyond this was a "distant and exquisitely blended view" at which Beltrami's pen was "struck motionless" until the *Virginia* ran through a forest fire whose light guided it for an entire night and of which the Italian wrote: "The flames towering above the tops of the hills and mountains . . . gave them the appearance of volcanoes at the moment of their most terrific eruptions; and the fire winding in its descent through places covered with grass, exhibited an exact resemblence of the undulating lava of Vesuvius or Ætna."

The little *Virginia* was not a true upper-river boat in that she drew over five feet when light. Later vessels specially built for the northern and western trades could have traveled on a heavy dew. Poles were needed to help the little craft through the upper rapids, and even then she became stranded and could not proceed until some of her cargo was portaged around the rapids. At the mouth of the Fevre River above the rapids the missionary, whom Beltrami described as "one of those good women who devote themselves to God when they have lost all hope of pleasing men," left to carry her message to the Winnebago, as did the Kentuckians, who were bound for Galena to prospect for lead. When he viewed the lead mines across the river at Dubuque, Beltrami made a shrewd prophecy of what the steamboat would do to all the northern-plains Indians: "The mines are so valuable and the Americans so enterprising that I much question whether the Indians will long retain possession of them."

Finally, after twenty days, the little vessel nosed into the mouth of the Minnesota and came to rest under the stockade of Fort Snelling to end its 700-mile voyage. The trip was neither as epic as that of the *North River* sixteen years before nor as exciting as that of the *New Orleans* twelve years earlier, but it led the way to the opening of a vast new territory to the white man's civilization. Beltrami, for one, was properly impressed with the awe-inspiring aspects of their accomplishment when he wrote, "I know not what impression the first sight of the Phoenician vessels might make on the inhabitants of the coast of

Greece; or the Triremi of the Romans on the wild natives of Iberia, Gaul or Britain; but I am sure it could not be stronger than that which I saw on the countenances of those savages at the arrival of our steam-boat."

For a few years after the *Virginia*'s first voyage, steamboat service on the upper river was sporadic. The principal customer was the government, which started to use steam instead of muscle-powered keelboats to transport troops and supplies to upriver forts. The little boats also carried traders and their goods to posts and Indian villages and brought back furs. They hauled a few venturesome settlers, and traffic related to the Indians soon became an important source of revenue.

As elsewher, the Indians on the upper Mississippi first feared and distrusted the "fire canoe." Beltrami described how, at the arrival of the *Virginia*, the redskins at Fort Snelling "took to the woods, men, women, and children, with their blankets flying in the wind, some tumbling in the brush which entangled their feet as they ran away." Sophisticated white men were highly amused at the antics of the primitives, although a European account tells that the peasants of Walachia, who proudly traced their lineage to imperial Rome, did exactly the same thing when the first steamboat appeared on the Danube seven years later. Unlike their eastern brethren the Indians on the upper Mississippi soon accepted the steamboat as a way of life, not realizing that it was an important factor in the usurpation of their lands by the white man.

Four years after the voyage of the *Virginia* three little steamers carried five hundred troops up the river to chastise the Winnebagos for attacking white settlers. In 1831 six companies steamed up the stream to quell disturbances among the Sauk and Fox. In the Black Hawk War that started in 1832, the *Warrior*, with a six-pounder in her bow, fought a skirmish with the Sauk chief and his braves that cut off their retreat across the Mississippi and pinned them down for the troops that defeated them at Bad Axe. Black Hawk was taken downstream in chains on the *Winnebago* in custody of Lieutenant Jefferson Davis. The red warrior said that the future President of the Confederacy "treated all with much kindness. He is a good and brave young chief, with whose conduct I was much pleased." Black Hawk again became a steamboat traveler when he was taken down the Mississippi and up the Ohio to Wheeling on the first leg of his journey to visit President Andrew Jackson. During the next few years it became quite the thing for the government to transport deputations of chiefs by steamboat to visit the Great White Father. It impressed the Indian leaders with the white man's power, and it was good propaganda for the people in the many river-bank towns where the vessels stopped to display their passengers as evidence that the government was doing something about the Indians.

The steamers also carried Indian deputations up and down the river to tribal conferences with each other and with the white man. Although at first the redskins accepted this form of transportation with some trepidation, they soon decided that it was fun. Many quietly slipped away from the vessels before reaching the council grounds, paddled rapidly downstream, and waited for a ride back upstream on another boat, which sometimes delayed the councils. The councils usually resulted in an agreement that the tribes would give up certain rights in their lands to the white man in return for annuities in food and goods, and these annuities became an important cargo for the steamboats. If a steamboat did not get through with an annual payment before the river froze, Indians starved to death.

Meanwhile, another cargo had become important for the upper-river boats—lead. The Kentuckians whom the *Virginia* brought to the mouth of the Fevre River to prospect for lead were the beginning of a trickle that became a stream and then a flood as the lead mines, which had been opened by the Indians, were taken over by the whites. The year after the *Virginia* made her trip about 175,000 pounds of lead came down the river, mostly in keelboats. Five years later the poundage was

With a six-pound cannon on her deck, the steamboat Warrior *helped end the Black Hawk War by preventing the Indians from crossing the Mississippi.*

14,000,000. During the first quarter-century of steamboating it was almost half a billion pounds—four fifths of the nation's supply—and was largely responsible for the establishment of regular steamboat service on the lower half of the upper Mississippi. Ten years after the *Virginia*'s first trip there were 175 steamboat arrivals at Galena.

By the 1830s Galena was a boom town and prospectors by the thousands roamed the levee at St. Louis seeking steamboat transportation to the diggings. There was profitable business for steamboats in both directions, bringing the prospectors and supplies upstream and the lead down. In the spring, when the ice broke, captains could ask and get their own prices for hauling the first passengers and supplies in and the winter's accummulation of lead out. In the fall there was an equal clamor to get in or out on the last boats. In the high-water periods of the late spring and early fall rates plummeted; in the low-water period of midsummer they soared. In various years and at different seasons the downstream rate varied from a high of eighty cents to a low of five cents per hundredweight.

On the whole, steamboating on the upper river was a more profitable business than on the lower, but the variation in rates and the risks of the river made it a chancy venture. A single trip might return the original cost of the boat, in an extreme instance. On the other hand, the boat might be lost, or delays, accidents, and unfavorable rates might cause a vessel to end up in the red for an entire season, as in the case of the *Lynx*, which made only $161.04 in 1844 and over $12,000 the following year. The largest single cargo of lead was taken out by the *Amaranth*—455 tons, although the vessel was rated at only 200 tons. That day a rate of 15¢ a hundredweight gave her owner a profit of $1,265. Two months later the rate had fallen to the point that the cargo would have netted him only $500. But at the low-water point of the same season he could have commanded $4,550—if he could have carried the load.

Lead was so heavy that most steamboats supplemented their carrying capacity by towing keelboats to spread the load over more hull space. At the rapids these might be cast off, poled through the fast water, and picked up below, and in low water some of the steamer's cargo might be transshipped to the keels for the run through the rapids. This was somewhat risky, for the lead-laden keels were hard to control and many had their bottoms ripped out and landed on the bottom of the river, but it was better to lose a keelboat load of lead then to lose the steamboat. One newspaper editorialized that the value of the lead lost in a single season in the upper rapids was greater than the cost of eliminating the rapids, but the government was not yet interested in river improvement.

Hauling lead was hard work. Galena had a reputation for infernal heat in the summer. It was said that after a rouster had picked up a seventy-pound pig from the shaded warehouse "he would start on the run for the boat, but the lead would melt and run down his back so that when he got on board he would have to cool the lead, after which the engineer would cut it off his person with a cold chisel." This was surely an exaggeration, but an ex-British naval captain turned writer, Frederick Marryat, attested to the summer heat on the upper river boats: "I have often heard the expression 'Hell afloat' applied to very uncomfortable ships in the service, but this metaphor ought to have been reserved for a small high pressure steam-boat in the summer months in America; the sun darting his fierce rays down upon the roof above you, which is only half-inch plank, and rendering it so hot that you quickly remove your hand if, by chance, you put it there; the deck beneath your feet so heated by the furnaces below that you cannot walk with slippers; you are panting and exhausted between these two

Diminutive in size and awkward in appearance, the early boats on the upper tributaries were a far cry from the "floating palaces" of the larger rivers. The above sketch, from Harper's Weekly, *compared the rustic* Anson Northup *to an Indian canoe.*

fires, without a breath of air to cool your forehead. Go forward, and the chimnies radiate a heat which is even more intolerable. Go—but there is no where to go, except overboard, and then you lose your passage. It is, really, a fiery furnace, and, day or night, it is vain to seek a cool retreat."

Until the 1840s there was little thought for the comfort of passengers aboard the upper-river boats. Prospectors, trappers, settlers, missionaries, soldiers, and Indians did not expect much in the way of travel amenities. Because of the low water, boats were generally smaller than their lower-river counterparts. During the early days stern-wheelers were more common than side-wheelers, and the vessels usually had only one high-pressure engine instead of a separate engine for each wheel, as in most side-wheelers. Generally the main deck was not roofed over forward, the cabin—such as it was—extending only about two thirds of the length of the boat. The wheels were much smaller than on the lower-river boats, usually not rising above the cabin floor. The private stateroom was a novelty that was not introduced on the upper river until 1837.

Much less is known about early travel conditions on the upper-river boats than on those of the lower river, perhaps because few of the upper-river passengers were of the type that wrote memoirs. One traveler of the 1830s wrote that his vessel was "a very small, dilapitated and filthy boat." But another reported that he traveled on "a high pressure steamer, whose puffing could be heard miles ahead. The cabin was plainly but substantially furnished, and kept very clean. There were no state rooms; but two tiers of bunks, containing the beds, ran along the side of the boat and were separated at night from the saloon by curtains. The fare was substantial, plentiful and good, and the officers were pleasant and gentlemanly."

A few missionaries reported on their travel experiences, all favorably. Of course, missionaries were usually easily pleased if the moral climate was right, and during the first half of the nineteenth century morality on the northern boats seems to have been on a higher plane than on the vessels of the East or South. There is little reference to gambling in contmporary writing and no mention of sex, undoubtedly because there were few women. The whiskey that flowed like water elsewhere seems to have been used somewhat more sparingly on the upper river, perhaps because all but the fur traders, who used it in their line of business, were wisely reluctant to mix whiskey and Indians.

Also, the gulf between deck passage and cabin passage did not yawn so widely on the upper-river boats. The cabin passengers do not seem to have fancied themselves as such privileged beings and the deck passengers and crew seem to have been of a more responsible type than on the lower river. There was no grub pile for roustabouts, who took their meals at a separate sitting in the cabin, as did those deck passengers who chose to pay a quarter for dinner. The mother of an English immigrant family of seven that traveled up the river in 1831 described the trip as both enjoyable and cheap, and wrote, "We had engaged to find our own provisions, but on account of their cheapness, or partly because I acted the part of matron to such as needed my assistance, we were frequently presented with young fowls, coffee, rice, etc., so that our food cost us very little on the river."

Some boats built for operation far up the Mississippi and on the northern tributaries—the Chippewa, the Wisconsin, and the Minnesota—were so small that they were the subjects of jokes about their diminutive size. It was said that when the seventeen-ton *Monitor* grounded on a reef on one side the pilot shifted his quid from one cheek to the other. If this did not get her off he took drastic measures and walked across the pilot house. If she grounded head on it was necessary for two men to get off, lift her up and carry her over. The captain of another midget vessel became incensed when some citizens of a town at which he stopped asked permission to put his vessel on a wagon so that they could run it up town and show it to a bedridden invalid.

Navigating the upper tributaries was a weird and wonderful experience if we can believe Henry David Thoreau, who, with Horace Mann, made a trip on a small steamboat up the winding Minnesota. Of this stream he said: "There was not a straight reach a mile in length as far as we went—generally you could not see a quarter of a mile of water and the boat was steadily turning this way or that . . . . Two or three times you could have thrown a stone across the neck of the isthmus while it was from one to three miles around it . . . . In making a short turn we repeatedly and designedly ran square into the steep and soft bank, taking a carload of earth, this being more effectual than the rudder to fetch us about again, so that we were obliged to run and break down at least 50 trees which overhung the water, when we did not cut them off, repeatedly losing part of our outworks, though the most exposed had been taken in. I could pluck almost any plant on the bank from the boat. Very frequently we got aground and then drew ourselves along with a windlass and cable fastened to a tree, or we swung round in the current, and completely blocked up and blockaded the river, one end of the boat resting on each shore . . . . It was one consolation to know that in such a case we were all the while damming the river and so raising it."

A new element was added to upper-river steamboating, started in the late 1830s, for which the artist George Catlin was at least partially responsible. In 1829 Catlin gave up a fairly profitable business in Philadelphia—painting portraits and miniatures of such luminaries as De Witt Clinton and Dolley Madison—and went west to paint that country and its Indians and thus gain an international reputation. For eight years he roamed the upper Mississippi and the Missouri River country and became enamored with the "magnificence of the scenes which are continually opening to the view of the traveller, and riveting him to the deck of the steamer, through sunshine, lightning or rain, from the mouth of the Ouisconsin to the Fall of St. Anthony."

Catlin later wrote, "The scenes that are passed between Prairie du Chien and St. Peters . . . will amply reward the tourist for the time and expense of a visit to them. And to him or her of too little relish for Nature's rude works to profit as they pass, there will be found a redeeming pleasure at the mouth of St. Peters and the Fall of St. Anthony. This scene has often been described, and I leave it for the world to come and gaze upon it for themselves; recommending to them at the

Popularized by painter George Catlin, the Falls of St. Anthony became a favorite attraction where tourists could "rough it" among friendly Indians and see the northernmost point of navigation on the Mississippi. Eight miles downstream was Pig's Eye, which was not renamed St. Paul until 1841.

same time to denominate the next 'Fashionable Tour,' a trip to St. Louis; thence by steamer to Rock Island, Galena, Dubuque, Prairie du Chien, Lake Pepin, St. Peters, Fall of St. Anthony, back to Prairie du Chien, from thence to Fort Winnebago, Green Bay, Mackinaw, Sault de St. Mary, Detroit, Buffalo, Niagara, and home."

The Fashionable Tour caught on with "in" people in the East and South and with foreign travelers. A growing stream of adventurous visitors flowed through St. Louis—"delightful and delighted tourists who were making an excursion considered more wonderful in those days than would be a trip to the Hawaiian Islands now." Their destination was Fort Snelling or, more specifically, a tiny settlement of crude huts called Pig's Eye, five miles from the fort. This community had been named for its original half-breed settler, who bore that unflattering appellation. The name was not changed to St. Paul until a priest erected a chapel dedicated to that holy man in 1841.

When the tourists debarked they found a stockaded fort, an American Fur Company trading post, and nearby Indian villages. To effete easterners there was the titillation of imagined danger in mingling with the savages. It soon became the custom for the redskins to don their best regalia and entertain the visitors with dances, ceremonies, and ball games. Then the tourists ignored their sensitive noses and slummed among the teepees, seeking to purchase the Indian's effects as souvenirs. They soon learned the truth that Beltrami had noted on the first steamboat visit: "Red men give nothing for nothing, any more than white men." The American Fur Company was pleased with tourist's patronage, of course, and the garrison of the fort—particularly the wives—put themselves out for this welcome company.

But the great event of the tour was a trip to the Falls of St. Anthony. The little settlement of the same name at the foot of the falls proudly proclaimed itself as the head of navigation of the Mississippi but, in truth, none but the very smallest boats could reach it. The real head was St. Paul and from there it was an eight-mile trip on foot or in any obtainable conveyance to the awesome sight of the rushing water of which Beltrami has given perhaps the best description: "Seated on the top of an elevated promontory, I see, at half a mile distance, two great masses of water unite at the foot of an island which they encircle, and whose majestic trees deck them with the loveliest hues . . . . From this point they rush down a rapid descent about two hundred feet long and, breaking against the scattered rocks which obstruct their passage, they spray up and dash together in a thousand varied forms. They then fall into a transverse basin, in the form of a cradle, and are urged upwards by the force of gravitation against the side of a precipice, which seems to stop them a moment only to increase the violence with which they fling themselves down a depth of twenty feet. The rocks against which these great volumes of water dash throw them back in white foam and glittering spray; then, plunging into the cavities which this mighty fall has hollowed, they rush forth again in tumultuous waves, and once more break against a great mass of sandstone forming a little island in the midst of their bed."

The Fashionable Tours from the South and East, supplemented by summer steamboat excursions from St. Louis and the growing cities above, brought increasing throngs of visitors to the head of the river through the 1840s and '50s. In 1854, only thirteen years after it had ceased to be Pig's Eye, St. Paul was described as having "brick dwellings and stone warehouses, a brick capitol with stout, white pillars, a county court-house, a jail, several churches, a market, school-houses, a billiard-room, a ten-pin alley, dry goods' stores, groceries, confectioners and ice-creamers, a numerous array of those establishments [saloons] to which the Maine law is especially hostile, and a glorious, boundless country behind."

The above was written by Charles A. Dana of the New York *Tribune*, one of the guests on the biggest tour to reach St. Paul, that

In 1854 a New York Tribune *writer described St. Paul as having several churches, eight saloons, and "a glorious, boundless country beyond."*

which was organized to celebrate the completion of the Chicago and Rock Island Railroad to the bank of the Mississippi. This was really not a Fashionable Tour. Rather, it was the first great publicity expense-account jaunt, which, said one eastern paper, "could not be rivaled by the mightiest among the potentates of Europe." Ex-President Fillmore was the prize catch of the railroad publicity men, but in addition there were congressmen and governors, four professors from Yale and one each from Harvard and Dartmouth, industrialists, socialites, editors, and magazine and newspaper writers without number. And, of course, wives and other pretty ladies.

The group arrived at Rock Island from Chicago aboard two nine-car special trains to find five steamboats awaiting them. When the five overflowed, two more were quickly recruited—there were apparently many gatecrashers. There was also some confusion. Dana wrote, "Staterooms had been allotted at Chicago, where the names had been registered; but many of the tickets had been lost, and many persons had none at all. Besides there had been some errors—husbands and wives were appointed to different boats, and several young fellows were obliged to part from the fair ladies about whom they had hitherto revolved with the most laudable devotedness." As a result some took trains back to Chicago, but more than 1,200 remained to pack the boats. The scope of this excursion to the head of the Mississippi was truly tremendous for the time. Today, even mighty General Motors would think twice before hiring two special trains and seven steamboats to take 1,200 people on a week-long publicity brawl.

To the crash of fireworks, the ringing of bells, the tooting of whistles, and the blare of bands on deck, the boats steamed up the river in line, furnace doors glowing in the night and sparks streaming from the stacks. Early next morning the fleet stopped at Galena for a visit to the lead mines and a picnic in the woods, where "wines of Ohio and of France stood upon the board . . . and glasses were drained to the health and prosperity of Galena and its citizens." At the frequent landings for wood the passengers went exploring and some were recovered only with difficulty. At one such stop President Fillmore's daughter found a horse and galloped to the top of a "mighty rampart" to the cheers of her fellow travelers. While passing through Lake Pepin (actually a wide place in the river) the boats were lashed side by side for visiting and dancing. Apparently nobody got much sleep during the two nights of the trip.

The visitors debarked at St. Paul and were trundled away in every conceivable kind of vehicle for a view of the Falls of St. Anthony. One editor described the expedition as follows: "Here was a Governor bestride a sorry Rozinante of which even the great Don would have been ashamed; here an U.S. Senator, acting the part of footman, stood bolt upright in the baggage boot of a coach, holding on by the iron rail surrounding the top, here the historian of which the country is justly proud, squatted on his haunches on the top of a crazy van, unmindful of everything but himself, his book, his hat and spectacles; there a hot house flower, nursed in some eastern conservatory, so delicate and fragile that a falling leaf might crush it, but a beautiful specimen of the feminine gender, withal, would be seated over the hind axle of a lumber wagon, supported on either side by opera glass exquisites, who only wondered 'why the h--l the people in this country didn't sent to New York for better carriages.' "

After speechmaking and banqueting at St. Paul, visits to Fort Snelling and entertainment by the Indians, the weary 1,200 started home to complete what the Chicago *Tribune* described as "the most magnificent excursion, in every respect, which has ever taken place in America" and of which President Fillmore said, "History had no parallel, and such as no prince could possibly undertake." Every newspaper account of the trip glowed with fulsome praise of the country, the river and the mode of travel; the Chicago and Rock Island's trip was an unqualified success in publicizing the area to which its shining rails ran. The nearest thing to criticism was a comment in a New York paper which said, "As the Upper Mississippi must now become a route for fashionable summer travel, it is only proper to say that those who resort here must not yet expect to find all the conveniences and comforts which abound on our North River steamers. Everything is very plain; the staterooms are imperfectly furnished, but the berths are roomy; the table is abundant, but butter-knives and sugar-tongs are not among its luxuries."

Despite the absence of sugar tongs, the upper-river boats had come of age by the 1850s. They would never reach the stage of luxury—real or sham—that characterized the eastern and southern boats of the later "floating palace" era, nor would they ever equal in size the vessels on wider and deeper rivers. A vessel 200 feet long was a good-sized upper-river steamboat; one like the *Die Vernon*, 255 feet long and costing $50,000, was rightly called a river queen. The *Ben Campbell*, with fifty staterooms, "rivalled in size and elegance of arrangement the Lake and Ohio steamers; the state-rooms were large, and generally furnished with double beds and wardrobes, and the fare was so excellent that one was naturally at a loss to conceive how passengers could possibly be conveyed four hundred miles, lodged and fed sumptuously, and provided with attendance for four dollars each." Of the *War Eagle* the Cincinnati *Times* said, "The cabins are furnished, with just enough of the gilt work to give them a cheerful appearance. All the modern steamboat improvements had been attached, and the barber shops, wash room, etc, are on a liberal scale."

Perhaps more typical of upper-river boats of the 1850s is this description of the *Red Wing*: "The walls, the ceiling, the beds, all are uniformly painted white. Even in the ladies' salon, there are none of the chandeliers, the lamp globes, the gilded scrolls and arabesques, the pianos, the sofas, and the couches which made the Lakes steamships so pleasant. A few red tables and yellow chairs, that is the total—except that in the ladies' salon there are some of those rocking-chairs which seem to be a sort of *sine qua non* of feminine existence everywhere in America. The only sign of luxury in the men's parlor is that the tables and parts of the floor are left uncovered so that the men can indulge to their heart's content in their favorite pastime of 'unrelenting, merciless spitting,' of which Mrs. Trollope speaks with such evident disgust. Their operations generally center about the two stoves, where they sit as silent as statues, each one chewing his tobacco."

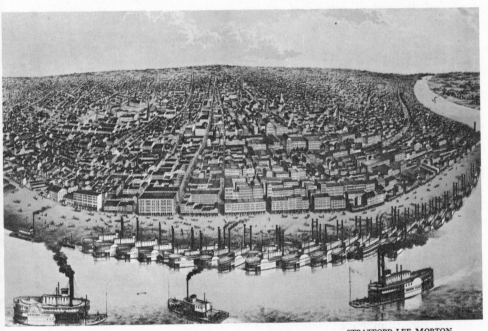

STRATFORD LEE MORTON

By 1858 St. Louis, the fur trading post that Pierre Liguest had established 94 years earlier near the mouth of the Missouri, was fully in the age of steam.

By the 1850s passengers had outstripped freight as a revenue source for upper-river boats. The Fashionable Tours and local excursions accounted for some of this but the bulk of travelers for twenty years, starting about this time, were immigrants who in a single generation changed the upper Mississippi Valley from a frontier to a populous and thriving agricultural area. They came from the east coast; they came from the older frontier in Ohio and Indiana; they came from the South; they came from Ireland, Germany, Switzerland, England, Holland, and Scandinavia. For a brief period it seemed that Iowa and Minnesota were twin meccas for a worldwide pilgrimage. Wrote Fredericka Bremer in 1852: "The people of Europe pour in through the cities of the eastern coast. Those are the portals of the outer court; but the West is the garden where the rivers carry along with them gold, and where stands the tree of Life and of Death."

They came to the upper valley by train, by covered wagon and by the Erie, Welland, and Illinois-Lake Michigan canals. They came down the Ohio and up the lower Mississippi. They came up the St. Lawrence and across the Great Lakes. And most of them, at some point, went up the river by steamboat.

When the railroads reached the east bank of the river they gave a great impetus to steamboat travel. During the last half of the 1850s seven separate east-west lines reached the river. But the iron horse did not reach St. Paul until 1867, and it was the late seventies before rails linked St. Paul and St. Louis. Until then the only north-south artery of the upper valley remained the river. Upper-river steamboating had its best years after southern and eastern water travel was starting to decline.

The horde of immigrants on the steamboats was reminiscent of gold-rush eras. Wrote one of the hundred passengers of a trip on the *Northern Belle*: "State-rooms were out of the question, and bunks upon the floor or seats at the table were at a premium. Standing at the lower end of the cabin, and gazing upon the hundreds of persons whose beds covered almost every foot of the cabin floor, I intuitively exclaimed, 'This is going West.'" And, said another, "What a scene is witnessed for the first two hours after the passengers begin to come aboard! The cabin is almost filled, and a dense crowd surrounds the clerk's office, just as the ticket office of a theatre is crowded on a benefit night. Of course, not more than half can get state-rooms and the rest must sleep on the cabin floor."

Under such conditions there were, of course, some complaints. Charles Francis Adams, son and grandson of Presidents, said the berths of the boat on which he traveled were so "dubious that I deemed it most prudent not to risk the reception of vermin. Hence I was awake most of the night." The busy pen of Mrs. Elizabeth Fries Ellet harped on the familiar theme of facilities for personal cleanliness. Women were expected "to perform their ablutions in a small wash-room, scantily supplied with water and towels, and allowed but a minute and a half for the duty, elbowed and grumbled at in the mean time by half a dozen impatient for the succession. This was uncomfortable enough for those who could be content with 'a wipe' over the prominent parts of the face, and an imperfect cleansing of the hands; but for us whom the habitual and plenteous use of the Croton had made absolutely dependent for life and comfort on a daily *bona fide* bath—the evil was intolerable."

All of these complaints were from cabin passengers. While there is some reference in contemporary journals to overcrowding on deck, conditions on the upper river seem to have been better than on the lower. This may have been due to the fact that the immigrants were of a somewhat more responsible type and few were destitute. Many of the early Irish and German peasants who poured on to the lower-river boats at New Orleans, fresh from the steerage of an ocean vessel, ended as rousters or farm hands or laborers somewhere along the bank of the river. Those who journeyed to the upper valley were, in the main, more substantial families, whether native or foreign, who brought household and agricultural effects and intended to settle in the new land. Many, particularly the Scandinavians, came in well-organized groups with sufficient funds to provide proper sustenance and leaders capable of demanding their rights.

Still, deck travel was fraught with hardship and some danger. On the upper as on the lower river cholera took its toll almost exclusively among deck passengers and the treatment of its victims was no better. Passengers aboard the *West Newton* saw six corpses floating in the river, deck passengers who had been thrown overboard "to save the trouble of burial and to escape quarantine regulations." The dead on the *Excelsior* were treated somewhat more kindly. One passenger wrote, "The first intimation I received of the presence of death in our midst was the tolling of the bell and the mooring of the boat at the foot of a high bluff on the Illinois shore. Soon some hands jumped ashore, a grave was speedily dug . . . [for] the infant which an hour before had breathed its last. We proceeded on our way and 'ere two days had passed we had buried five deck passengers . . . victims of cholera no doubt aggravated or induced by filthiness, exposure, fatigue and improper diet."

A few of the immigrants who arrived on the upper river were victims of real-estate swindles perpetrated by eastern confidence men. The captain of the *Nominee* was approached by a group that wanted to book deck passage to the town of Rolling Stone. When the captain said that he had never heard of it they produced maps of a well-laid-out com-

The upper-river boats never equaled the elegance of the eastern and southern boats, nor were they glamorized by painters. Most are depicted

only in rather poor photographs dating from the early days of photography.

munity in which they had purchased land. So far as the captain could determine the mythical Rolling Stone was located in the Minnesota Territory on land still owned by the Indians, far from any white settlement. Still, the immigrants insisted on going there and the captain reluctantly put them off in the wilderness. Some died, others made their way back to civilization; there is today no trace of Rolling Stone.

Travelers bound for the mythical community of Ninninger possessed not only maps and deeds to the land which they had bought, but a picture of the town showing a busy levee lined with steamboats and backed by warehouses, church steeples, and a newspaper building. They also had copies of a Ninninger newspaper, full of accounts of the doings of fictional people and advertisements for nonexistent stores. When they arrived at the site they found at the edge of the forest only the dilapitated shack in which the newspaper had been printed.

While immigrants were going up the river by the tens of thousands, logs by the million were coming down. Logging in the upper Mississippi wilderness lasted from the mid-1830s until 1915, with the greatest era of the industry from about 1850 to 1890. During those four decades the steamboats brought out most of the forests of Minnesota and Wisconsin and brought in the people who converted the land to pasture, grain fields, and orchards.

In the early days the logs were merely floated down in rafts borne on the spring crest of high water. Individual tree trunks from far up the tributaries first floated to rafting works on the banks of the Mississippi. The greatest of these was Beef Slough, at the mouth of the Chippewa, and Read's Landing, at the foot of Lake Pepin. Each log bore its owner's brand; the XX for Weyerhaeuser is still in use. Behind a boom at the rafting works the timber was sorted and formed into brails—loose logs end to end in an oblong framed of larger logs lashed together with cables. Three brails made a "half a raft," a platform of logs perhaps 700 feet long and 135 feet wide. Depending on the level of the water, two, three or sometimes as many as six half-rafts were lashed together to make a raft containing as many as three acres of tree trunks.

This watercraft, which would dwarf today's largest aircraft carrier in deck area, was taken downstream by a captain, pilot, cook, and a crew of about twenty-four men who slept, ate, worked, and played on the logs. In all respects raftsmen, who were mostly Irish and French-Canadian, were reminiscent of the keelboat men of yore, hard-working when they worked, hard-drinking and hard-fighting at other times. There were 21 saloons at Read's Landing, and it was a rare night when there was not a fight in each of them. The rafts floated along silently, controlled by long sweeps at sides, bow, and stern and with polemen at the four corners. "Sometimes," recalled Mark Twain, "in the big river where we would be feeling our way through a fog, the deep hush

EMIGRATION

UP THE MISSISSIPPI RIVER.

The attention of Emigrants and the Public generally, is called to the now rapidly improving

TERRITORY OF MINNESOTA,

Containing a population of 150,000, and goes into the Union as a State during the present year. According to an act of Congress passed last February, the State is munificently endowed with Lands for Public Schools and State Universities, also granting five per cent. on all sales of U. S. Lands for Internal Improvements. On the 3d March, 1857, grants of Land from Congress was made to the leading Trunk Railroads in Minnesota, so that in a short time the trip from New Orleans to any part of the State will be made in from two and a half to three days. The

CITY OF NININGER,

Situated on the Mississippi River, 35 miles below St. Paul, is now a prominent point for a large Commercial Town, being backed by an extensive Agricultural. Grazing and Farming Country; has fine streams in the interior, well adapted for Milling in all its branches; and Manufacturing **WATER POWER** to any extent.

Mr. JOHN NININGER, (a Gentleman of large means, ideas and liberality, speaking the various languages,) is the principal Proprietor of **Nininger.** He laid it out on such principles as to encourage all **MECHANICS**, Merchants, or Professions of all kinds, on the same equality and footing: the consequence is, the place has gone ahead with such rapidity that it is now an established City, and will annually double in population for years to come.

Persons arriving by Ship or otherwise, can be transferred without expense to Steamers going to Saint Louis; or stop at Cairo, and take Railroad to Dunleith (on the Mississippi). Steamboats leave Saint Louis and Dunleith daily for **NININGER**, and make the trip from Dunleith in 36 to 48 hours.

NOTICES.

1. All Railroads and Steamboats giving this card a conspicuous place, or *gratuitous insertion* in their cards, AIDS THE EMIGRANT and forwards their own interest.

2. For authentic documents, reliable information, and all particulars in regard to Occupations, Wages, Preëmpting Lands (in neighborhood), Lumber, Price of Lots, Expenses, &c., apply to

THOMAS B. WINSTON, 27 Camp street, New Orleans.
ROBERT CAMPBELL, St. Louis.
JOSEPH B. FORBES, Dunleith.

A well-planned real-estate swindle. Settlers lured by this advertisement were furnished not only with maps and deeds to the land they had purchased but with pictures of the town showing a busy levee lined with steamboats. The city of Nininger, however, simply did not exist.

would be broken by yells and a clamor of tin pans, and all in an instant a log raft would appear through the webby veil—and we had to pile on steam and scramble out of the way."

Rafting changed in the 1860s when steamboats were first used to tow or, rather, push them. Although called towboats, the rafting steamers never pulled their load. The first attempt to control a raft with a side-wheel steamer failed; the vessel was too small and the raft ran away with it. Then, in 1869, the Weyerhaeusers built the *J. W. Van Sant*, a rugged and powerful stern-wheeler that set the pattern for more than a hundred specialized rafting boats on the upper Mississippi.

Unique to rafting steamers was the "midship nigger," a double-drum horizontal capstan which was used to steer the raft. The towboat put its nose against a "butting block" on the middle of the stern of the raft. Lines were run from each drum of the "midship nigger" to a stern corner of the raft. When one drum took in the line on one side the other slackened the line on the opposite side. This slanted the boat and caused it to act as a rudder for the raft. Sometimes steering was aided with a "bow boat," a small steamer lashed to the front of the raft at right angles to its length. This moved the head of the raft from side to side by going forward or back.

The captains, pilots, mates, and crew of rafting boats were a group of rivermen apart, highly skilled in performing a variety of complex operations. The most interesting of these was double-tripping. There were points on the river where there were rapids and railroad bridges that were narrower than the rafts. Here the boat would moor the raft to the bank above the narrow point, split it in half, and take one half through. This would then be moored below while the boat went back for the other half. Below the bottleneck the halves were rejoined and towed—or pushed—on down the river.

With the coming of the steam towboat the raftsmen changed. When Mark Twain returned to the river in the early 1880s he recorded somewhat wistfully that on the upper river "we met massed acres of lumber-rafts coming down, but not floating leisurely along, in the old-fashioned way, manned with joyous and reckless crews of fiddling, song-singing, whisky-drinking, breakdown-dancing rapscallions; no, the whole thing was shoved swiftly along by a powerful stern-wheeler, modern fashion; and the small crews were quiet, orderly, men of a sedate business aspect, with not a suggestion of romance about them anywhere."

The pattern of accidents from snags, bars, fires, and boiler explosions was not materially different on the upper and lower rivers, although, for some unknown reasons, there were far fewer boiler explosions; the first did not occur until 1837, fourteen years after steamboats came to the region. Fires, too, were less frequent, possibly because there was no highly flammable cotton. But the greatest single fire in steamboat history was at the junction of inland river traffic, St. Louis.

About 10 P.M. on the evening of May 17, 1849, the steamer *White Cloud*, moored at the St. Louis levee, mysteriously caught fire and the flames quickly spread to the *Endors*, above, and the *Edward Bates*, below. The latter boat was cast adrift in an ill-considered attempt to restrict the further spread of the blaze. A strong wind blew the floating vessel back to the levee at several points and every time it touched it ignited another boat. Then boats below that had not caught fire were cast adrift in an attempt to save them. The perverse *Edward Bates*, a floating torch, now outsped the other drifting craft, touching them one by one and communicating her flames to each. The river below St. Louis soon carried a sizable fleet of burning steamboats slowly downstream. Meanwhile, flames from the vessels that had not been cast adrift spread to buildings on the water front. Before the fire subsided, twenty-three steamboats and the entire business section of the city had been consumed.

Racing was a sometime feature of upper-river steamboating, but as with boiler explosions and fires, it was not as prevalent as on the lower river—perhaps there was some connection. The most memorable upper-river speed contest, between the *Grey Eagle* and the *Itasca*, is usually referred to as a race, although in fact it was not, because one skipper did not know that he was being challenged until the last few miles.

The event came about when Captain Daniel Harris decided that his *Grey Eagle* would be the first to bring a message from England's Queen Victoria to St. Paul. The completion of the Atlantic telegraph cable was a subject of keen interest in 1858, particularly since the cable had been lost on the first two attempts to lay it. News of the event and the first messages exchanged between the Queen and President Buchanan were avidly awaited. The press in Dubuque and other upriver cities chided St. Paul because the city at the head of the river was the only one not yet linked to the eastern seaboard by telegraph. Other cities would have the royal message seconds after it was received in New York, but St. Paul would not.

The *Grey Eagle* was scheduled to leave Dubuque at 9 A.M., the same time that Captain David Whitten's *Itasca* was due to depart from Prairie du Chien, 60 miles north. The *Itasca* had a reputation as "the fastest on the river." It would be quite a feather in Harris' cap if he could reach St. Paul with the news before Whitten, running 265 miles in less time than it took the rival boat to run 205.

Both boats carried a full load of freight and passengers but the *Grey Eagle* had, in addition, quantities of highly combustible pitch, rancid bacon, and grease. Harris kept his boat at top speed, stopping only when he had to. He offered way passengers a free trip up the river and back to their destinations to avoid stops, carried some freight up and back, and delivered the mail by swinging in toward the bank and throwing the sacks ashore. By dusk he had cut the *Itasca*'s normal nine-hour lead to three hours.

Next morning, when the *Grey Eagle* slid into the Prescott levee, the *Itasca* was heard whistling for Hastings, just two and a half miles ahead. As the trailing boat passed Hastings, Harris could see his rival's smoke ahead. Whitten, too, saw smoke that did not belong behind him, and from the density and sparks it was obviously being made by a boat traveling under pressure. He ordered flank speed for his own vessel although he did not know, until both vessels reached a straight stretch in the stream, that the upcoming boat was the *Grey Eagle*, now but a mile behind him and ten hours ahead of schedule.

At Merrimac Island the gap had narrowed to three quarters of a mile; at Newport a half mile intervened; as they passed Dayton Bluff there was only a boat's length between the two vessels, and St. Paul was but a mile away. As they neared the St. Paul levee, with passengers and crews of both boats in a frenzy of excitement, the bow of the *Grey Eagle* overlapped the stern of the *Itasca*, but Whitten had the inside track, the *Grey Eagle* would have to cut across his bow to dock first. Harris did not quite make it, as the vessels were abreast when the *Itasca* pulled into the levee, but Harris did deliver the news first. While Whitten was lowering his gangplank a rouster on the *Grey Eagle* threw a Dubuque newspaper wrapped around a billet of wood to Harris' agent on the levee.

The *Grey Eagle* made the 265-mile run in twenty-four hours and forty minutes, a fraction over eleven miles an hour, including time for twenty-three landings and to take on thirty-five cords of wood on the fly. It was estimated that the *Grey Eagle* made about thirteen miles an hour while under way, and that was the fastest time ever made by an upper-river steamboat, upstream, during their heyday.

Mountain Boats

and Grasshoppers

I have seen nothing more frightful." So wrote the Jesuit Jacques Marquette in 1669 when he first set eyes on the muddy torrent of the Missouri River pouring into the Mississippi. Things did not change much during the next two centuries. In 1843 John James Audubon wrote of the Missouri, "All is conflict between life and death .... All around was the very perfection of disaster and misfortune."

The Missouri was not a smooth-running road. Everything bad that can be said about the Mississippi must be doubled for its greatest tributary. The Missouri was crookeder; it was muddier; it was shallower; the current was swifter; it had more snags and bars; there was frequently a wind that ruffled the surface to confuse the pilot and sometimes literally blow a boat out of the channel, which changed almost from day to day; and the eddies of the Mississippi were whirlpools in the Missouri. Of this frustrating stream it was said, "Of all the variable things in creation the most uncertain are the action of a jury, the state of a woman's mind, and the condition of the Missouri River."

Daniel Boone, who had led the parade of westward migration on foot, lived to see the first steamboat pass his son's home on the bank of the Missouri the year before he died in 1820. By that time there were scattered settlers as far as Franklin, Missouri, 200 miles from the river's mouth. Beyond were only Indians and the forts of the fur companies. In 1819 the *Missouri Intelligencer* recorded, "with no ordinary sensation of pride and pleasure," the arrival at Franklin of the steamboat *Independence* with a cargo of flour, whiskey, sugar, and iron castings. Cannon joyfully boomed from the boat and the shore to mark "the grand *desideratum*, the important *fact* is now ascertained, *that steamboats can safely navigate the Missouri River*." The *Intelligencer* was a little premature. It exulted that the *Independence* had made the 200-mile trip in seven sailing days, but did not mention the six days that she had spent grounded at various places. And Franklin was only one tenth of the way up the river.

While the *Independence* was making the pioneer voyage, six other steamers were gathering at St. Louis for a mass assault on the river as far as the mouth of its principal tributary, the Yellowstone, with a great military and scientific expedition that was to establish a post at that point. The Missouri was to be conquered with a bang; it turned out to be a dull thud.

In 1818 Congress and the administration of James Monroe were in a rather belligerent mood. The Missouri Fur Company had been virtually put out of business by the aggressions of the Blackfoot Indians, and Washington was sure that the nefarious British were behind this. The lawmakers felt that the Indians needed to see the Stars and Stripes and learn who were their masters, and that the far Northwest, about which Lewis and Clark and written such a fascinating journal, should be mapped and further explored. A thousand troops were assigned for the first purpose, a group of the country's leading scientists for the second. There were high hopes and great enthusiasm for the expedition. *Nile's Register* said that it would "go to the source and root of the fatal British influence which has for many years armed the Indian nations against our Western Frontier . . . . The Northwest and Hudson Bay Companies will be shut out from the commerce of the Missouri and Mississippi Indians; the American traders will penetrate in safety the recesses of the Rocky Mountains in search of its rich furs, a commerce yielding a million per annum will descend the Missouri." A more imaginative editor wrote that the expedition would open a "safe and easy communication to China," over which "we shall have the rich productions of that country transported from Canton to the Columbia, up that river to the mountains, over the mountains and down the Missouri and Mississippi, all the way (mountains and all) by the potent power of steam."

Congress was also in an expansive mood. It decreed that the troops should be carried to the mouth of the Yellowstone in steamboats, of which they rented five from a Colonel James Johnson of Kentucky. Secretary of War John C. Calhoun also undertook to build one for the use of the scientists. This was the government's first involvement with steamboats.

Johnson's boats were a complete fiasco. Two of them never got past St. Louis, a third was snagged and sank thirty miles up the Missouri, and the other two never reached Franklin, to which point Colonel Atkinson had moved his troops while awaiting the steamers. For this he had devised some paddle-wheel keelboats, the wheels turned by soldiers laboring at cranks. There was surely some hanky-panky about the Johnson contract. Although not a soldier ever set foot on one of his boats he asked for and was paid a quarter of a million dollars for the enterprise.

The government-built boat—the *Western Engineer*—was not much more successful, but it was, in appearance, the most unusual steamboat ever built. It is best described in a contemporary letter: "The bow of this vessel exhibits the form of a huge serpent, black and scaly, rising out of the water from under the boat, his head as high as the deck, darted forward, his mouth open, vomiting smoke, and apparently carrying the boat on his back. From under the boat at its stern issues a stream of foaming water, dashing violently along. All the machinery is hid. Three small brass field pieces mounted on wheel carriages stand on the deck. The boat is ascending the rapid stream at the rate of three miles an hour. Neither wind nor human hands are seen to help her, and, to the eye of ignorance, the illusion is complete, that a monster of the deep carries her on his back, smoking with fatigue, and lashing the waves with violent exertion. Her equipments are at once calculated to attract and to awe the savages. Objects pleasing and terrifying are at once placed before him—artillery, the flag of the Republic, portraits of the white man and the Indian shaking hands, the calumet of peace, a sword, then the apparent monster with a painted vessel on his back, the sides gaping with portholes and bristling with guns. Taken altogether, and without intelligence of her composition and design, it would require a daring savage to approach and accost her with Hamlet's speech: 'Be thou a spirit of health or goblin damned, etc.' "

The Western Engineer *was built by the government to explore far up the Missouri and draped with a huge serpent to frighten Indians along the way. She failed in the first purpose, and there is no evidence that she did better in the second. But one Indian did comment on her morality: "White man, bad man, keep a great spirit chained and build fire to make it work a boat."*

There is no record as to how well the *Western Engineer* served its purpose in awing the Indians, although one redskin was critical of the white man's morality when he said, "White man, bad man, keep a great spirit chained and build fire under it to make it work a boat."

The government boat was a good Missouri River vessel for its day, drawing only nineteen inches. The fact that it failed to reach even the halfway point on its voyage to the Yellowstone was apparently due to poor management rather than the deficiency of the vessel. It reached Fort Lisa, near present-day Omaha, before laying over for the winter. By the next spring Congress had lost interest in the expedition. The *Western Engineer* came back downstream, made a short and purposeless trip up the Mississippi to the foot of the Des Moines rapids and then disappeared from history.

The Missouri was not conquered to the mouth of the Yellowstone by steam for more than a decade after the abortive government expedition. Then, in 1830, Pierre Chouteau, manager at St. Louis for the American Fur Company, wrote to his New York office proposing that the company build "a small steamboat for the trade of the upper Missouri. We believe that the navigation will be much safer in going up, and possibly also in coming down, than it is by keelboat . . . . Such a boat as we require we think will cost in Cincinnati or Marietta about $7,000." When John Jacob Astor gave his consent, the 130-foot *Yellowstone* was built by the fur company and started for the river for which she was named. On the first trip she was stopped by low water at Fort Tecumseh, which was renamed Fort Pierre in honor of Pierre Chouteau, whose contribution to Missouri steamboating is commemorated in the name of South Dakota's capital city.

On her second trip, in 1833, the little vessel reached the fur company's Fort Union at the mouth of the Yellowstone and returned to St. Louis "with a full cargo of buffalo robes, furs and peltries, besides ten thousand pounds of buffalo tongues." John Jacob Astor congratulated Chouteau from Paris, writing, "Your voyage in the *Yellowstone* attracted much attention in Europe and has been noted in all the papers here." Of more consequence was the attitude of the Indians. Many who had been trading with the Hudson's Bay Company started to come to the American fur post, saying, "The British might turn out their dogs and burn their sledges, as they would no longer be useful while the Fire Boat walked on the waters."

Twenty-seven more years would elapse before steamboats reached the head of navigation of the Missouri at Fort Benton in the foothills of the Rockies of western Montana. The fur company vessels *Chippewa* and the *Key West* first ascended the river to this distant point, 3,600 miles from the mouth of the Mississippi and 3,300 feet above sea level, in 1860. In all, it took over forty years to evolve the boats, the experience and the maneuvers required to navigate the Missouri.

Most of these maneuvers had to do with getting off or over sand bars. Upriver travel, except in the highest water, was slow and laborious work. The most pedestrian means of getting through low water was to lighten the cargo in barges towed for the purpose or double-trip it by piling half on the bank and making two trips through the low spots. Virtually all the vessels were stern-wheelers, and when one grounded it was sometimes possible to get off by reversing the wheel to send a rush of water under the boat and so lift the bow. Or a boat might pull itself through

Built by the American Fur Company, the 130-foot Yellowstone *was the first steamboat to reach Fort Union at the upper end of the Missouri River. Indians who had formerly traded with the Hudson's Bay Company began bringing their furs to the American post, saying that the British dogs and sledges "would no longer be useful while the Fire Boat walked on the waters." In the above picture the* Yellowstone *is shown at St. Louis.*

by warping. Because large trees were not common on the banks of the upper Missouri, vessels carried a "dead man,"a heavy timber to the center of which was fastened a cable. This was taken forward to a point on the bank and buried, and then the capstan hauled in on the cable and dragged the vessel through the mud or sand.

When these techniques were ineffective a boat might be walked over a bar by "grasshoppering." In this interesting engineering feat two large iron-tipped spars were set up by the vessel's derricks off the bow, with their points firmly embedded in the bar. Near the top of each spar was a block through which a line attached to the side of the bow ran to the capstan. When power was applied these lines lifted the bow of the boat at the same time the stern wheel pushed the vessel forward. It was then set down on the bar, the spars moved forward, and the operation repeated until the vessel had cleared the obstruction by a series of grasshopper-like jumps.

Piloting on the Missouri was a more advanced art than on the Mississippi because it was based more on a "sixth sense" technique than on memory of the channel. There was little point in memorizing a channel that was constantly changing. This propensity of the Missouri to move around was amusingly described, somewhat later, as follows: "Time after time it has gotten out of its bed in the middle of the night, with no apparent provocation, and has hunted up a new bed, all littered with forests, cornfields, brick houses, railroad ties and telegraph poles. It has flopped into this prickly mess with a gurgle of content and has flowed along placidly for years . . . . Then it has suddenly taken a fancy to its old bed, which by this time has been filled up with suburban architecture, and back it has gone with a whoop and a rush, as happy as if it had found something really worth while."

The trip to the mountains on the Missouri was the most dangerous of all steamboat journeys. Snags resulting from trees toppled into the stream by the shifting channel were more plentiful on the Missouri than elsewhere, and there was no Henry Shreve to drag them out. There was a mountain boat namd the *Henry M. Shreve* whose captain recorded, on a single trip to Fort Benton, passing eight vessels that were breached, snagged, stranded or otherwise wrecked. During the fifty years of active steamboating on the Missouri nearly 500 vessels were lost between St. Louis and Fort Benton.

Another problem was fuel. On much of the river bank it was not readily available, and often as much time was spent in wooding as in traveling. One captain carried a team of oxen to haul logs for his vessel. The fur companies frequently changed the locations of their forts, and the stockades of abandoned ones were used for fuel. The Indians went into the wood business, and John James Audubon told of a boat on which

The course of the Missouri River through Monona County, Iowa,
1804 to 1894. The dotted and broken lines trace the changes in the
channel in the 90 years since it was first charted by Lewis and
Clark (solid lines).

he was traveling buying eight cords of wood from the savages for five cups of sugar and three of coffee, worth about a quarter in St. Louis. But the redskins soon learned better and sold their wood for what the traffic would bear, sometimes up to $15 per cord. The fuel bill for the *Henry M. Shreve* was over $6,000 for one trip upriver.

Unique steamboat obstructions on the Missouri were herds of buffalo. Boats were frequently held up for many hours waiting while hundreds of thousands of the shaggy beasts, in herds stretching as far as the eye could see, forded the stream. Buffalo meat was a staple on the river boats and passengers and crew played their parts in almost exterminating the species. A more serious hazard were the Indians, particularly the Sioux and Blackfoot, who frequently attacked boats or wooding parties. The pilothouses of mountain boats were armored with boiler iron to protect their exposed occupants from Indian bullets.

For the first thirty years, until the 1850s, steamboating on the upper river was entirely in the hands of the fur companies, which hauled their provisions, trade goods, and *engagés* up in the spring and brought furs and buffalo hides down. After the first treaty was made with the western-plains Indian tribes in 1850 they also hauled the Indian annuities. In addition to the fur company people, passengers included missionaries, scientific explorers like Audubon, adventurers like Catlin, military men, prospectors, some settlers, and Indian delegations en route to or from St. Louis.

The distinction between deck passage and cabin passage was less on these boats than elsewhere. VIPS might sleep in a bunk while *engagés* slept on the deck, but otherwise it was share and share alike, and every man was expected to turn out to repel an Indian attack or lend a hand in other emergencies. There is no mention of private staterooms nor of "sumptuous fare." Until the vessel reached game country the menu usually consisted of pork, corn, and navy beans. Every boat carried a hunter whose sole responsibility was to supply the table with fresh meat at wooding stops.

The typical mountain boat, after the first decade of steamboating on the upper Missouri, was a stern-wheeler drawing less than thirty inches when loaded with 400 tons of freight and up to 200 passengers. She was built to take punishment, with a rugged hull, a single powerful engine, and a shallow, spoon-shaped bow that helped her back off when she ran aground. There were never any "floating palaces" on this stream. Upper Missouri vessels bore the same relation to those of the same era on the lower Mississippi and the Hudson as did the Model T Ford to the Packard and Pierce Arrow of its day—they were purely utilitarian.

At the height of the fur trade steamboating on the Missouri was highly profitable because of its extreme risks. Cabin fare for the trip from

St. Louis to Fort Benton, which might take up to two months, was $300 and the freight rate 12½¢ a pound. Costs were equally high. The crews were capable frontiersmen as well as steamboat men; there were none of the loitering rousters of the lower-river boats here. The job of captain and pilot was frequently combined in one individual, who was sometimes paid as much as $2,000 per month. One of the most famed captains, Joseph LaBarge, made an annual four-month trip to the mountains commanding an American Fur Company boat for which he was paid $8,000. The high cost of fuel has already been mentioned.

Still, boats could make fabulous profits, and several boats paid for themselves in a single trip. The *William J. Lewis* cleared $60,000 in her first season, the *Peter Balen* $65,000 in the same year. The *Waverly* made only one trip before she was snagged, but she grossed $50,000. Her downstream cargo included 508 bales of buffalo hides, 5 bundles of antelope skins, and 37 wolf pelts.

Whiskey was an important, though contraband, cargo on upriver boats. Long before the Eighteenth Amendment created the expression "rum-runner," Missouri River boats were engaged in smuggling liquor. Whiskey was far and away the most important item of trade goods. Blankets, trinkets, and manufactured goods were of little concern to the Indians in comparison with liquor. They wanted whiskey and would trade with anybody who supplied it. A government edict of 1832 prohibiting the introduction of liquor into the Indian country would have put the American Fur Company out of business had it been strictly enforced.

On her third trip up the river the *Yellowstone* carried a still and a quantity of corn to Fort Union, and the trader there, McKenzie, established a corn plantation at the mouth of the Iowa. McKenzie soon wrote to Chouteau in St. Louis: "Our manufactory flourishes admirable. We only want corn to keep us going. The Mandan corn yields badly but makes a fine, sweet liquor. Do not load the boat too heavily at St. Louis, that a few hundred bushels of corn may be placed on board at the Bluffs . . . . I have a good corn mill, a respectable distillery, and can produce as fine a liquor as need be drunk. I believe that no law of the United States is thereby broken . . . . But liquor I must have or quit any pretension to trade in this part." Whether or not the law actually forbade distilling in the Indian country, the St. Louis agent of the Indian Department chose to so interpret it. When jealous competitors rushed to him with an account of McKenzie's still, he threatened the company with the loss of its license unless it stopped making firewater.

After that, smuggling whiskey was a regular practice aboard the steamboats. As long as the army was in control this did not present much difficulty. The American Fur Company was far more responsible in dealing with the Indians than their many little fly-by-night competitors who operated off the beaten trail with pack trains. It would have been impossible to prevent them from smuggling whiskey, and if the fur company had been unable to supply ardent spirits the trade would have shifted to these less responsible traders. If there were to be drunken Indians the army wanted them at the fur company forts, where they could be policed, rather than off in the remote villages from which they might run amok, so the practical army officers looked the other way when boats came through with liquor. Not so the agents of the Department of Indian Affairs. Some of these were ministers who, quite rightly, were more concerned with the physical and moral welfare of their charges than with the practical economics of the frontier or the problems of the army.

John James Audubon, in his journal of a trip upstream on the *Omega* in 1843, tells an amusing story of his participation in a bootlegging operation. The minister-agent at Bellevue was absent when the vessel stopped there, and the army did not search her. Upon the agent's return he insisted that a captain and a squad of dragoons gallop upstream after her to seize any liquor aboard. When he caught the *Omega* the army captain regretfully told the boat captain that he would have to search the vessel. Audubon had a permit to carry spirits, presumably to preserve his bird specimens, but it did not distinguish betwen the kind of spirits that are good for birds and those that are palatable to men.

The naturalist suggested that there was no hurry about searching the boat—the captain must first join him for lunch. By the time the meal was over Audubon's stock of preservative had been diminished and the captain and his men had lost whatever interest they ever had in searching for liquor. Meanwhile, the crew had loaded the boat's cargo of contraband on the car of a little cargo-carrying tramway that ran up one side of the shallow hold and back the other. While the military stumbled through the dark cargo space, going aft from the hatch on one side and forward on the other, crewmen quietly pushed the tramcar ahead of them in the dark. The boat was given a clean bill of health and proceeded on its not-quite-uneventful way. A few miles upriver it was fired on by a party of Santee Indians. Audubon preserved two of the spent bullets among his souvenirs. Later it had to make its way through the decaying carcasses of thousands of buffalo that had drowned in a spring freshet while fording the stream and of which the stench was almost unbearable.

On the next trip upstream Joseph LaBarge, who was piloting the *Nimrod*, was ready for the zealous minister at Bellevue. The whiskey was packed in the center of barrels of flour consigned to the fur company manager at that point. These were unloaded as soon as the nose of the vessel touched the river bank, before the Indian Affairs agent made a thorough search. Clean as a whistle, the *Nimrod* was authorized to proceed but, strangely, LaBarge seemed in no hurry to resume his trip. Somewhat suspicious at a boat lying beside the bank with its steam up, the minister stationed a guard. LaBarge had to wait until that worthy fell asleep in the wee hours before he reloaded the whiskey barrels and carried them to the thirsty Indians.

The remainder of this trip, too, was not entirely uneventful. At one point while LaBarge was prospecting for a channel in the yawl ahead of the steamer he was captured by a raiding party of Pawnees. Fortunately this was one Indian tongue he spoke and, in return for some of the illicit firewater, they let him go. Later the boat met four bull buffalo swimming in the river. The crew wounded two and launched the yawl to lasso one of them and bring it aboard. The mate, who was handling the lasso, was a veteran of the Royal Navy who knew a lot about ropes but nothing about buffalo. He dropped the noose over the neck of one of the un-wounded beasts, which promptly took off with the yawl behind it to give the crew a South Dakota version of a New Bedford sleigh ride, with a buffalo instead of a whale as the motive power. Fortunately the stem post of the yawl gave way before it had been dragged too far across the prairie. The *Nimrod* then reached her destination without further inci-dent except a hail-and-wind storm that broke all the glass in her cabin and carried away the pilot house. The boat went on with a buffalo-skin roof to cover the wheel. Incidents such as these were more or less regular features of Missouri River steamboating.

While the fur trade dominated steamboating on the upper reaches of the Missouri, a more diversified business developed on its lower reaches. The river runs almost due west for 400 miles across the state of Missouri before it swings north, and at the western border where Kansas City and St. Joseph now stand were the termini of two great overland routes—the Sante Fe Trial to the Southwest, Mexico, and lower California and the Oregon Trail to Great Salt Lake, the western mountains, and the Pacific coast. This vast area might be likened to a fan of which the stretch of the Missouri River between St. Louis and Kansas City was the handle. The ribs of the fan were outstretched from Sante Fe in the south to Fort Union at the mouth of the Yellowstone in the north. There were several modes of travel along the ribs, from the upper-river boats to Fort Union to covered wagons or pack trains to Sante Fe, but travel along the handle was usually by river boat. By the 1840s there was regular packet service acorss the state carrying travelers and their equipment and supplies to the eastern ends of the trails. This business gained impetus in 1846 when, during the Mexican War, the river boats carried troops to Forts Leaven-worth and Kearny for expeditions against New Mexico and California. It swelled to a flood when "the Forty-Niners" hit the trail and with the migration of the Mormons.

After being harried from New York to Ohio to Missouri, the Mormons, by 1841, had settled in Illinois and built the substantial city of Nauvoo. Their preference for polygamy and their potential political power soon caused trouble there, which resulted in the mob murder of the sect's founder, Joseph Smith. In 1846 the new leader, Brigham Young, decided that there would be no peace for his band in the United States and decided to migrate west, into what was then the Republic of Mexico. Young and the vanguard of Mormons reached Great Salt Lake in July 1847, but two large colonies remained on the bank of the Missouri near the present sites of Omaha and Council Bluffs. For the next decade these settlements were the jumping-off points for the major Mormon migrations, and the steamboats carried thousands of the faithful with their chattels, cattle, and supplies to the beginning of their overland trek to their final home.

The lower river as far as Council Bluffs, Iowa, was really a separate trade, with vessels that were not mountain boats. Most of these were side-wheelers, larger than the upper-river craft. One of the most famous, the *Emilie*, was built by Captain LaBarge after he left the fur company in 1859. The *Emilie* was 225 feet long, 32-feet abeam with a 6-foot hold, and could easily carry 500 tons. The most famous cargo that the *Emilie* carried was Abraham Lincoln, who visited Council Bluffs in 1859. He had not yet been mentioned for the presidency and his trip was supposedly nonpolitical, but he did make a speech. Said the Council Bluffs *Weekly Nonpareil*, "The distinguished 'sucker' has yielded to the earnest importunities of our citizens,—without distinction of party,—and will speak upon the political issues of the day, at Concert Hall, this evening . . . . Go and hear 'Old Abe.' " The Great Emancipator also bought a building lot in Council Bluffs and asked LaBarge to send him a fine buffalo robe.

Two years later the lower river would have its counterpart to the upper river's Indian attacks when both sides in the Civil War started to harass steamboats. The principal offenders were Confederate guerrillas on the south bank of the river, ruthless gangs who were far more interested in loot than in the southern cause. One such band attacked the *Sam Gaty* while she was going upstream with some paroled Union soldiers among her passengers and forty free Negroes in her crew. The ruffians boarded the vessel, threw the freight overboard, robbed the passengers, broke open the safe, and shot such of the paroled soldiers as they could

Southern guerrillas attack a steamboat that has come in for a night landing on the Missouri. Some gangs fought for the southern cause; others, for loot.

identify. The Negroes were taken ashore, where those who were not killed started their journey back to slavery.

Captain LaBarge had the misfortune to be persecuted by both sides. At St. Joseph his *Emilie* picked up some southern sympathizers as passengers, and they gave a loud cheer for Jefferson Davis as the boat pulled into the river. Word of this was wired to Fort Leavenworth, where a group of irate citizens decided, quite unreasonably, to hang LaBarge when his vessel arrived. The lynch mob was waiting on the levee when a friend of LaBarge's jumped aboard before the gangplank was lowered to warn him not to land. The prudent captain made no further stops until he reached the safety of St. Louis. On another occasion when his vessel was under contract to the Union forces, the Confederates seized it and forced him to return upstream to convey General Price, who was ill, to safety. Although LaBarge obtained a letter from Price saying that he had acted under duress, Union General Lyons placed him under arrest when he returned, and the confiscation of his vessel was prevented only by a good friend on Lyons' staff. In the no-man's-land of Missouri during the Civil War no steamboat was safe, but the profits were tremendous.

In the early 1850s mountain men in the far Northwest, perhaps inspired by the California gold strike, started poking into the ground and rooting around in streams. Gold was discovered on the Salmon and Clearwater rivers in Idaho, and a small stream of prospectors began to flow up the Missouri and the Columbia and to trek overland from Salt Lake. Then a strike was made in Montana about fifty miles from present-day Butte, and some of the parties headed for Idaho decided to go to this new location. The business built slowly until, in 1863, a rich lode was uncovered at Alder Gulch on the Jefferson Fork of the Missouri. The next year a still richer strike was made at Last Chance Gulch and the Montana gold rush started. Overnight Virginia City sprang up at Alder Gulch and attained a population of 10,000 in two years. The town that arose at Last Chanch Gulch was named Helena and outdistanced her Alder Gulch rival to become the state capital.

During the last half of the 1860s steamboating to the head of navigation became a bonanza business. Only six boats arrived at Fort Benton during the four years after the *Key West* and the *Chippewa* made the initial voyage. In 1866-67 seventy boats reached the outpost, bringing twenty quartz mills and ten thousand gold-hungry passengers. The *Deer Lodge* wintered at Fort Benton in 1866. On her way down in the spring she passed forty boats struggling up the stream packed to the guards with people, oxen, mules, wagons, tools, food, and other freight. There was an alternate route to the mines from the east, the overland Montana Road that ran from Fort Laramie on the North Platte River to the headwaters of the Yellowstone. The Sioux and Cheyenne prevented travel along this route so successfully that it was practically abandoned in 1866, leaving the Missouri, which ran within a hundred miles of the diggings, as the only access to the golden wealth of the mountains.

A picture of steamboating during the gold rush was left in the memoirs of Captain Grant Marsh, who brought the *Luella* to Fort Benton in the spring of 1866. Before the precious metal had been found near it, the fort had been a quiet, well-ordered place, with discipline maintained among both Indians and whites by the fur company. Now it was a sprawling, muddy collection of tents, shacks, warehouses, and saloons selling whiskey at forty cents a drink and offering girls who were *persona non grata* in more civilized communities. There was no official law; such order as existed was ruthlessly maintained by a Vigilante Committee. One of the *Luella*'s crew who stole a bottle of high-alcohol-content patent medicine was flogged almost to death, and the vigilantes told Marsh that they had come within three votes of hanging him.

Shortly after her arrival the *Luella* performed a mission that, though it was not evident at the time, marked the beginning of the end of fur trade on the Missouri. Fort Union at the mouth of the Yellowstone had long been the greatest Indian trading post in the United States—Fort Benton was an outpost. Now the fur company was closing the lower post and the *Luella* went down to pick up its supplies.

Marsh made another short downstream trip to rescue the cargo and passengers and salvage the machinery of the stranded *Marion*. Profits from the gold-rush trade were so enticing that some deeper-draft lower-river boats tried to share them by going upstream where they did not belong. The *Marion* was one of several that did not make it.

The *Luella* was the last boat to leave Benton in September 1866, and carried the largest single shipment of gold dust ever brought down the river—$1,250,000 worth—and the 230 miners to whom it belonged. Although the cargo was light, the *Luella* was a long time loading. Each handful of the supposedly golden grains with which the miners paid their fares had to be washed before the clerk's vigilant eye to make sure that it had not been adulterated with sand. The miners carried their wealth in money belts around their waists. When the *Luella* first grounded, a passenger who engaged to help the crew get her off fell overboard. The water was only two feet deep but the current was strong and the weight of his hard-won wealth was so great that he was swept downstream and drowned.

Near the abandoned Fort Union the *Luella* was hailed by a beautiful Cuban girl astride a horse on the bank. The presence of a luscious Latin at the mouth of the Yellowstone was due to the army's decision to build little Fort Buford near the site of Fort Union; the girl on horseback was a captain's wife who had ridden from the fort when she heard the approaching vessel. The hazards of the country were pointed up when the captain's wife, while riding the short distance back to the fort to tell her husband that they had company, was ambushed by Indians, and only a sharp application of her spurs saved her from what was then seriously described as "a fate worse than death."

The *Luella* herself had her brush with Indians a few miles farther downstream. The savages had probably been following the vessel at some distance back from the river bank, waiting for her to get into trouble. Their chance came when the *Luella* grounded under a high bluff in a manner that required grasshoppering. As the crew started to set the spars the Indians attacked from the bluff, shooting down to make the deck untenable. The best shots among the passengers crouched behind the stacks and the pilothouse and picked off those redskins rash enough to expose themselves to fire while the crew returned to its work.

The gold rush introduced the last phase of steamboating on the upper Missouri and its tributaries—serving the army in the Indian Wars that were at their height during the 1860s and '70s. The white man's lust for gold contributed the final straw to the red man's accumulated injustices. Supposedly iron-clad treaties reserved to the Indians the lands in which the gold was found, except for white traders. But treaties could not stop gold-hungry immigrants, and when the army came to protect them the Sioux and Blackfoot took to the warpath.

In the several campaigns against the Indians, steamboats figured large in the logistics. The first big expedition against the Sioux, in 1864, involved some 4,000 men, under General Sully, and eight steamboats: the *Marcella, Sam Gaty, Chippewa Falls, General Grant, Isabella, Tempest, Alone,* and *Island City.* They neither fought nor chased Indians, but served as movable supply bases for the horse soldiers who did the fighting and chasing, and they connected and supplied the many far-flung river-bank outposts the army established in the Indian country. As Sully's horsemen moved overland from stream to stream, the steamers pushed far beyond previous civilization to replenish their rations and ammunition and take out the wounded.

This campaign ended on the Yellowstone when, in mid-August, the weary, heat-crazed troopers reached the bank of that shallow stream and found the *Chippewa Falls* and the *Alone* awaiting them with much-needed food. The *Island City* was supposed to be there, but it had been snagged at the mouth of the tributary and had sunk, taking with it the material with which Sully had planned to equip a fort up the stream. After feeding the army the two vessels ferried it across the river for its march back to Fort Union. Then the army had to help the boats. The water had fallen so low that it was necessary to use cavalry horses to drag them over low-water spots on their voyage back to the Missouri.

The vessel of greatest renown in the Indian wars was the *Far West*, captained by the same Grant Marsh who had taken the largest gold shipment down the Missouri. This vessel's claim to fame was based primarily on her minor involvement in "Custer's Last Stand" in 1876. She began the campaign as a supply vessel for the command of General Terry, of which Custer's cavalry was a part. Terry's troops had marched out from Fort Lincoln at Bismarck, North Dakota, to rendezvous with General Gibbons' command on the Yellowstone at the mouth of the Powder River. As soon as the ice permitted, Marsh brought the *Far West* up to Fort Lincoln, loaded her with 200 tons of supplies, and set out for the camp on the Yellowstone.

Grant Marsh had been selected for this assignment because he was the only steamboat captain who knew the Yellowstone. The preceding year General Philip Sheridan, in extreme command in the West, had sent him exploring up that stream in another vessel, the *Josephine*. The logistics of the coming campaign were to be determined by how far steamboats could get up the Yellowstone to supply the troops. There was also a scientific aspect to the expedition, which included several professors from the Smithsonian Institution.

Beyond its lower reaches the Yellowstone was virgin territory for a steamboat, but the *Josephine* had no great difficulty getting up to the mouth of the Big Horn. The current was fairly swift, four to six miles an hour, but the water was at its spring crest with a minimum depth of eight feet. As the vessel plowed along the scientists measured the length of the river in a rather ingenious manner. The hurricane deck was 150 feet long. Two men stationed at the front of it took turns walking to the stern, carefully keeping abreast of an object on the shore. Each time a man reached the stern the vessel had traveled 150 feet. The number of trips from bow to stern, multiplied by 150, indicated the length of the river.

When the Big Horn River was reached the explorers were surprised at its size and volume. It was fully 450 yards wide and had a powerful current. Marsh pushed the nose of the *Josephine* 12 miles up this stream out of curiosity and then returned to his assigned task of further exploring the Yellowstone. Beyond the Big Horn travel on the main stream became more difficult. The current at one place raced at nine miles an hour, a torrent which the *Josephine*, under a full head of steam, could barely match. She was sparred through to quieter water and steamed on to Pompey's Pillar, a landmark famed from the Lewis and Clark expedition. High on this tall tower of yellow sandstone, rising from the floor of a valley, was carved "Wm. Clark, July 25th, 1806." Marsh climbed up to engrave below this, "*Josephine*, June 3rd, 1875."

The vessel pushed on with increasing difficulty, repeatedly warping and sparring her way through rapids and inching through island-hemmed chutes that were scarcely wider than her hull, until she finally struggled through a stretch of white water that her crew named Hell Roaring Rapids. A party that reconnoitered ahead on foot reported that the river beyond this point was so broken up by islands that the vessel could not get through. The *Josephine* was then 483 miles from the mouth of the Yellowstone and within 60 miles of the northeast corner of what is now Yellowstone National Park. Marsh's report to General Sheridan to the effect that the Yellowstone was readily navigable in the spring to the mouth of the Big Horn determined the strategy of the 1876 campaign, which would take the troops into the heart of the Indian country.

When, during this campaign, the *Far West* reached the rendezvous point at the mouth of the Powder River she found Gibbons' command on one side of the Yellowstone and Terry and Custer on the other. She unloaded

FREDERICK WAY, JR.

Remembered chiefly for her role in Custer's Last Stand, the supply vessel Far West *served on the upper Missouri during the Indian Wars. In her cabin General Custer planned his campaign against the Indians in 1876, and two days later Custer's Indian scout, Curly, returned to the* Far West *with the first reports of the massacre.*

her supplies, returned downstream for more, and then became Terry's headquarters. In her cabin Generals Terry, Gibbons, and Custer planned the tactics that would lead the impetuous cavalry commander to his death in one of the most famous battles in American history. The battle plan was simply a pincer movement by Custer's cavalry and Gibbons' infantry that would envelop the Indians, whose trail had been discovered leading into the valley of the Little Big Horn River. While the brass conferred in the cabin a more tense battle was waged around a poker table in the pilot-house, involving Marsh, Custer's younger brother Tom, and three infantry officers. According to Marsh, Captain Crowell of the Sixth Infantry walked away from the game in the wee hours of the morning richer by several thousand dollars.

After Custer marched out with twelve troops of the Seventh Cavalry the *Far West* ferried Gibbons' troops across the river and then followed them upstream to the mouth of the Big Horn, where eight days' rations were issued from the supplies on the boat. Then General Terry ordered the vessel to proceed up the Big Horn, if possible to the mouth of the Little Big Horn, to establish a forward supply base. After the first few miles, which Marsh had traversed the previous year, this proved to be an almost continual process of warping against the strong current. Troops carried a cable along the shore and fastened it to a tree, and the capstan pulled the boat forward. On the second day the river became so narrow that cables were put ashore on each bank and both port and starboard capstans were used to pull the boat up the middle of the river. While the men were sweating at this work they watched tall columns of smoke in the sky farther up the valley, caused, they believed, by the burning of Indian tepees by the victorious white troops.

On the afternoon of the second day the *Far West* reached the mouth of the Little Big Horn and was moored to an island in midstream to guard against attack, after which everybody started to fish for the salmon, pike, and catfish with which the river abounded. They were so engaged when a mounted Indian broke through the willows on the bank, saving himself from being shot by a trigger-happy trooper by frantically making the peace sign. The redskin proved to be Custer's scout Curly. On the deck of the *Far West* the Crow scout, who spoke no English, drew a diagram of a little circle full of dots that he indicated were white men, surrounded by a larger circle with many more dots to which he pointed as he repeatedly said, "Sioux, Sioux." He then made signs for being hit by bullets and scalped, and crossed out the dots in the little circle. Thus, on the deck of the *Far West*, was filed the first report of Custer's Last Stand.

The next day an exhausted white courier, pursued by Indians to within sight of the boat, arrived with news from the infantry column that had reached the battlefield to find the scalped and mutilated bodies of Custer and five troops of the Seventh Cavalry. Major Reno, Custer's subordinate, and the remaining seven troops of the Seventh Cavalry had fought another action a few miles from the massacre site and held the Indians off for two days until relieved by the infantry. The *Far West* was to prepare to receive Reno's wounded and take dispatches back to civilization. Under the direction of a doctor who was aboard, the crew and soldiers cleared the open deck aft of the boilers and piled it eighteen inches deep with fresh grass cut from the marshlands along the river, over which they placed tarpaulins to form a gigantic, soft bed. Then, as night fell, parties went up the valley to make fires at intervals to light the stretcher bearers and guide them to the vessel. About two o'clock in the morning the sad column stumbled through the flickering firelight to lay fifty-two groaning wounded on the king-sized bed of the *Far West*.

Before the *Far West* pulled out a lieutenant of the Seventh Cavalry who had been detached with Terry appeared on the bank with the sole survivor of the Custer massacre, the horse Comanche, mount of one of the troop captains. A grass-carpeted stall was hastily constructed at the stern of the vessel and the wounded animal was tenderly led aboard.

The dispatches that the *Far West* brought out from the mouth of the Little Big Horn to Bismarck, North Dakota, were the world's first news of the Custer massacre. The vessel then crossed the river to Fort Lincoln to carry the tragic news to the twenty-eight newly bereaved widows at that outpost.

Grant Marsh was not finished with the aftermath of the Custer massacre. Sitting Bull, who commanded the Sioux, had fled to Canada. When he voluntarily surrendered with a few destitute followers six years later, the *W. J. Behan*, commanded by Marsh, brought the captives down the Missouri. In Canada the Sioux chief had learned to write his name. He had also learned the value of money. When crowds gathered at each stop the vessel made he regally acceded to requests for his autograph—at a dollar per signature. Somewhere along the line Captain Marsh was presented with a handsomely carved pipe, to which Sitting Bull took a fancy. As Marsh told the story, the Indian offered to buy it. Not wanting to sell a gift, Marsh set a price of fifty dollars. Through an interpreter the chief grunted that fifty dollars was too much money. "Tell him," said Marsh to the interpreter, "that he has kept me scared for twenty years along the river and he ought to give me something for that." With dignity Sitting Bull retorted, "I did not come on your land to scare you. If you had not come on my land you would not have been scared, either."

It took forty-one years, from 1819 to 1860, for steamboats gradually to work their way up to the head of navigation of the Missouri. It took about thirty years for steamboating to wither away on that stream as the railroads inexorably reached farther and farther upstream. As elsewhere, the initial effect of the railroad was to give an impetus to the steamboats that carried people and goods on from the railhead, but as the railhead advanced, steamboating languished behind it.

The Hannibal and St. Joseph Railroad reached St. Joseph, on the western boundary of Missouri, in 1859, at which time that city partially supplanted St. Louis as the terminal for the upper-river traffic. True, a line of packets briefly flourished running south to Kansas City and north to Sioux City, but when the Sioux City and Pacific Railroad reached the latter city in 1868, lower-river steamboat traffic again declined. And so it went through the 1870s and '80s. Immediately after the famed golden spike was driven at Ogden, Utah, to complete the Union Pacific Railroad in 1869, a freight spur was thrown up to Helena. In 1872 the Northern Pacific reached Bismarck. The final blow was delivered in 1883 when the main line of the Great Northern Railroad reached the upper Missouri valley and fostered the town of Great Falls, Montana, a few miles above Fort Benton and beyond the reach of the steamboats. The great fur-trading and gold-mining days when the old post was the commercial center were gone; it declined (present population 1,500) as its new rival on the shining rails grew. The last steamboat left Fort Benton in 1890.

Bonanza Boats

It all happened within a single decade. In 1839, when ex-papermaker Johann Augustus Sutter, a Swiss, sailed the schooners *Nicholas* and *Isobel* up the Sacramento River from the Russian settlement of Fort Ross at its mouth to establish his inland empire of New Helvetia, there was nothing else on the river but Indian boats woven of tule reeds and the dugouts of Spanish missionaries. In 1849, when a Hudson River side-wheeler, the *Senator*, churned its way over the same route, California had changed from a Mexican state to an independent republic, the Russians were gone and their fort had become the boom town of San Francisco, and Sutter's Fort was about to become Sacramento.

The *Senator* was enticed to the distant California waterway by the lure that brought all steamboats up all rivers—profit. When carpenter James Wilson Marshall scraped some shining yellow flakes from Sutter's millrace in 1848 he started a frantic pilgrimage for gold to the valleys of the Sacramento, its tributaries the Feather and American, and the San Joachin. Conveying and supplying this pilgrimage was a bonanza in which scores of steamboats rushed to share. During the next ten years the Golden State's rivers became busy traffic arteries up which varied vessels chugged to serve the newly arrived populace of California's great inland valley.

The *Senator* was not the first steamboat on the Sacramento. In 1847 a Russian bark, the *Naslednich*, moored at Fort Ross and disgorged from her hold the hull sections, engine, and wheels of the steamer *Sitka*. The little Russian vessel was not much of a steamboat, being only 37 feet long, and she was not new, as the Russians had been using her in Alaska. But when she plowed up the Sacramento to Sutter's New Helvetia, she brought steam power to California's rivers for the first time. She took more than six days to cover the 125 miles between Fort Ross and Sutter's Fort, and *Daily Alta California* reported that she was beaten by an ox team on the the downstream voyage. It is possible that this was her only river trip. Two months later she sank in San Francisco Bay.

The gold rush brought steamboats converging at the Golden Gate from various points on the east coast, and local entrepreneurs were quick to start a native boat-building industry. The *Senator* was not the first bonanza boat to reach western waters. There was a *Sacramento* that arrived in the hold of a brig in July 1849; another *Sacramento*, a scow with an engine, that may have been built locally; and the *Lady Washington*, which was assembled at Sutter's Embarcadero and took to the water on August 9, 1849. But the *Senator*, which left New York on March 10 of that year, was the first river boat to round Cape Horn and the earliest respectable steamer in California.

The 220-foot side-wheeler *Senator* was not built for any waters rougher than those of Long Island Sound; she surely had no business in the Straits of Magellan. But gold is where you find it and when her owner, who had purchased the vessel from "Deacon" Daniel Drew, found a skipper who was willing to risk the trip—a navy lieutenant named LaFayette Maynard— he took off with one paying passenger, a lawyer who envisioned a personal bonanza in San Francisco settling disputes over mining claims.

With fuel piled high on her deck, the river boat hugged the Atlantic coast, wallowing in the waves on rough days when the seas sometimes canted the vessel so violently that one wheel would spin madly in the air. She touched a few ports below the Mason-Dixon line and in the West Indies for fuel and then made a daring crossing to hedgehop down the coast of South America, with frequent pauses for fuel. Fate was kind to her as she rounded treacherous Cape Horn, and she reached Panama without serious mishap. Here she found her first bonanza in a horde of treasure seekers who had come across the isthmus and were clamoring for transportation northward. The *Senator* took 200 of them aboard at $500 a head and proceeded on to San Francisco, reaching the Golden Gate seven months and seventeen days after she had left her slip in New York's East River.

The *Senator* immediately started to ply between San Francisco and Sacramento, making in eight or nine hours a trip that had taken sailing craft days or sometimes weeks. On each trip she was jammed with prospectors eager to pay $45 to $65 for the 125-mile voyage, and loaded with freight at $40 to $80 a ton. She could gross perhaps $50,000 for a one-way trip. Although competition quickly put an end to such lush profits, before this happened the *Senator* probably earned more money than any steamboat in history. Perhaps an even better instance of the fabulous profits of gold-rush steamboating was an unnamed scow fitted with an engine that had been intended for a dredge. For two months this makeshift vessel carried bricks up the Feather River at a dollar per brick and lumber at $150 per thousand board feet. It was then sold at auction for $40,000.

The *Senator* was but one of a parade of river boats that made the perilous passage round the Horn, almost all of them successfully. The *Sarah* and the *California*, which competed on the run from Haverhill to Newburyport, Massachusetts, shifted their competition to the Sacramento. From "down east" came the *W. J. Pease* and the *Governor Dana.* From Long Island Sound came the *Hartford*, the *Commodore Preble*, the *General Warren*, the *Antelope*, and others. The biggest and plushest vessel to make the long ocean trek was the 530-ton side-wheeler *New World*, which was snatched from the claws of the law to make the trip. A New Yorker named William Brown started to build this floating palace in 1849, with the idea that she would excel anything on the Sound or the Hudson in magnificence. Unfortunately, his ideas were bigger than his pocketbook. Her gilt mirrors, crystal chandeliers, marble-topped tables, and other luxurious appointments were in place and she was almost ready for her shakedown trip when some of Brown's creditors decided that they wanted their money. Pieces of legal paper were tacked up on her pilothouse door and deputy sheriffs lounged on her ornate sofas to attest that the vessel had been attached.

By blarney or bribery Brown convinced the law officers that the vessel would be more valuable to the money men whose minions they were if she had been proved. The deputies agreed that the *New World* could be taken for a trial run in the river and did not realize their mistake until the vessel entered the Narrows at the foot of New York's upper bay, outward-bound for the Pacific coast. By that time it was too late to do other than accept the captain's offer of a dinghy in which they could row back to Staten Island, and the *New World* continued on to her new world in the Far West. She plied the Sacramento for a decade to make Brown a wealthy man, then moved up to the Columbia and ended, 29 years after she stole away from New York, as a San Francisco Bay ferry. Whether or not Brown ever paid the creditors who had seized her is not part of the record.

Many smaller steamers, which could not risk the ocean trip, came to the Golden Gate in the holds or on the decks of sailing vessels. Most of these were shipped in sections, to be reassembled on arrival, but a special carrier was constructed to convey the *S. B. Wheeler* to the west coast in one piece. This 110-foot stern-wheeler was built in St. Stephens, New Brunswick, specifically for the gold-rush trade. On neighboring ways the sailing bark *Fanny* took shape and was launched, minus a deck and masts, before the *Wheeler*. Spectators thronged to watch as the *Fanny* was slowly sunk in deep water off the end of the *Wheeler*'s ways. The latter was then launched and floated over the submerged *Fanny*, which was raised to encase the steamer snugly in her hold. She was then decked and rigged, and spread her sails for the long ocean trip. When the bark reached its destination the process was reversed and, as the *Fanny* sank beneath her, the

Wheeler floated into San Francisco Bay. The *Fanny* was then again raised, rerigged and returned to the sea lanes while the steaming child of her womb churned up and down the San Joachin River between San Francisco and Stockton.

The eastern boats, with their relatively deep draft, could reach Sacramento, the jumping-off point for the diggings, with ease, but as the demand increased for transportation on the upper Sacramento and its tributaries, the locally built craft developed into a compromise between eastern and Mississippi steamboats. They were usually stern-wheelers with high-pressure engines and hulls that were similar to but somewhat deeper than western river boats. The boilers, the furnaces, and the base of the engine were in the hull and extended up through the main deck, which was devoted almost entirely to cargo. The boiler deck supported the main cabin and dining room, a few staterooms, and the bar. As on the Mississippi boats, there were a texas and a pilothouse above all. There was no ladies' cabin on the early boats—there were no ladies—but the California vessels had a passenger space unique to that area, the "China hold" in the bow for Oriental passengers.

During the brief bonanza period the boats came downstream lightly laden with little but gold dust; everybody wanted to get in, not out. Upstream they carried prospective miners who could afford the tariff, building machinery, mining equipment, food, and everything else needed to maintain the mushrooming communities. The first owners on the scene could command their own prices for freight; with eggs selling at a dollar apiece at the mines and whiskey at forty dollars a quart, shippers were not prone to argue about freight rates. An unusual item of freight was cats—common cats. Rats were such a plague at the diggings that their feline enemies sold for twenty-five dollars.

In the hectic and lurid situation of the gold rush the rivers naturally produced some colorful characters. A minor west coast Mike Fink was Captain William Corlett, who reached the Sacramento in 1849. Because of his rugged individualism and the heavy fists with which he expressed it, Corlett changed vessels frequently, but his ability always procured him a new berth. His prodigious strength was legend, although it is doubtful that he ever actually saved a purebred bull from a flooded island by swimming from shore to boat dragging the animal behind him by the tail. There may be truth in the story of the time he caught two Chinese rifling his office, tied their queues together, dunked them overboard, and then hung them up on the texas to dry; and he may, as legend avers, have picked up under each arm the two "ladies of the evening" whom he found plying their trade on his boat and dropped them quietly overboard within wading distance of the bank.

Corlett is credited with the first improvement to the channel of the

The first river boat to round Cape Horn, this Hudson River side-wheeler was lured

to California by the rush for gold in 1849. The painting is by James and John Bard.

Sacramento River. He tied a half dozen plows together, lowered them over the side at the end of a hawser, and drove his steamer up and down in front of the levee at Sacramento. The current flushed away the sand that his underwater plowing loosened and removed the bar that blocked the channel.

The bonanza period for steamboats on the California rivers lasted less than two years. By 1851 California yards were turning out boats so fast that shipping space exceeded even the boom demand. As on the Hudson, rate wars resulted. In the early 1850s the fare to Sacramento tumbled from thirty dollars a head to ten, to five, to one, and finally to a dime. In other respects the business resembled that on the Hudson in the 1830s. Western runners were perhaps somewhat more vigorous than their eastern brethren in extolling the speed, safety, and comfort of their respective vessels; fist fights were common between runners, and it is said that if two of them latched on to the same prospect the traveler was lucky if his arms were not pulled from their sockets.

The solution, again as on the Hudson, was an association of the principal owners, formed in 1854, called the California Steam Navigation Company, which stabilized fares at ten dollars from San Francisco to Sacramento. Fights between independent and monopoly boats were frequent throughout the 1850s, with deliberate rammings, a few instances of gunplay, and temporary rate wars during which passengers were carried free; but the Navigation Company had such a well-filled war chest that none of the independents lasted long. Another situation reminiscent of the Livingston monopoly on the Hudson was the pressure applied in San Francisco by the politically potent Navigation Company to prevent independents from getting licenses to carry passengers into the city. The owner of the *Defiance* lived up to the name of his boat by defying the port officials, who refused to let him "carry" passengers into their domain. He transshipped his passengers to barges outside the city limits and, with band playing and passengers disdainfully jeering the authorities, towed them in.

By 1860 steamboating on the Sacramento had settled down to a fairly well-ordered business. The boats now connected what was rapidly becoming a metropolis at the mouth of the stream with a thriving community 125 miles above, and the trade had become very similar to that between New York City and Albany, with one dramatic exception. In April 1860 the first Pony Express rider threw his saddlebags aboard the ex-Long Island Sound steamer *Antelope* at Sacramento and she streaked downstream to complete the coast-to-coast mail service. The *Antelope* also carried a lot of gold dust for Wells Fargo's Express and thus earned the name *The Gold Boat*.

1860 also saw the birth of the most famed California steamboat, the *Chrysopolis*, which Bret Harte, proud of his knowledge of Greek, properly called the *Golden City*. By this time the "floating palaces" had made their bow on eastern waters. When Captain James Whitney returned from a honeymoon trip to New York and described these luxury craft to California steamboat owner John North, the latter resolved that San Francisco should have a vessel that would outshine them. He went north where the giant trees grew to select timbers for his craft, dragging them through the streets of the bayside city with twelve-horse teams. There was a war on back east, but North's quarter-million dollars enticed skilled labor to the Pacific coast and brought a mammoth low-pressure engine around the Horn. His slim princess grew to a length of 245 feet and a breadth of 40 feet, and her wheels stood as tall as a three-story house. Her white paint was enlivened with much red velvet, shining brass, gleaming mirrors, and glistening gold leaf. She could carry 1,000 passengers and 700 tons of freight between San Francisco and Sacramento in five hours and ten minutes at a speed of almost twenty-three miles an hour.

For fifteen years the *Chrysopolis* made a daily trip between the two cities, up one day and down the next, the toast of prideful San Franciscans. Her specialty was "the conveyance of bridal parties," and she was widely recognized as "the carrier of the elite." As elsewhere, the railroad ended her career as a luxury packet. In 1875 she was sold to the Central Pacific Railroad, rebuilt as a double-ender, renamed the *Oakland*, and set to shuttling back and forth between Oakland and San Francisco as a ferry. During the next fifty-five years she carried millions of Californians to and from work, few of whom knew they were riding on the one-time queen of the river. The Bay Bridge retired her as a ferry in 1930, and ten years later she was broken up for scrap. But the *Chrysopolis* outwitted the junkmen. They got her engine and other ironwork out, but before they could break up the hull a spark from an acetylene torch found its way into her old timbers and the eighty-year-old river queen was cremated.

The California river boats were not the only inland steamers to share the bonanza of the gold-rush days. There were three ways to get to the mines from the East: overland in a covered wagon; around the Horn in a deep-water vessel; or across the isthmus of Central America. This last route was the fastest, and on it American river boats played a dramatic part. Most of the vessels that brought prospectors to the east coast of the isthmus, and those that took them up the west coast, were oceangoing ships, although some river boats were pressed into service. "Liveoak" George Law secured a contract for carrying mail to Panama and put his *Central America*—formerly the *George Law*—on this run. She was one of the unlucky seagoing river boats. In a September gale, en route from Panama, she went to the bottom of the Atlantic, carrying $280,000,000 in gold dust and 423 souls, a misadventure that inspired this doggerel:

The *Central America,* painted so fine
Went down like a thousand of brick
And all the old tubs that are now on the line
Will follow her two at a lick.

George Law had a monopoly on the isthmus crossing at Panama, but Cornelius Vanderbilt could not miss out on this profitable gold-rush business. He organized the Accessory Transit Company, secured a franchise from the Nicaraguan government, and undertook to transport gold pilgrims to Greytown, Nicaragua, in steamships and up the San Juan River and across Lake Nicaragua in river boats. From the head of navigation it was but twelve miles on muleback to the Pacific side of the isthmus.

By this time the millionaire commodore employed many "experts," all of whom assured him that the San Juan River was not navigable by steamboats. So the Commodore went there himself, towing the river boat *Director* behind his new ocean steamship *Prometheus,* which would bring passengers from New York to Greytown. The San Juan presented no greater difficulties than the upper reaches of many rivers in the Mississippi Valley. The *Director*'s safety valve had to be tied down to provide power for the first rapids, and the vessel had to be warped through the Castillo rapids where the river fell eight feet in a hundred yards, but she reached calm Lake Nicaragua and steamed triumphantly across it to within twelve miles of the western coast. Vanderbilt promptly towed other little steamers from the States to provide regular service across the isthmus.

His activities almost caused a war between the United States and England. The Commodore's deal with the Nicaraguan government, under which the country received a percentage of the profits, granted him free and exclusive access to Greytown. When the *Prometheus* was about to sail, a group of native officers came aboard and demanded $123 in port fees. Vanderbilt refused and cast off, but the *Prometheus* was quickly brought up short by a shot across her bow from a British sloop-of-war. It seems that the officers who wanted the port fee represented the king of the Mosquito Indians, who claimed that the port was in his domain. Great Britain had established a protectorate over the Mosquito kingdom, and the captain of the British sloop was protecting the king's rights with round shot. The incident caused a widespread furor in the United States, with demands for punitive action against England for firing on an American ship and violating the Monroe Doctrine. The commotion died down when Secretary of State Daniel Webster's stern note to the British was answered with an apology and a disavowal of the naval captain's action; at the time England was too busy in the Crimea to fight over Central American Indians.

A more serious threat to Vanderbilt's profits from the Nicaraguan water route was a fabulous character named William Walker. Before he became a self-styled "man of destiny," Walker had been successively a doctor, lawyer, and editor. He started his career of conquest in 1853 by invading Lower California and the Mexican province of Sonora at the head of forty-five gringo adventurers. The Republic of Sonora, of which Walker declared himself president, did not last long after his men finished their looting and drifted away. Their leader got back across the border only two jumps ahead of Mexican troops.

Walker's next target for conquest, in 1855, was Nicaragua, which, as usual, was in the throes of revolution—it had had 15 presidents in 6 years. Walker made a deal with the leader of the liberal "outs," recruited 58 American desperadoes, and captured the town of San Juan del Sud, the Pacific coast terminal of the Transit Company route. From here, with his own forces and native revolutionists, he marched the 12 miles to Lake Nicaragua, seized two of Vanderbilt's steamers, and made a successful amphibian attack on Granada, the Nicaraguan capital. All the country's other communities were on the lake or the river and, as long as he controlled the steamboats, Walker could attack at will. This shortly led to the complete defeat of the conservatives, followed by the convenient death of the liberal leader from smallpox. Walker declared himself President of Nicaragua.

The country's most valuable asset was the river-lake route to the gold fields, as 2,000 prospectors were crossing the isthmus along it every month. Claiming that Vanderbilt had not paid Nicaragua its full share of the profits, Walker voided Vanderbilt's franchise and gave a monopoly, on more favorable terms, to two Americans named Morgan and Garrison. Also, in taking over the country, Walker had been aided by money and arms from "Liveoak" Law in neighboring Panama, who was gleeful at this opportunity to contribute to the woes of his long-time steamboat competitor.

The double indignity of lost profits and Law's derisive laughter at his discomfiture threw Vanderbilt into a rage. He immediately hired a little army of his own, led by an English soldier of fortune, and placed it at the disposal of Costa Rica, which was at war with Nicaragua. The Commodore also suspended steamship service to both ends of the isthmus route and induced the U.S. Navy to dispatch a steam frigate to San Juan del Sud to completely isolate Walker from recruits and supplies.

In two weeks of bloody fighting Vanderbilt's janizaries, spearheading Costa Rican troops, defeated Walker's mercenaries and the Nicaraguan forces and seized the river and lake steamers. It was evident that the side which controlled the steamers controlled the country, and Walker escaped the venegeful Costa Ricans by surrendering to the U.S. Navy.

Walker returned to Nicaragua in 1857 on another filibuster expedition and again captured the steamboats, but this conquest was nipped in the bud by a frigate full of U.S. Marines. His final fling at being a "man of destiny" was a third attempted invasion of Nicaragua through Honduras in 1860. This time he was captured by a British man-of-war and turned over to the Honduran government, which promptly shot him. Meanwhile, Vanderbilt's trans-isthmus bonanza petered out when a railroad was completed across Panama. As usual, the Commodore did not leave empty-handed. As he had in the early days on the Hudson, he made a deal with local steamboat interests under which they paid him $56,000 to stay off the San Juan River and Lake Nicaragua.

The first hectic years of the California gold rush had scarcely passed when gold was discovered to the north near Pikes Peak, then in Idaho, and finally in Montana. The latter two finds led to a little bonanza for steamboats on the Columbia River, or at least changed a rather casual means of transportation into a flourishing industry.

The first steamboat on the Columbia was a British craft, the *Beaver*, built on the Thames near London in 1835 for the Hudson's Bay Company. After her launching she was rigged as a brig, her wheels were tucked in her hold, and her boiler was filled as a spare water tank, and she sailed for the Columbia via Hawaii. She came up the river to Fort Vancouver, where she was met by a most unsympathetic Scotsman named John McLoughlin, the Hudson's Bay Company factor at this point. McLoughlin had little use for steamboats. He considered the *Beaver* esthetically unpleasant and economically unsound; God's free wind appealed to his thrifty Scottish soul.

After she was rigged for steam the *Beaver* was demonstrated for the dignitaries of the fort, their ladies, and some missionaries and visiting mountain men by means of an excursion trip a few miles down the Columbia and up its main tributary, the Willamette. Everybody was pleased with the trip and the picnic on the river bank, and one of the party, the Reverend Parker, recorded his philosophical thoughts on the coming of steam to the far Northwest: "We conversed of coming days, when with civilized men, all the rapid improvements in the arts of life, should be introduced over this new world, and when cities and villages shall spring up on the west, as they are springing up on the east of the great mountains, and a new empire shall be added to the kingdoms of the earth."

But McLoughlin had no interest in adding to the kingdoms of the earth. His vision was limited to a trading post on the Columbia River, at which he did not want a steamboat. He generously gave the *Beaver* to his opposite number, Dr. Tolmie, at Nisqually on Puget Sound. The little steamer was used as a combination trading vessel and man-of-war. She carried an armament of four six-pounders and the decks were protected by boarding netting to prevent access by natives. Large groups of

Indians were not allowed on deck unless they were accompanied by their wives and children.

The *Beaver* served the Pacific Northwest faithfully in this capacity and later as a tugboat for more than 50 years until, in 1888, she hit the rocks at the entrance to the harbor of Vancouver, British Columbia. She lay on what became known as Beaver Rock for five years, waiting for someone to pull her off and patch her up, but nobody ever did. Finally the swirling wake of one of the new, fast Puget Sound steamers washed the relic off her rock and she sank quietly out of sight.

Long before this, the first American steamboat had come to the Columbia when, in 1850, a group of businessmen at John Jacob Astor's defunct trading post, Astoria, near the mouth of the river, built the *Columbia*. Nobody involved knew much about steamboats, and the result reflected their ignorance. The *Columbia* was a side-wheeler 90 feet long and 16 feet wide and, as one passenger said, she was "not at all a harbor of comfort for her passengers." She had a tiny cabin but no bunks and no galley; passengers provided their own provender and blankets and paid $25 for deck space on the 100-mile trip to Portland, near the mouth of the Willamette River. The *Columbia* was far from a floating palace but as the only steamboat on the river she did a capacity

The stern-wheeler Wide West *was the first locally built "floating palace" on the Columbia River. She was described as being "fast, luxurious, and magnificent," and she provided "sumptuous fare."*

OREGON HISTORICAL SOCIETY

business, which continued even after a more pretentious craft, the *Lot Whitcomb*, was launched six months later. The *Whitcomb* was a good boat, a hybrid of Hudson and Mississippi design 160 feet long and 24 feet wide. A contemporary description calls her "simple and unostentatious, but tasteful and elegant," with a paneled main cabin and a nicely decorated ladies' cabin and dining hall.

The Columbia River was unique as a running road in that it was, until the twentieth century, divided into three sections, each with its separate river boats. From the mouth to the Cascades, a distance of about 150 miles, there was a fine, deep channel. On this stretch, steamships from San Francisco could compete with river boats to Portland or beyond. No boat could cross the Cascades, but there was another stretch of good water for 50 miles above these first rapids to a second set—The Dalles. With the coming of the first prospectors in the mid-1850s and when the army moved its outpost from the Cascades to The Dalles to protect them, steamboats were built above the Cascades to serve this short section. Beyond The Dalles the Columbia turns north at Wallula, 315 miles from its mouth, and flows some 900 miles through the state of Washington into Canada. The Snake River joins it a little north of the Washington boundary and flows east into the Idaho gold country. As the boom developed, shallow-draft steamboats were built on the banks of the upper Columbia and the Snake or carried in sections above the rapids and assembled.

In 1856 an enterprising individual named Bradford built a wooden tram railway for the eight-mile portage around the Cascades. After the lower-river boat owners got together in 1860 as the Oregon Steam Navigation Company, this near-monopoly ran a regular service from the mouth of the river to The Dalles in two separate sets of boats, assisted by mule-powered flatcars which portaged freight and passengers around the Cascades. When the gold rush was at its height in 1864 these vessels carried 36,000 passengers and almost 22,000 tons of freight upstream to The Dalles.

Some of the lower-river boats were locally built; more came up from the California rivers, where the gold rush had subsided. One such was the *Wilson G. Hunt*, which had originally been built in 1849 to carry excursionists to what was becoming a fashionable New York seaside resort—Coney Island. After one season in this trade she was caught by the gold fever, made the trip around the Horn, and entered service on the Sacramento until a reoccurrence of the fever brought her to the Columbia. Another two-time bonanza boat was the delinquent *New World*, which moved from California to Oregon in 1864. There is a report that she once carried a ton of gold down from the Cascades, but since there are not many tons of gold outside of Fort Knox this probably meant a ton of gold-bearing ore.

The equivalent of the *Chrysopolis* as the pride of the Columbia was the *Wide West*, a 236-foot stern-wheeler built in Portland to which all of the usual floating-palace adjectives were applied. She was fast, luxurious, magnificent, and provided "sumptuous fare." The *Wide West* was unique in that her cabin was done "tastefully in delicate shades of lilac and the floors covered with mosaic oil cloth" instead of the Brussels carpet beloved in the East. She also had brass beds in her staterooms, which, said a local editor, "contrast favorably with the cramped up little dens called staterooms on eastern steamboats." Perhaps the vessel's greatest claim to fame was the auxiliary engine, which pumped a continuous flow of water through what on deep-sea vessels are called the heads, "so that no offensive effluvia taints these sumptuous cabins."

There was no such luxury above The Dalles in gold-rush days. On the little local boats that pushed up the Snake comfort was of no concern so long as the vessel reached as near as possible to the diggings around Boise. The *Yakima*, the *Webfoot*, the *Tenino*, the *Nez Perce Chief*, the *Spray*, and the *Okanagon* went as far as Lewiston, across the Idaho border, above which they were stopped by the canyon of the Snake. One large vessel, the *Shoshone*, was built above the canyon. Drawing only two feet of water, she reached the mouth of the Boise River on her maiden voyage in 1866, but by that time the railroads had opened a shorter route to the mines. The bonanza days were over and the *Shoshone* lay beside the bank far into the Indian country in Idaho for two years before she was disassembled and taken down the river.

But steamboating had come to stay on the Columbia, at least until the Grand Coulee Dam put much of the upper river under a lake. For all practical purposes the head of navigation of the three-stage river trip was Wallula, where the river turned north. Travelers headed upstream from Portland had to get up early; the river boats left at 5 A.M. so that the first two stages of the trip could be accomplished in a single day. The lower-river boat reached the Cascades at 11 A.M. Here the voyagers loafed around while through freight was transshipped to the narrow-gauge railway, which now boasted a little engine instead of mules. Then they boarded colorful cars for the short trip to the upper end of the Cascades. They looked at the rushing water and the rugged scenery until the freight was loaded on the second boat and, in the early afternoon, steamed up to The Dalles, which they reached before evening.

At the lower end of The Dalles they might stay overnight at the Cosmopolitan Hotel or the Umatilla House, the latter being preferable because it had two baths for its 123 rooms and a lavatory in the basement. The Cosmopolitan was smaller and less gaudy, but it did have a pool table and a piano. Next morning they were up betimes at catch a 5 A.M. train that would take them around Tumwater Falls in an hour and a half, if sand had not blown across the track. At Celio, above the falls, they boarded their third boat and reached Wallula late that afternoon, having traveled for two days on three boats and two railways to cover 229 miles—but this was by far the easiest and fastest way to travel that 229 miles. From Wallula the traveler could take a narrow-gauge railway to Walla Walla or a stage to Boise or Salt Lake City and the East.

The final gold-rush boats found their bonanza on the Yukon River in Alaska in 1897. In 1869, two years after the United States acquired "Seward's Ice Box" from Russia, the first steamboat appeared on the Yukon, which winds across Alaska from east to west for 2,000 miles from the Bering Sea into British Columbia. The river is navigable for most of its length, but only from June to October; at other times the approved transportation for much of this area before the airplane was snowshoes or dog sleds.

The first vessel, the *Youkon*, was a forty-seven foot stern-wheeler twelve feet wide, built in San Francisco for the Alaska Fur Company, which took over the business of the Russian Fur Company when Alaska became a United States territory. There is no detailed description of the *Youkon* nor anecdotes of her career, except that on her first voyage she carried a Captain C. W. Raymond of the army who was traveling upstream to find out what Secretary of State Seward had bought—specifically, to determine whether Fort Yukon should be garrisoned by American or British troops; he learned that the post was 120 miles inside Alaska. The *Youkon* and other early Alaska steamers sometimes faced a variation of one of the problems of the upper Missouri River boats—on occasion they were driven aground by herds of swimming moose.

During the next three decades a score or more steamers appeared on the Yukon; some came from San Francisco, and a few were built at St. Michael on the shore of Norton Bay near the many-mouthed delta of the river. They carried explorers, trappers, missionaries, and their supplies in and some furs out.

In the spring of 1897 when the first Coast Guard cutter of the season reached St. Michael from "outside," a little river boat came downstream with twenty-five bearded and boastful prospectors and a half-million dollars in gold dust. The prospectors reported that far up the Yukon there was gold for the taking in the beds and banks of the Klondike River and of Bonanza and Eldorado creeks. While the cutter, the famed

Bear, pushed northward on patrol, the steamship *Excelsior* streaked for San Francisco, bringing out the proverbial "ton of gold dust" and the magical news: "Gold in the Klondike."

When the *Bear* returned to St. Michael in the early fall the sleepy northern settlement was unrecognizable. Tents stretched from the village to the mouth of the Yukon and thousands of would-be prospectors milled on the beach offering all they possessed for passage up the stream on anything that would float. The existing boats could handle but a fraction of the trade. Hammers were ringing and saws were singing at new shipyards at St. Michael and Unakleet, a few miles up the coast. New river boats for the Yukon were abuilding at San Francisco, Portland, Tacoma, and elsewhere on the coast. Boats that had seen better days on the Sacramento and the Columbia were churning across the Bering Sea to participate in the new bonanza. Neither that summer nor the next could they keep pace with the gold-hungry pilgrims. In all the previous gold rushes prospectors could reach the diggings by foot, horse, or covered wagon; the only way to the Klondike was by boat.

The *Bear* had to defer its return to the States so that it could police St. Michael and the mouth of the Yukon, as there was no other law. Almost all the prospectors were tenderfeet who did not know how to care for themselves in the North, and many were the victims of ingenious swindles perpetrated by steamboat owners as well as some men who sold passage upriver but did not even own a steamboat. Some gold-seekers at St. Michael held tickets on nonexistent boats for which they had paid handsomely in San Francisco without reading the fine print that committed them to help build the boat. Passengers the boats could get in plenty, but workmen to build them were scarcer than the gold upstream. Many tenderfeet who held tickets and berths on existing boats found that rectangles marked on the deck in chalk were their "berths," in which they had a one-third interest; the same deck sleeping space had been sold to three prospectors, each to have it for eight hours a day.

The Coast Guard had all-powerful law-enforcement authority in the sub-Arctic. The officers of the *Bear*, after a quick look at the several steamers under construction, instituted an on-the-spot inspection and licensing service. It was obvious that some of the jerry-built craft would founder before they got through the river's delta. The Coast Guardsmen refused to let any boat leave that they considered unsafe, an act that did not endear them to the gold-hungry prospectors, who would risk passage on anything afloat. The Coast Guard later built a river boat, the *Nunivec*, to carry law and order up the river.

An admittedly incomplete list of bonanza boats on the Yukon contains the names of eighty-four vessels. The North American Transportation Company—an attempt by some principal boat owners to set up a monopoly similar to those on the Sacramento and Columbia—had been organized before the Klondike excitement, and their boats, plus some others, were respectable craft. The *Cudahy*, built at Unalaska in 1898, was typical of the better vessels; it was a stern-wheeler 192 feet long and 33 feet wide, rated at 481 tons. The *Cudahy* was reputedly the fastest boat on the river and made a record round trip to Dawson, head of navigation for the diggings, in twenty days, a feat that inspired a long poem in the St. Michael *Aurora Borealis*, the literary merit of which can be judged by these last two stanzas:

> Full proud she seemed as she came in
> Her screaming whistle made a din;
> Her Captain was congratulated
> His vow he kept, as I have stated.

> Oh! the "Cudahy" is a record breaker
> May her fortune good, ne'er forsake her;
> Keep all her flags a flying free,
> She's the joy and pride of the N.A.T.

Two brothers named Moran built a dozen boats at Seattle and sailed them as a fleet up the coast, escorted by three seagoing tugs. All the Moran boats were identical; one officer said that they were "built by the mile and cut apart in proper lengths." One boat was lost on the ocean voyage, but the brothers said that the others paid their cost with the first load of freight taken up to Dawson, and justified their high rates by adding that "there would have been a shortage of food and much suffering in the country if the eleven cargoes of food had not been taken up the Yukon in 1898 by the Moran fleet."

It was common for a boat to return its cost plus a handsome profit in a single trip during the bonanza days. The *Leah* took 300 passengers to Dawson in the spring of 1898—125 on the boat and 175 on a barge that she pushed. At $220 a head they paid her owners $66,000. Six hundred tons of freight at $100 per ton added another $60,000, and 70 downstream passengers $15,000 more, for a total of $141,000. The *Leah* and her barge had cost $70,000, wages were $3,000, and food and fuel $27,000, for a total of $100,000. After recouping their entire investment the owners made $41,000 on the *Leah*'s maiden voyage.

During the first two hectic years of the gold rush, upriver boats were so crowded that passengers almost literally traveled like subway straphangers and ate in shifts around the clock. Food was no problem on the way up, as the vessel's freight consisted largely of food and whiskey, but eating on the downstream voyage was another matter. A story is told of the *Merwin*, which started down in the summer of 1899 with 200 passengers—by that time the outward flow of disappointed prospectors equaled the influx of new hopefuls. Because the downstream rush was unexpected, the *Merwin* had few supplies aboard and could buy no food in Dawson nor at Circle City, which could supply the craft with only a barrel of whiskey. Despite the shortage of edibles, one passenger reported that the whiskey gave out first, then the "hooch," then the cigars, chewing tobacco and peanuts, until they were left with nothing but corn meal. The last of the "hooch," which was apparently a locally produced beverage, was consumed by a white man who came aboard at a way stop with three Indians, who watched him passively until he passed out and then soberly carried him ashore after he had quenched his long winter's thirst. The whole incident took about fifteen minutes.

During the eight months of the year when the river was ice-bound,

THE MARINERS MUSEUM, NEWPORT NEWS, VA.

The Seattle water front in the 1880s. The George E. Starr *(foreground, right) was a popular Columbia River vessel, but not a fast one, as this doggerel of the period indicates:*

Paddle, paddle, George E. Starr,
How we wonder where you are.
You left Seattle at half past ten
And you'll get to Bellingham
God knows when.

steamers wintered in creeks flowing into the lower reaches of the streams; there was no breakwater on Norton Sound. Some, loaded with freight, pushed part way up the river to find a winter haven so as to get a head start up stream in the spring and secure the high prices commanded by the first vessels at Dawson. These plans sometimes went awry when the river froze while the boats were en route and forced thm to stay where they were caught. In 1898 the river froze so fast that the *Weare* became ice-bound at the river bank while she was wooding. Her crew built a log breakwater in front of her to protect the vessel from the spring ice jam and relaxed for eight months.

Robert W. Service painted a stark picture of wintering-in in the sub-Arctic in "The Shooting of Dan McGrew."

> With only the howl of the timber wolf, and
> you camped there in the cold,
> A half-dead thing in a stark, dead world,
> clean mad for the muck called gold.

That may have been true for miners, but the crews of ice-bound steamers seldom faced such hardships. In the long winter dusk they watched the aurora borealis from beside a hot stove, replete with food and whiskey. When tired of the northern lights they played black jack or hired an Aleut dog team to take them to some settlement or mission. The Indians were quick to find and serve a trapped boat. A lazy, leisurely life is usually associated with palm-fringed South Sea islands, but few tropical beachcombers ever led such a thoroughly carefree existence as the crew of a steamer trapped in the ice of the Yukon.

Stateside papers carried sensational stories of the bonanza boats being robbed by river pirates and Indians, who looted the gold, massacred the passengers, and kidnapped the dance-hall girls. One Hearst paper published a picture of pirates firing on a vessel from the bank with an old muzzle-loading cannon. Despite such imaginative tales, there is no authenticated instance of piracy on the Yukon. The nearest thing to it was an incident at Circle City. There was a food and clothing shortage upstream in 1898 because many of the boats brought liquor instead of grub, believing that it would be a more profitable cargo, as whiskey was selling at a dollar a drink in Dawson. When one boat arrived at Circle City with food and clothing consigned to upstream Dawson a posse of citizens boarded it and forced the purser to disgorge at gunpoint, but these goods were delivered to a company store and paid for by the miners.

The bonanza days ended for the boats on the lower river in 1899 when the White Pass and Yukon Railway was completed. A few vessels continued to operate up the coast to Nome, where there was a later rush, but most of them were left to rot along the river. On the upper stream a trickle of steamboat traffic continued that was not usurped by either railroads or automobiles. The Yukon craft were the only river boats to bow to the airplane.

Some seventy years after the first gold rush a few of the Sacramento River boats had another brief bonanza that had nothing to do with gold. The motion-picture industry had moved from the East to Hollywood, and in those days their location shooting was still governed by the eastern axiom, "A tree's a tree, a rock's a rock—shoot it in Central Park." When the script called for a river, the Sacramento was handy and became the Mississippi in many pictures and the Yangtze in at least two. Several old river boats were taken out of mothballs and returned to brief glory in these river epics, one of which starred Will Rogers, another Bing Crosby. The first such picture was *Jim Bludso*, based on the legend in John Hay's poem. The stern-wheeler *Grace Barton* played the role of the Mississippi vessel in which the valiant engineer was cremated and played it with impressive realism. The fire effects got out of hand and the boat actually burned.

River Boats at War

To many casual readers of American history it may seem that the Civil War took place largely in Virginia. Contemporary newsmen reported at length on the deadly and dramatic struggle between the Army of the Potomac and the Army of Virginia as they lunged at each other's capital cities, and popular historians have since penned untold millions of words detailing the masterful leadership of Robert E. Lee and the dramatic accomplishments of such colorful lieutenants as "Jeb" Stuart and "Stonewall" Jackson. Actually, in the big picture of the war, the fighting in Virginia was almost a detail in the corner of the canvas. If all events are placed in proper perspective, the struggle for control of the midwestern river valleys was far more meaningful to the final outcome than that for the capital cities, and the battles of Fort Henry, Fort Donelson, and Island Number Ten were of greater strategic importance than the better-known and bloodier conflicts at Manassas, Fredericksburg, and Chancellorsville. The result was that steamboats on the western rivers, unsung in popular history, were more potent factors than Stuart's dashing horsemen or Jackson's lean, fast-marching foot cavalry.

As with all other war matériel, the Confederacy was deficient in river warships. Although the Mississippi River steamboat is usually associated with the South, it was actually a product of the North; at least its vital engines were made in northern machine shops. And the South's small capacity for producing fighting ships was misdirected, as far as the river war was concerned, by the shipbuilding policy adopted at the beginning of the conflict by Confederate Naval Secretary Stephen Mallory.

Mallory realized that the South could not begin to match the North in building conventional warships. The solution, as he saw it, was the construction of a few vessels more powerful and less vulnerable than any Yankee craft: ironclads. The first result was the vessel generally known as the *Merrimack*, although its proper name was the *Virginia*. It consisted of a heavy, sloping-sided iron casemate armed with broadside guns mounted on the deep-water hull of the captured Union steam frigate *Merrimack*. Whether or not this type of vessel might have been effective in salt-water fighting if the North had not devised a superior ironclad of the *Monitor* type is beside the point, as it certainly was not a river boat. Yet the only river warships the South tried to build were of this type— heavy, slow, cumbersome vessels that could hardly have breasted the river current and that drew from eleven to fourteen feet. The Confederates started to construct eight of these on the western rivers, most of which, because of material shortages, were captured or destroyed to prevent capture before they were finished. Only one of them, the *Arkansas*, took part in a river battle, before she, too, was destroyed.

For the rest, the Confederate inland navy consisted of about thirty converted existing river steamers. Because the South had little iron, most of these were armored in their vital parts by two heavy timber bulkheads with compressed cotton bales between them. The principal weapon was an iron ram below the water line at the reinforced bow. Carrying only one or two guns, these craft were relatively fast, and it was hoped —unrealistically—that their speed would compensate for the heavier armor and firepower of the northern vessels.

The North's river navy was started by a man named James B. Eads, who was also interested in ironclads. Eads had retired in St. Louis after making a fortune salvaging wrecked steamboats with specially equipped snag boats that he called "Submarines." He had read of the use of ironclad floating batteries by the French in the Crimean War and rushed to Washington with plans to convert one of his "Submarines" into an ironclad. His idea was approved by Lincoln's cabinet, and naval designer Samuel Pook was assigned to draw up the plans—until War Secretary Cameron confused the issue by insisting that boats on rivers were in the army's jurisdiction rather than the navy's. He did not want Eads' "Submarine," but he did accept designs from Pook for somewhat similar vessels to be built from scratch, and contracted with Eads to build seven of them.

These were true river boats, flat-bottomed stern-wheelers 175 feet long and 52 feet wide. Wheel, engine, and armament were protected by an oaken casemate with sloping sides two feet thick. Since the boats were expected to do most of their fighting head-on against Confederate forts at the bends of rivers, the casemate was armored with two-and-a-half-inch iron only at the bow and beside the engine. The stern and most of the sides were unarmored. Each vessel mounted three powerful guns facing forward, four lesser weapons in each broadside and two light guns at the stern. Named *St. Louis*, *Carondelet*, *Cincinnati*, *Louisville*, *Mound City*, *Cairo*, and *Pittsburgh*, the vessels collectively were always called the "Pook Turtles." Eads later converted his *Submarine No.* 7 and a river ferry into larger versions of these—the *Benton* and the *Essex*.

Meanwhile, Navy Lieutenant Commander John Rogers had appeared in St. Louis and induced General McClellan to let him buy three river steamers, the *Lexington*, the *Tyler*, and the *Conestoga*. He cut each one of these down to the boiler deck, removing the cabin and the texas, braced the main deck to carry guns, and plated the sides with five inches of oak plank. These "timberclads," plus the nine ironclads, formed the initial Union river-boat fleet of which Flag Officer Andrew Foote took command in January 1862, nine months after the war had started.

The Confederate defense plans for the river valleys were based on the European concept of controlling rivers by forts on their banks. Confederate President Jefferson Davis was proud of his West Point diploma, and this was good textbook theory. They built their northernmost fort on the east bank of the Mississippi at Columbus, Kentucky, a few miles below the Mississippi's confluence with the Ohio. Almost due east from Columbus the Tennessee and Cumberland rivers were but twelve miles apart. On the former stream the Confederates built Fort

Shortly after the Civil War broke out, Union Secretary of War Cameron ordered the construction of seven identical armored river boats. Called "Pook Turtles" after their designer, Samuel Pook, they all looked like the Cairo, below: flat-bottomed stern-wheelers with three powerful guns facing forward and four lesser ones on each broadside. The "Pook Turtles" were 175 feet long and had sloping sides 2 feet thick. They were "ironclad" only at the bow and beside the engine.

LIBRARY OF CONGRESS

Henry, on the latter Fort Donelson. A few miles below Columbus, above New Madrid, the Mississippi made an S curve in the center of which was Island Number Ten. This was fortified with eleven entrenched batteries on the banks and the island and with a large floating battery. Farther south, defending Memphis, was Fort Pillow, and far below this the strongest bastion of all, Vicksburg. The mouth of the Mississippi was defended by Forts Jackson and St. Philip, each on a bend in the river about 75 miles below New Orleans.

By subduing these fortifications and gaining control of the Mississippi the North could cut the Confederacy in two, isolating the important food-producing area west of the stream. Also, control of the tributaries was vital to logistics. Federal forces and supplies could be moved and concentrated rapidly by water.

It was fortunate for the Union cause that, at about the same time that the river fleet was assembled at Cairo, Illinois, Brigadier General U. S. Grant was selected to make a reconnaissance in force toward the Confederate defenses. It was further fortunate that Grant and Flag Officer Foote got along together; neither talked much and both were more interested in results than in textbook theories. It was obvious to Grant that boats would be handy in fighting around rivers. He loaded his troops on all the idle steamboats at Cairo and asked Foote to precede him up the Ohio and Tennessee with the river-warship flotilla for a joint attack on Fort Henry.

With the three timberclads and four of the ironclads—there were no crews available for the others—Foote steamed to a point below the fort. While the army was slogging its way from a swampy landing on the river bank, the inland navy opened fire at long range and slowly advanced to within 500 yards of Henry's earthen parapets. Here they "stood on their wheels" and the green gunners on both sides exchanged shots for an hour. The ironclads in the fore were hit repeatedly, but only the *Essex* was badly hurt when the current swung her sideways and a shell came through the unarmored casemate and pierced a boiler, sending her drifting downstream out of control.

The southerners were taking a more serious beating. By the end of an hour everything burnable in the fort was afire and only four guns were fit for service. When Grant arrived with his muddy troops, he found the Stars and Stripes flying above the fort and Confederate General Tilgham enjoying a friendly drink with Foote aboard the *Cincinnati* after his surrender.

While Grant got his troops out of the swamp and started marching overland toward Fort Donelson, Foote steamed back to Cairo to replace the battered *Essex* and *Cincinnati* with the *Louisville* and the *Pittsburgh* and sent his three timberclads up the now undefended Tennessee River to Muscle Shoals. This was merely a raid, but the Yankee river boats destroyed all Confederate shipping and supplies on the river, burned a railroad bridge, and captured one of the partially finished southern ironclads, the *Eastport*, which was later finished and added to the northern fleet.

Meanwhile Foote, with four Pook Turtles, hastened up the Cumberland River hoping to repeat his performance of reducing a fort before the army arrived. Based on his success at Henry, he threw his four ironclads forward to within 250 yards of the fort, keeping two of the timberclads that had rejoined the group in the rear to lob shells into Donelson at long range. He soon learned his mistake. Donelson was not only better armed than Henry, but its guns were on a bluff rather than, as at Henry, near the water line. Although the Yankees piled coal, hawsers, chains, and other hard material atop their casemates, this was not proof against the plunging fire from above. Within minutes the *St. Louis'* pilothouse had been carried away, and she was hit sixty-five times before she drifted downstream. The wheel ropes were shot away on the *Pittsburgh* and the *Louisville*, and they circled helplessly as they followed the flagship down the river. The *Carondelet* continued the battle singlehanded for an hour until she was leaking so badly from fifty-four hits that she had to limp away. The fleet licked its wounds and buried its dead while Donelson surrendered to Grant's land attack from the rear two days later.

The repulse of the river warships at Donelson was a tactical failure, but the combined operation was, over-all, a brilliant success that, in two weeks, had placed the Union in control of all of northwestern Tennessee and the valleys of the Cumberland and Tennessee rivers. Outflanked, the strong Confederate fortifications at Columbus were abandoned, and the southerners established a new line anchored at Chattanooga on the right and Fort Pillow on the left, leaving Island Number Ten projecting northward to prevent the Yankees from coming down the Mississippi and sweeping inland.

A vital point on the center of this line was Corinth, a transshipping point on the Charleston and Memphis Railroad, and here the Confederates assembled their scattered forces. At St. Louis, Grant gathered eighty-two steamboats to transport his army up the Tennessee to attack them. Among these was the old *John J. Roe*, which Mark Twain had once piloted and of which he had said: "For a long time I was on a boat that was so slow we used to forget what year it was we left port in . . . . This boat, the *John J. Roe*, was so slow that when she finally sank in Madrid Bend, it was five years before the owners heard of it . . . . She was dismally slow; still, we often had pretty exciting times racing with islands, and rafts, and such things. One trip . . . I think we changed

watches three times in Fort Adams reach, which is five miles long." The
mate of the *Roe* was the same Grant March who would later explore the
Yellowstone River in the *Josephine* and bring the news of the Custer
massacre via the *Far West*.

The *Roe* and her consorts plowed back and forth for a week, building
up troops and supplies around Pittsburg Landing and Savannah on opposite banks of the Tennessee twenty miles from Corinth near little
Shiloh Church. On Easter morn the river bank was as busy as the St. Louis
levee when heavy firing was heard from the direction of Shiloh. Grant,
aboard his command boat, the little *Tigress*, streaked toward Pittsburg
Landing. En route he met a courier aboard the *John Warner* with news
that the Confederates were attacking in force at Shiloh.

The fighting on the first day at Shiloh was disastrous for Grant's forces,
and defeat might have been total but for the timberclads *Tyler* and
Lexington, which were there to protect his transports. By midafternoon
the Union troops had been driven back nearly to the river bank, with the
left wing protecting the landing. The *Tyler*, with grape and canister from
its thirty-two pounders, smothered the artillery support of a strong
Confederate attack on his wing, and, with enfilading fire down a
ravine that led to the river, disorganized the two Confederate brigades

*The campaign to control the midwestern river valleys began when Gen-
eral Grant moved his troops by steamer to attack Fort Henry on the
Tennessee River. The ability of the Union to move forces fast and in
strength was an important factor in winning the war in the West.*

that were making the attack. When night fell the Union forces still held the landing and reinforcements in the form of General Don Carlos Buell's Army of the Ohio had reached the opposite bank of the river.

Through the night the steamboats carried Buell's fresh troops across the river and up to the landing—the *Roe* took an entire brigade on a single trip—while the timberclads continuously shelled the Confederate bivouacks in the woods. At dawn the reinforced northerners attacked and swept the weary Confederates back toward Corinth. That night, the *John J. Roe* steamed downstream with 600 wounded on her decks, the first shipment of the 13,000 Union casualties at the Battle of Shiloh.

Meanwhile, Flag Officer Foote had taken the ironclads and some mortar rafts down the Mississippi to support Union General John Pope in an attack on Island Number Ten. The terrain was such that the Confederate fortifications could be pinched off from their supplies if a ribbon of high ground below the fort on the Missouri side of the river were occupied. But Pope was above the fort, the river was high and the neck of the peninsula that was between him and New Madrid, below the fort, was a vast swamp. When Pope asked his engineers to build him a road through the swamp they offered him, instead, a canal, which they built with an ingenious sawing device that cut tree trunks off under water so that troops could be floated above the stumps in barges. Within three weeks Pope was in New Madrid; if he could get across the river the southern fort would be isolated, but Confederate field batteries on the opposite bank, which his light guns could not reach, prevented his crossing. He asked Foote whether he could run one or two Pook turtles past the bristling batteries of Island Number Ten to knock out the Confederate artillery and ferry his men across.

After their experience at Donelson the captains of the ironclads were properly respectful of plunging fire from big guns in forts, and Island Number Ten had many more such guns than Donelson. A boat trying to pass them would expose its unarmored side to a murderous fire and, if it were disabled, would continue to float slowly past the remaining batteries, rather than away from them as at Henry and Donelson. But time was of the essence. The South was building two mighty ironclads at Memphis—the *Arkansas* and the *Tennessee*. If either were finished Pope's position would be untenable. Captain Henry Walke volunteered to try to run the gantlet with the *Carondelet*.

In preparation for her dangerous passage the deck and the most exposed side of the *Carondelet* were protected with makeshift armor. Planks from a wrecked barge covered her deck, a heavy hawser was wound around her pilothouse, cordwood was stacked around her boilers, and a barge loaded with coal and baled hay was lashed against the side toward the island guns so that, said Walke, "she looked like a farmer's wagon." The night selected for the daring run—April 4, 1862—was dark, and as the *Carondelet* cast off a violent thunderstorm broke. This was both good and bad; the storm would make the Confederates less alert and might drown out the noise of the steamer, but a flash of lightning might disclose it to a wet sentry.

For a time the good outweighed the bad. The *Carondelet*, its black smoke lost in the black night, steamed past the first Confederate batteries unchallenged. It seemed as though she might get past unseen, until two tall pillars of flame jetted from her stacks to light the boat and the landscape. To make her engine more silent, escape steam had been vented through the paddle-wheel housing instead of the stacks, and dry soot in the latter had ignited to form temporary twin torches.

The flame died, but not before the southerners had been alerted. Muskets cracked, rockets arched, and gunners poured out of their shelters to their wet guns, which had been deflected to keep water out of the barrels. If the Confederates had left them that way, they might have blown the *Carondelet* out of the water; but, conscious that the weapons were at maximum deflection, officers ordered gunners to elevate the muzzles to aim at where they thought the dark target might be. As a result, scores of shells whistled above the heads of the Yankees crouched aboard the running ship, but only one was found imbedded in a bale of hay when the *Carondelet* rounded the bend into New Madrid. Two nights later another storm gave the *Pittsburgh* a chance to run past the fort unscathed. The two ironclads drove the Confederate batteries from the bank below the fort and towed Pope's men over in their barges. On the same night that the Confederates retreated from Shiloh, Island Number Ten surrendered.

The next fortified point was Fort Pillow above Memphis, where mighty guns frowned down from strong bastions high on Chickasaw Bluffs. The river warships could not hope to subdue this alone, and Pope's forces were recalled to join Grant in an attack on Corinth. While waiting for an army, four ironclads and the mortar rafts dropped downstream to annoy the garrison at Pillow. This was done by stationing a mortar raft behind a point protecting it from the fort and lobbing shells into the works at intervals. One ironclad stood off the point to guard the mortar raft; the others anchored upstream.

The Yankees knew of the two ironclads that were abuilding at Memphis, but they did not know that there was a Confederate fleet in being at that city—eight of the cottonclad rams that had come up from New Orleans. On a misty Saturday morning Confederate "Commodore" J. E. Montgomery decided to take his rams up and cut out the mortar raft and its guardian ironclad. This was not an easy decision to carry out because of the nature of the command situation in the Confederate River Defense Fleet and its officers and crews.

The ram fleet had nothing to do with the Confederate Navy. Montgomery was an ex-river captain who had been authorized to convert, equip, and man the boats. His officers and operating crews were also river men, and remained rugged individualists throughout their combat service. Theoretically, Montgomery was under the command of General Lovell, who indicated his opinion of the system by writing, "Fourteen Mississippi captains and pilots woud never agree about anything after they had once gotten under way . . . . There is little or no discipline or subordination, too much 'steamboat' and too little of the 'man-of-war' to be effective."

Other than the operating crew, the vessels were manned by soldiers who volunteered for or were assigned to this duty. They would take no orders from river men and frequently walked off the boats if they were displeased. The Union had equal trouble using soldiers aboard river warships, which they usually had to do, at least as gunners. On one occasion when 250 troops were assigned to a fleet of mortar rafts and their accompanying steamboat, the major in command and his adjutant positively refused to board the boat without their horses.

But on the misty morning of May 10, 1862, Montgomery did get his cottonclads steaming up the river. The *Cincinnati* was guarding the mortar raft that day and its crew was calmly hanging out its wash when the rams appeared out of the mist. The ironclad got off one volley before the leading ram, the *General Bragg*, crashed into her side. As the *Cincinnati* recoiled the *Sumter* crashed into her stern and wrecked her steering gear. When the *Colonel Lovell* opened a large gash in her other side, the *Cincinnati* quietly sank in water up to the floor of her pilothouse.

The other Union vessels upstream could see none of this, but they got under way and steamed toward the sound of the guns. As the *Mound City* rounded the point behind which the action had taken place the ram *Van Dorn* met her head on to hole her so badly that the ironclad ran aground and sank. The *Benton* and the *Carondelet* had their bow guns blazing when they rounded the point and, when a shot from the latter burst a boiler of another ram and sent it drifting after the *Bragg,* the Confederate vessels dropped down the river while the Union ships stood by their sunken sisters, unable to pursue without coming under the guns of Fort Pillow.

The Confederate rams had proved potent weapons against the slow-moving ironclads, but at this point, like the cavalry arriving in the nick of time, Colonel Charles Ellet, Jr., appeared on the scene with a fleet of Union rams. Ellet was a civilian engineer who was obsessed with the idea that the ancient ram of row-galley days was still a worth-while weapon. He presented his plan to War Secretary Stanton so effectively that he was commissioned as a colonel in the army and authorized to procure nine vessels, convert them in accordance with his ideas, and man them.

Ellet's vessels were basically bigger and faster than the southern rams, and his method of conversion made them more effective weapons. Instead of merely reinforcing the bows he ran three heavy bulkheads parallel to the length of each vessel, strongly braced against the sides and deck with iron rods, making the hull immune to longitudinal shock and so stiffening it that the weight of the entire boat would be behind the ram at the bow when it hit the target vessel. He sacrificed armor and armament to speed; his craft were capable of about 13 miles an hour in still water,

U.S. NAVY

The Union's river-boat navy first demonstrated its worth in the attack on Fort Henry in 1862. An hour after they had opened fire, the four ironclads and three timberclads had set the fort on fire and destroyed all but four of its guns. When General Grant's land forces arrived, they found the Union flag flying above the fort and Confederate General Tilgham, surrendered, aboard the Cincinnati.

but were armored only with an oak shield around the engines and boiler iron around the pilothouse as proof against sniper fire. They carried no guns.

Ellet's personnel consisted of civilians and soldiers—and Ellets. He commissioned a brother, sons, nephews, and cousins as army officers to command his vessels and hired civilian crews of river men to operate them. For a fighting force of about 20 men per vessel to repel boarders he recruited his own army unit with posters that were headed:

MISSISSIPPI MARINE BRIGADE.
Soldiering made Easy!   No hard Marching!
No carrying Knapsacks!
$100 BOUNTY!

The glowing inducement went on to emphasize the good beds and fine cooking in the river marine corps, but said not a word about fighting.

The first of Ellet's rams joined the fleet above Fort Pillow on May 26, 1862. Ellet had been instructed by Secretary Stanton to secure the "concurrence" of the senior naval officer present for any operation, who by then was Navy Captain Charles Davis, who had replaced Foote. Ellet proposed that they run past Fort Pillow and attack the southern fleet. Davis did not approve, nor would he assist, but, in Ellet's mind at least, he "concurred." The senior Ellet sent his brother in the ram *Monarch* downstream to reconnoiter. The younger Ellet returned to say that there was no danger in running past Pillow—it was deserted. Three day earlier Union forces had captured Corinth, and Pillow, outflanked like Columbus, had been quietly evacuated. The Union fleet of four ironclads and four rams dropped down toward Memphis, where the *Benton, St. Louis, Cairo,* and *Carondelet* were anchored boldly abreast in midstream while the rams moored behind them on the bank.

On June fifth Confederate Commodore Montgomery held a council of war with his civilian captains and all agreed that the next day they would go out and sink some ironclads—they knew nothing about the Union rams. The army officer commanding the gunners aboard the southern vessels did not agree, so all the soldiers marched off the boats, which probably did not make any difference in the ensuing action. On June sixth the citizens of Memphis lined the low bluffs above the city to watch the fun, the women carrying parasols against the hot sun and slave boys lugging picnic baskets. They saw the shortest completely decisive naval battle in history.

The four Union ironclads opened fire as the eight southern rams charged toward them. Through the smoke the Union ram *Queen of the West* charged past the line of ironclads, the senior Ellet waving his hat from atop the pilothouse. The *Queen* and the Confederate *Colonel Lovell* tore toward each other, head to head, until the southern vessel swerved at the last minute. The fast *Queen* hit her amidships, cut her in two, and sent her to the bottom. The Union *Monarch* struck toward Confederate *Price* and was in turn charged by the Confederate *Beauregard*. The *Monarch* slipped between the two southern ships and the *Beauregard* crashed into the *Price* tearing off her port wheel and sending her into the bank. The *Monarch* spun around and crashed into the *Beauregard* at the same moment that a shell from the *Benton* hit the southerner's engine. Gunfire had also disabled the *Little Rebel*, which staggered to the bank, and set the *Jeff Thompson* afire. The Confederate *Van Dorn* wisely fled downstream while the *Bragg* and the *Sumter* streaked for the banks and surrendered. It was all over in 20 minutes, with two Confederate vessels sunk, one

CHICAGO HISTORICAL SOCIETY

One of the most decisive battles in the war lasted only 20 minutes. While spectators watched along the river banks, the city of Memphis was captured by a Union fleet of four rams and four ironclads. Within minutes seven Confederate rams had been sunk, burned, or forced to surrender. An eighth, the Van Dorn, *fled to safety downstream. The above painting is by Alexander Simplot.*

burned and four captured; only the *Van Dorn* escaped. Before one of Ellet's sons went ashore to raise the Stars and Stripes above the Memphis post office the southerners burned their uncompleted ironclad, the *Tennessee*. The *Arkansas,* complete except for her armor, had been towed down the Mississippi and up the Yazoo after the fall of Island Number Ten.

The Mississippi was now open to the Union forces down to Vicksburg —and up to Vicksburg. Late in April, Admiral Farragut had run past the forts at the mouth of the river with a deep-water fleet and captured New Orleans. The only river boats in Farragut's command were five ferries that were brought to the Gulf to tow his big vessels over the bars at the mouths of the delta. Of the few Confederate converted river boats that futilely opposed Farragut one is worthy of mention, the unique ironclad *Manassas.*

The *Manassas* was the screw towboat *Enoch Train* until a syndicate of New Orleans speculators converted her into what they hoped would be an invulnerable privateer by placing an iron-covered turtleback over the entire vessel. A short smoke stack stuck out of the top and a single large retractable gun poked through a covered port at the bow; a small hatch at the stern provided the only access to her stuffy interior. When it was learned that the weight of her armor made her too slow for privateering she was taken into the Confederate River Defense Fleet and became the first American ironclad to see action, five months before the famed battle of the *Monitor* and the *Merrimack.*

This happened one dark night in October 1861 at the Head of Passes, a stretch of water fifteen miles above the Gulf from which the many mouths of the Mississippi Delta branch. The Union navy had learned that the Mississippi could not be blockaded in the Gulf without vessels covering each of its outlets, so they had sent a big steam sloop-of-war, the *Richmond,* two smaller sailing sloops and a tug armed with popguns up to Head of Passes, sure that four ships with a combined fire power almost equal to that of the entire Confederate navy could blockade a stretch of water two miles square.

The officers of the squadron shared this confidence and were peacefully asleep, guarded by only an anchor watch, when the little *Manassas* steamed down from New Orleans to attack them. Behind the ironclad were three barges loaded with combustibles acting as fire rafts and towed abreast by two tugs. Behind these were five of the converted cottonclads, each with one heavy gun in the bow. The plan was for the *Manassas* to sneak up and ram the *Richmond* and then fire a rocket as a signal to ignite and release the rafts. Aiming by the light from the rafts, the cottonclads were to hang back and shell the Yankee squadron at fairly long range as it would have been suicidal for these flimsy craft to come under the broadsides of the real warships.

All this might have happened except that the *Richmond* was coaling from a barge on the side from which the *Manassas* made her attack. The little ironclad hit the front of the barge and was deflected, making only a small hole in the big sloop. Further, the hawser lashing the barge to the sloop cut off her smokestack flush with the turtleback, filling the latter's interior with smoke, and the shock of the crash threw one of her engines off its mount. For several minutes the crew was too busy trying to save itself from asphyxiation to send up a rocket, and during that time the Union vessels fired broadsides madly into the darkness, slipped their cables, and tried to obey the conflicting lantern signals from the flagship. By the time the rafts were lighted the Yankee ships were drifting downstream faster than the fire boats, and the cottonclads were too far away to do much damage. The little *Manassas* limped back upstream.

Meanwhile, the *Richmond* had entered one of the passes sideways and coud not straighten out. She floated fifteen miles and went aground on a bar at the mouth of the pass. One of the smaller sloops, the *Vincennes,* also went aground, her stern pointing up the channel. When two of the cottonclads poked their noses down to see what was going on the skipper of the *Vincennes* cut holes in her taffrail to bring two guns to bear; then he changed his mind, ordered the crew into the boats, and had a slow match laid to the magazine to blow her up. He had himself rowed over to the stranded *Richmond* with, for some unexplained reason, an American flag draped around his shoulders. Fortunately, a gunner ignored the order to light the slow match and the *Vincennes* did not blow up. Both ships jettisoned their guns and stores to get off the bar and sailed away to complete the most disgraceful performance in the history of the U.S. Navy.

Farragut passed the forts below New Orleans on April 24, 1862, a dark night that was lighted by flashes from bursting shells and flames from blazing fire rafts, all of which did little damage to the Union vessels. Above the forts two unfinished giant ironclads plus eleven converted river boats represented the Confederate naval defenses, all of it ineffectual. The ironclad *Mississippi* was unarmed and had to be burned by its builders; the ironclad *Louisiana* was armed but engineless and, after serving as a floating battery, was blown up to prevent its capture. The fast Union vessel *Varuna* got ahead of the line and sent the Louisiana State river boat *General Quitman* into the bank aflame, and was then herself sunk by the other Louisiana boat, the *Governor Moore,* which was in turn destroyed by a broadside from the *Pensacola.* Six of the Confederate rams with civilian captains were driven ashore by the Union *Cayuga* and were abandoned and fired by their crews, most of whom did little fighting. One, the *Defiance*, did none at all. Her drunken captain burned her before the *Cayuga* had a chance to shoot at him. The most powerful southern vessel, the *McRae*, was crippled and sunk in a single-ship action with the Union *Iroquois*; the *Stonewall Jackson* limped upstream a few miles, so badly crippled that she had to be destroyed—and that left only the little *Manassas*.

As the Union warships swept past the forts in column the little ironclad valiantly charged at the towering *Brooklyn*, firing her single gun and pushing her ironclad nose against the side of the giant. Because of her slow speed and light weight she did little damage. As the northern vessels slowed to dispose of the other Confederate craft, the *Manassas* crawled back up the line firing her popgun and vainly seeking a chance to ram. The *Pinola, Richmond, Pensacola*, and *Wissahickon* all shot at her, cutting off her stack and piercing her armor in places. Then dawn disclosed the pesky little vessel to Farragut, who ordered the *Mississippi* to ram her. (There was a *Mississippi* on each side.) The big side-wheeler missed the little target with her rush, but not with her broadside. Afire and with her armor a sieve, the *Manassas* was driven into the bank and her crew took to the woods as the *Mississippi* hit her with another broadside, dislodging her from the bank. She floated downstream, burning until she exploded.

After pausing to raise the Stars and Stripes above undefended Baton Rouge and Natchez, Farragut steamed on to Vicksburg. Washington had ordered him to move against this last Confederate bastion on the river, although it could never have been taken by naval force alone. The guns on its bluffs 250 feet above the river were too high to be reached by naval artillery other than mortars. As a gesture toward taking the offensive, and to prove that he could run past forts at will, Farragut took three of his big ships and eight sloops and gunboats above the city, where he was met by Ellet and four of his rams. Davis with four ironclads shortly joined them, and the river and seagoing fleets were united.

The Confederates had little left afloat except the *Arkansas* up the Yazoo, which emptied into the Mississippi a few miles above Vicksburg. When she was taken upstream the unfinished ironclad had two engines, homemade in Memphis, that drove twin propellers, an iron beak for a ram, and an odd assortment of ten guns—two in the bow, two in the stern and three in each broadside. Confederate Naval Lieutenant Isaac Brown was ordered to complete her armor, but was not supplied with men, money, or materials. Using local labor, Brown sent wagons around the countryside to tear up railroad spurs. He placed one course of rails upright around the vessel's casemate, with the bar of the T down, and drove another course between these, bottom side up, to form an effective three-inch armor plate. The vessel was rust colored simply because the rails were rusty and Brown had no paint.

By the time the *Arkansas* was finished the Yazoo was falling and, unless he wanted to stay until next spring, Brown had to take his makeshift vessel out. As the Confederate craft started downstream, Farragut ordered three Union ships up the river to investigate the southern ironclad. The *Carondelet*, the ram *Queen of the West*, and the timberclad *Tyler* were moving upstream abreast when the rusty *Arkansas* came around a bend above them. Unable to ram effectively against the curent, the unarmed *Queen* turned and frankly ran. Acting independently, the skippers of the other two Union craft each made the same unwise decision—to run and fight a rear action going downstream, expecting that the racket would help bring the rest of the fleet, seven miles away in the Mississippi.

The small cannon on the sterns of the northern vessels did no damage to the *Arkansas* other than to pierce her stack and decapitate an Irishman in the crew who stuck his head out a port to see how the battle was

The Union steamer Mississippi *attempts to ram the converted towboat* Manassas *in a battle below New Orleans. The* Mississippi *missed with her bow, but hit the little ironclad with her guns. The* Manassas *was driven to the bank, where her crew escaped to the woods. She then floated downstream, burning, until she exploded.*

On the night of April 16, 1863, Admiral David Porter, in the flagship Benton (right), led a fleet of six ironclads, a ram, and a few transports through the southern blockade at Vicksburg. The southerners discovered them and lit up the river with floats of tar and turpentine. In the exchange

that followed, all the Union boats got through except for the transport
Henry Clay (second from left). The city finally fell on July 4, opening
the entire Mississippi to the North.

going. The *Tyler* took some damage before she got out of range, and southern shells streamed into the unarmored stern of the slower *Carondelet*, crippling her steering, piercing her boiler, and finally driving her to the bank, where her crew scurried to safety.

The sound of the battle up the Yazoo had not alerted the Union fleet, whose officers thought the gunfire was an attack on shore batteries. Not a ship had steam up or guns loaded when the *Arkansas* appeared at the mouth of the river. The Union rams were behind the line of larger ships and Brown laid a course close to Farragut's vessels so that the rams could not get up speed to be effective. The day was so calm that smoke hung motionless in the air and the fighting soon became a matter of firing at flashes. The *Arkansas* discharged her bow guns at the *Hartford* and a broadside at the *Kineo* as she passed, receiving a clanging return of shells on her iron rails. Her stack was so cut up that she was soon reduced to a speed of about one mile an hour and could not ram the *Benton* when that vessel was presented as a target. The Union ram *Lancaster* got loose and started a run, but a shot in her boiler disabled her. The southern vessel drifted through the entire northern fleet to safety under the guns of Vicksburg.

At dusk Farragut's fleet ran past the southern ironclad, now moored against the bank below Vicksburg, each vessel firing a broadside as it passed. But a rust-colored ship against a red clay bank made a poor target, and only one shell pierced the Arkansas. Next morning the infuriated Farragut called the *Essex* down to engage the southerner and the *Queen of the West* to ram her. Soldiers who had handled the *Arkansas'* guns on the trip down the Yazoo had left when the vessel reached Vicksburg. Brown now had only enough men left to man two guns, but one of them drove the *Essex* off with disabled engines, and the other chased the *Queen* away after she had delivered a glancing blow. At this point Farragut gave up and returned to New Orleans for much-needed refitting, taking the *Essex* and leaving the other river boats above Vicksburg.

The *Arkansas* was repaired, after a fashion, and ordered to support a Confederate army attack on Baton Rouge, and the valiant vessel started downstream to meet an ignominious end. Never strong, her homemade engines failed several times on the trip downriver. Near Baton Rouge the *Essex* came up to meet her. As they were about to close, the *Arkansas'* port engine stopped, and the vessel swung into the bank in a position from which her guns could not bear on the *Essex*. When the northern ship took position to pound the helpless southerner, her commander ordered the crew ashore and personally fired the ship. Brown later wrote, "With colors flying the gallant

Arkansas, whose decks had never been pressed by the foot of an enemy, was blown into the air."

There followed almost a year of stalemate in the Union drive for complete control of the Mississippi. While waiting for an army to move down to attack Vicksburg the Union river navy grew. More ironclads of the Pook Turtle type were added and both double- and single-turret river monitors were built, although none was finished in time to do much fighting. Another type of vessel was added— "tinclads." These were new or converted river boats armored only with boiler iron to protect them against small-arms fire, armed with twenty-four-pound deck howitzers and manned with a contingent of sharpshooters. On patrol on the main river and up the tributaries, they harassed southern shipping and protected northern transports and supply ships against attack from the banks. There were ultimately about seventy of them, more vessels of a single class than the U.S. Navy ever had until the world wars.

During this year Congress ordained that the river boats should be transferred from the army to the navy with an order that caused some confusion because it referred to the "gunboats" that the army had built on the rivers. Since Ellet's rams carried no guns their skippers maintained that they were not covered by the order and could go their merry, undisciplined way. Abraham Lincoln finally had to settle this matter with an executive order. When the rams were taken into the navy the marine brigade was expanded and, with field artillery and cavalry added, horses were carried on the vessels for use in landing operations. These were the first true "horse marines."

A base behind Vicksburg, flanking its northern bastion at Haine's Bluff, was much to be desired. With the rivers in flood in mid-March, the new commander of the inland navy, Admiral David Dixon Porter, thought this might be accomplished by taking a fleet through the woods that separated the Mississippi and the Yazoo to reach a point above the Confederate defenses. Followed by General Sherman and 10,000 troops on land, Porter set out with five of the original Pook Turtles and four tugs.

This was perhaps the most bizarre naval expedition in history. The two rivers were roughly parallel at this point, separated by low land cut up with bayous and creeks. There was about fifteen feet of water in the bayous at the time, but there was no channel; a forest of trees stood in the water. The ironclads felt their way between the trees, from which the coons, wildcats, and snakes that had taken refuge from the flood dropped atop their casemates while branches broke their skylights and knocked down their stacks. During the first day they made eight miles and ended with four vessels pointed in as many directions. Then the *Cincinnati* learned that she could make a channel by ramming trees to knock them over and the boats got in line.

The bayous were bounded by high dikes on which cotton burned to throw a pall of smoke around the vessels. The Confederates set gangs of slaves to cut trees in their path which the tugs had to haul away before the fleet could proceed. Still they inched forward until the fourth day, when they came to a smooth stretch of water green with willow withes. The *Cincinnati* was soon stuck fast with the willows wound in her wheel. While all hands were trying to clear her, the fleet was attacked by field artillery firing from behind the bayou banks.

Two other boats finally pulled the *Cincinnati* loose and the fleet's guns were elevated as howitzers to drive off the rebel artillery, but sharpshooters then took its place. Negroes reported that the Confederate troops were gathering in force and the frightening thought occurred to someone that by damming the stream up ahead with cotton bales, the southerners might lower the water in the bayou and leave the navy sitting in the woods. The fleet squirmed back to the protection of Sherman's marching men and all hands returned to the Mississippi. The ironclads picked up some $300,000 worth of cotton on the way out, which helped pay for the damage to the boats.

At about the time the river boats returned from their abortive campaign through the woods, Grant settled on the plan of attack that would finally subdue Vicksburg, which involved the close support of the inland navy. While the army marched down the west bank of the river to get below the city, Porter prepared his fleet to run past Vicksburg, shielding the vulnerable sterns with logs and bales of hay and piling cotton topped with bags of grain around the engines. At ten o'clock on the dark night of April 6, 1963, four of the ironclads, two new ones, a ram, and a few transports silently started to drift past the fortress. They almost reached the halfway point before the Confederates discovered the moving fleet and lit up the river with blazing tar barrels on the bank. There was much noise, glare, and confusion as the southern guns on the bluffs belched and the cannon of the ironclads, elevated as high as possible, returned the fire. But when it was all over the fleet had passed the batteries with the loss of but one transport. A few nights later Porter brought down another line of transports and the river boats ferried Grant's army across the Mississippi for the final phase of the subjugation of Vicksburg.

The river warships joined with the army in three fruitless assaults on the city and then settled down to a forty-seven-day siege, during which the *Cincinnati* was lost when she went in to silence a water battery that was preventing Sherman from extending his flank. The general told Porter that he thought the big guns had been taken from the battery. He was wrong, and a shot from a ten-inch cannon went through the top of the casemate and out the ship's bottom. This was the last naval casualty in the Vicksburg campaign; on July 4, 1863, the city surrendered and Lincoln rejoiced that "the Father of Waters once more flowed unvexed to the sea," while General Sherman proclaimed: "Now the river of our greatness is free, as God made it."

The war would last for the better part of another two years and the inland navy, particularly the tinclads, was kept busy on patrol, but there was but one other naval expedition on the rivers, this one up the Red River toward Texas. The inspiration for this was largely political. French troops were in Mexico supporting the Emperor Maximilian in total defiance of the Monroe Doctrine. There was not much the United States could do about it at the moment, but Secretary of State Seward believed that it was important for Union forces to occupy some part of Texas, if only to prove that it was still part of the country.

Twenty thousand troops under General Banks were to gather at Shreveport supported by a fleet that was to go up the Red River on the spring flood in March 1864. This was the largest river fleet that had ever been assembled, and included most of the old Eads ironclads, some new ones, three river monitors, and six tinclads. The difficulty lay with the spring flood—it turned out to be the lowest in twenty years.

Porter left most of his fleet in Grand Ecore, about four-fifths of the way to Shreveport, and went on with the *Eastport*—the captured Confederate ironclad—and two tinclads. At Springfield Landing, forty miles below Shreveport, he was stopped by a big steamer that had been placed crosswise in the stream, filled with mud, and then broken in half. As he was planning how to deal with this obstacle, word reached him that Banks' army had been decisively defeated and was retreating to Grand Ecore. Also the river, which should have been rising, started to fall. Porter turned around, but it was too late. After striking a mine the *Eastport's* keel wedged in a bed of sunken logs. As there was no hope of getting her loose, she was blown up.

Meanwhile, panicky General Banks announced that he was leaving Grand Ecore, caring not whether the navy was stranded near the Texas border. The fleet kept pace with the retreat down to Alexandria, where the vessels, some of which drew seven feet, were faced with two sets of falls with a depth of three feet. Guns were taken out and portaged around and armor was stripped off and thrown into the river, but even without armor and armaments the larger vessels could not hope to cross the falls. At this point Colonel Joseph Bailey of the

Fourth Wisconsin Infantry stepped forth to save the day. Colonel Bailey had been a lumberman before the war. He had no experience with boats, but knew a lot about floating logs downstream, and the same methods used to float logs might float boats.

Banks grudgingly lent Bailey 3,000 men, who started to dam the river above the lower falls. This would back up water to give sufficient level at the upper falls and when the vessels had passed this, the center of the dam would be broken so that the fleet could dash through the lower falls on the surge of water. The structure consisted of a wing dam extending from each bank with a center section of three barges that could be cut loose to break the dam. The work was almost complete, and the water above the upper falls had risen over five feet, when the pressure tore out two of the barges. The *Lexington*, the only vessel with steam up, made a run for it. Pitching down the rushing torrent, she hung briefly on a rock and then bobbed through the gap in the dam to float safely in deep water while the watching army cheered.

Undaunted, Bailey started to build again, this time two wing dams above the upper falls. He reasoned that the narrow gap between the wings would form a channel in which the water would be deep enough for the boats, which now drew about six feet, and he reasoned well. When the troops finished the dams in three days, working to their armpits in water, there was a six-and-a-half-foot channel on which the ironless ironclads floated bumpily but safely through the falls and hastened to the bosom of the Mississippi.

War work for the river boats did not end with Appomattox. The western troops had to be brought home, and hundreds of thousands of them were safely returned to the northern states on rivercraft. This did not include an undertemined number of the men who were crowded aboard the *Sultana*. The explosion and burning of that troop-laden vessel was probably the greatest disaster, in terms of fatalities, in marine history—"probably" because no one knows the number burned, drowned, or scalded to death.

The *Sultana*, a big new boat, left New Orleans on April 21, 1865, twelve days after Lee's surrender. She was rated to carry 376 persons, but on this trip she carried only about 100 passengers, a crew of about 80, 100 hogs, 60 mules, and 100 hogsheads of sugar. The trip was uneventful until she reached Vicksburg, where the engineer reported a leak in one of her four boilers and she laid over a day to have it fixed.

Behind Vicksburg was a hastily improvised camp to which the beaten Confederacy was delivering Union prisoners, thousands of half-starved scarecrows who had been incarcerated in the prison stockades at Cahaba and the infamous Andersonville. As soon as possible after they were received the men were placed aboard northward-bound steam-boats, about 1,000 to a boat. Before the *Sultana* arrived, the *Henry Ames* had cleared with 1,300 and the *Olive Branch* with 700, and a nasty rumor had spread that one Union officer was accepting a dollar per head, under the table, to put the men aboard the boats owned by one certain company. To gainsay this assertion, the officer in charge of forwarding prisoners ordered that all the rest in camp were to be put aboard the *Sultana*, although two vessels of the suspect owner arrived while she was loading.

They came to the river bank on a little railroad, they came in wagons, and, when no other transportation offered, they walked in small groups. At first the loading officers tried to keep rolls and put the men aboard in an orderly manner—Ohio troops on the open hurricane deck, Indiana troops on the promenade around the cabin on the boiler deck, Michigan troops forward on the main deck, etc. But the crowd soon got out of hand as men climbed aboard wherever they could find standing room. When the camp was empty and the *Sultana* full nobody knew how many men were aboard. As the vessel steamed toward Cairo her clerk told one Union officer that there were 2,400 soldiers aboard plus 180 civilians; if the *Sultana* reached Cairo safely—which he seemed to doubt—it would be the greatest trip, in terms of people carried, ever made on the Mississippi.

The steamer arrived at Memphis at 7 P.M., eighteen hours after leaving Vicksburg. While some of the troops helped unload the sugar, others sneaked ashore to buy or cadge drinks in Whiskey Chute. A few lucky ones undoubtedly passed out from the long-deferred libation and remained in Memphis saloons. One survivor told the ironic tale of missing the boat and paying a Negro two dollars to row him across the river to catch it where it was coaling. The *Sultana* got under way for Cairo about midnight. Two hours later she was in the center of the spring-flooded river, picking her way through a group of islands called the Hen and Chickens, when a boiler exploded.

The blast hurled lethal splinters and iron shards into the closely packed sleeping bodies on the main deck and steam scalded others near the boilers. Sleepers above the blast on the boiler and hurricane decks were hurled into the air and rained back on to the boat or into the river, whole or in pieces. The texas, the forward part of the cabin, and one stack collapsed into the hull, pinning many men in the wreckage, where they slowly roasted in the fire that quickly spread. The flames, starting about one third of the way from the bow, licked at the remains of the cabin above and were swept aft by a downstream wind.

It would seem that almost every survivor later told his personal tale of the event, and they were suprisingly similar horror stories: ". . . men who were scalded and bruised were crawling over one another to get out of the fire . . . . it seemed as if some were coming out of the fire and from under the boiler . . . . men who were buried beneath the wreck were crying for help . . . . men caught in every conceivable manner . . . screaming in their agony . . . . flames were madly rushing through the broken kindling of the boat cabin . . . . the stench of burning flesh was intolerable." The panic-ridden crowd was perhaps more deadly than the explosion: ". . . the heat was intense, driving the men back, those in the center and nearest the fire crowding those on the outer edges into the river . . . men were trampling over each other in their endeavors to escape . . . the men rushed to the bow of the boat . . . to the stern . . . and jumped overboard as fast as they could, tumbling into the river upon each other and going down into the deep by the hundreds."

Swimming ability was of little help, as even the strongest swimmers were pulled down by frantic flounderers. Some remained calm enough to wrench off a door to float on before diving in; others were lucky to be blown into the water near life-saving wreckage. One section of the boiler deck hit the water intact with nine men who were sleeping

No one knows for certain how many people were crowded aboard the steamer Sultana *nor how many were killed when her boiler exploded on her northbound trip from Vicksburg after Lee's surrender. The official figure is that 1,547 lives were lost—a greater number than went down with*

THE MARINERS MUSEUM, NEWPORT NEWS, VA.

on it and they clung to their improvised raft as it floated off. Some 500 persons remained on the bow of the burning craft for almost an hour, apparently safe—until one of the wheel housings burned through and collapsed, which caused the vessel to swing around. Thus the wind blew the flames toward the bow, and the men were forced to jump.

An hour and a half after the explosion the *Bostonia*, coming downstream, rounded a bend and discovered the blazing boat, now deserted. She anchored, lowered her yawl, and picked up about a hundred survivors before proceeding to Memphis. Some survivors had floated to that city before the *Bostonia*'s arrival and were being hauled from the water by small boats, including those of the *Essex* and the *Tyler*. Three river boats hastened to get steam up to join the search for the hundreds of survivors spread over miles of swollen river clinging to wreckage, or others in the branches of trees on its banks. By afternoon the boats were bringing in more dead bodies than live ones and Memphis' public buildings were turned into hospitals or charnel houses.

It is probable that the dead of the *Sultana* disaster topped 1,500, although an army review board, seeking to minimize the tragedy, placed it at 1,238. They claimed 765 military personnel and 12 to 18 civilians

the Titanic. *Left is the only photograph of the* Sultana *as she left Memphis, her last port of departure. Below is a drawing of fires sweeping her decks, with troops on the foredeck and in the water.*

THE MARINERS MUSEUM, NEWPORT NEWS, VA.

had been saved and arrived at their conservative estimate of fatalities by estimating the number of soldiers aboard at 1,866. All the testimony before a Memphis court of inquiry put the figure much higher. Three witnesses who claimed to have made a count agreed on 1,966 as the number of paroled prisoners, plus a full-strength guard company of about 200. These figures, plus civilians made the boat's total complement close to 2,400, of whom about 800 were saved. The United States Customs Service at Memphis gave out an official figure of 1,547 dead, which would make this the greatest marine disaster in history, topping by thirty the death toll of the *Titanic*.

The most surprising thing about the *Sultana* disaster is the extent to which it was ignored by the press. The front pages in the north were devoted to more prominent corpses—that of Lincoln wending its slow way toward Illinois on the funeral train, and of John Wilkes Booth, lying with a hole in its head on the deck of the monitor *Montauk* in the Potomac. The more than 1,500 dead of the *Sultana* received but a five-inch story on page four of *The New York Times* on the day after the disaster.

Floating Palaces

Immediately after the initial cruises of John Fitch's *Steamboat* up and down the Delaware in 1790, his backers insisted that a cabin be erected on the stern of the vessel. It was planned by one of them, Dr. William Thornton, who would gain fame as an architect by designing the nation's Capitol. Fitch objected that the structure would interfere with the operation of the boat, but he was overruled and it was built, painted, and carpeted—and, although the expression does not appear in contemporary writing, somebody undoubtedly then called the vessel a "floating palace." A few years later Fulton's *North River* was so dubbed in the press when she got a cabin with curtains at the windows.

It might be said that most river boats that were called floating palaces were so only in the eyes of the beholder. Mark Twain pointed out that Charles Dickens refused to agree with the popular conception that steamboats were "magnificent" or that they were "floating palaces," and, he continued, "Mr. Dickens's position was unassailable, possibly; the people's position was certainly unassailable. If Mr. Dickens was comparing these boats with the crown jewels; or with the Taj, or with the Matterhorn; or with some other priceless or wonderful thing which he had seen, they were not magnificent—he was right. The people compared them with what *they* had seen; and, thus measured, thus judged, the boats were magnificent . . . . The steamboats were finer than anything on shore. Compared with superior dwelling-houses and first-class hotels in the valley, they were indubitably magnificent."

In *Life on the Mississippi* Twain then described a fine home of the day and contrasted it with a steamboat of the floating-palace type. The home, he said, was a "big, square, two-story 'frame' house, painted white and porticoed like a Grecian temple—with this difference, that the imposing fluted columns and Corinthian capitals were a pathetic sham, being made of white pine, and painted . . . . Within, an uncarpeted hall, of planed boards; opening out of it, a parlor, fifteen feet by fifteen." Here, below a chromo of "Washington Crossing the Delaware," were "horsehair chairs, horsehair sofa which keeps sliding from under you. Window-shades, of oil stuff, with milkmaids and ruined castles stenciled on them in fierce colors . . . . Bedrooms with rag carpets; bedsteads of the 'corded' sort, with a sag in the middle, the cords needing tightening; snuffy feather-bed—not aired often enough; cane-seat chairs, splint-bottomed rocker; looking-glass on wall, school-slate size, veneered frame, inherited bureau; wash-bowl and pitcher. . . . Nothing else in the room. Not a bathroom in the house; and no visitor likely to come along who has ever seen one."

It was in relation to such a background that the midwesterner viewed the best of the river boats with awe and dubbed them floating palaces. "When he stepped aboard a big fine steamboat, he entered a new and marvelous world: chimney-tops cut to counterfeit a spraying crown of plumes—and maybe painted red; pilot-house, hurricane-deck, boiler-deck guards, all garnished with white wooden filigree-work of fanciful patterns; gilt acorns topping the derricks; gilt deer-horns over the big bell;

THE MARINERS MUSEUM, NEWPORT NEWS, VA.

The era of the "floating palaces"—a Currier & Ives print of the Mississippi in the postwar years.

gaudy symbolical picture on the paddle-box, possibly; big roomy boiler-deck, painted blue, and furnished with Windsor armchairs; inside, a far-receding snow-white 'cabin'; porcelain knob and oil-picture on every stateroom door; curving patterns of filigree-work touched up with gild-ing, stretching overhead all down the converging vista; big chandeliers every little way, each an April shower of glittering glass-drops; lovely rainbow-light falling everywhere from the colored glazing of the sky-lights; the whole a long-drawn, resplendent tunnel, a bewildering and soul-satisfying spectacle! In the ladies' cabin a pink and white Wilton carpet, as soft as mush, and glorified with a ravishing pattern of gigantic flowers. Then the Bridal Chamber . . . . whose pretentious flummery was necessarily overawing to the now tottering intellect of that hosan-nahing citizen. Every stateroom had its couple of cozy clean bunks, and perhaps a looking-glass and a snug closet; and sometimes there was even a washbowl and pitcher, and part of a towel which could be told from mosquito-netting by an expert."

Mark Twain was describing the floating palace of the midwestern valley, but his premise held true elsewhere, more so in the Far West, less in the East. As in earlier days, the eastern boats were superior craft in all respects; dependability, speed, comfort, and decor. Many people equate the phrase "floating palace" with the high, squarish, gleaming-white, twin-stacked Mississippi River boat. Actually, there was never a boat on western waters that compared with the later Hudson River and, particularly, Long Island Sound boats. The most pretentious Mississippi boat cost less than $400,000 to build; its eastern counterpart cost over $2,000,000.

The era of the true floating palace, East or West, started after the Civil War. Having said that, one must note exceptions. On the Mississippi the *Eclipse*, launched in 1852, was entitled to the appellation floating palace if only because of the exuberance of her 300-foot-long saloon, particularly its ceiling. In this and other boats it was the handling of the ceiling and its supporting members that gave rise to the term "steamboat Gothic," although *Eclipse*'s was actually a blending of Gothic and Norman styles. The top of the saloon was divided into dia-monds by the crossing of Gothic arches, with gilt pendants of acorns entwined with oak leaves at the intersections. Above were large stained-glass skylights through which streamed multicolored light on a sunny day. At night, the richness was made brilliant by the light of six massive, richly gilded oil-burning chandeliers. When the visitor could tear his eyes from the awe-inspiring magnificence above, he found the rest of the saloon in keeping with its covering. The door of each of the state-rooms that lined the main cabin was embellished with a landscape, and at the forward entrance to the cabin were large paintings of the vessel's patron cities, Louisville and New Orleans. At the men's end of the long hall was a gilt statue of Andrew Jackson and at the women's a matching replica of Henry Clay. The floor was covered with the ubiquitous Brussels carpet upon which rested the final touch of opulence, a piano.

On eastern waters pre-war floating palaces included the *New World* (not the one which took her magnificence to the gold rush in 1849) and her bitter rival, the *Francis Skiddy*, which stayed on the Hudson to become the most famous boat of the 1850s. The "in" people of those days did not merely go to Albany; they "took the *Skiddy*," as movie stars and other notables "took the *Super Chief*" to Los Angeles a few years ago. And in that same decade on the Hudson was the *Empire State* of which an English female traveler wrote in *Hunt's Magazine* in 1853:

The word boat gives a very imperfect idea of this floating palace, which accommodates . . . from five to six hundred American citizens and others, of all classes, in a style of splendor that Cleopatra herself might envy. There is little to remind one of machinery, for the paddle wheels are covered, and the engine is rendered invisible by being surrounded with glass and drapery. . . . I followed a crowd of five hundred up a handsome staircase, through splendidly furnished saloons covered with carpet of velvet pile, to the upper deck. Tea being served, we all adjourned to the gentlemen's cabin. . . . At the entrance we were met by tall swarthy figures, clothed in white linen of unspotted purity, who conducted us to our seats. There were three tables, the entire length of the room, covered with everything that was beautiful; but nothing that seemed eatable, except the pineapple and some small delicate, delicious-looking things that, for want of a better word, I shall call rolls, though it vulgarized them sadly. Notwithstanding this unreal appearance, you no sooner wished for anything than a ministering spirit was at your elbow to gratify you. At his touch pineapples became butter, pyramids tea cakes, and magical boxes of savory pies; tongue, ham, all kinds of delicacies issued from their flowery retreats at his bidding.

To quote Captain Andy, of radio *Show Boat* fame, this was "only the beginning." In 1861 the most famed Hudson River Queen of all time, the *Mary Powell*, made her bow. Hudson Valley historian Carl Carmer wrote in 1939: "The Hudson valley loved the *Mary Powell*. People who are more than thirty years old still love her, for her slim white image moves, swift and quiet, on waters called back to mind from long oblivion. 'She was a lovely boat,' they say. 'Her bell had a silver tongue. Her whistle was a golden sound.'" The *Mary Powell* made no pretense at being a floating palace in the ordinary sense. Her owner and captain, Absalom Anderson, deplored the rococo jigsaw that, to him, made a boat look like a fancy woman instead of a lady. The *Mary* was 300 feet of long, clean lines, neat but not gaudy, and built for speed and comfortable travel. It was said that Absalom had a little black boy whose sole duty was to keep flies from lighting on her rail and slowing her down by their weight. Captain Anderson had other ideas unusual among steamboat men. The *Mary* never traveled on Sunday and had no bar. Further, a passenger who was obviously "under the influence" was not permitted aboard and if a "painted hussy" tried to travel on the vessel she would be stopped at the gangplank by Absalom, standing as the angel Gabriel. If a daughter had to travel on the Hudson unchaperoned she was placed—perhaps unwillingly—in the strict charge of Captain Anderson.

The *Mary Powell*'s regular route was between New York and Kingston, making a round trip every day. She handled so readily that her pilot bragged that no lines were needed to hold her at a landing; he could keep her immobile with a slight movement of her wheels. The only time she gave trouble, it was said, was on her occasional trips to Albany. When she passed the mouth of Rondout Creek at Kingston

THE MARINERS MUSEUM, NEWPORT NEWS, VA.

From the day she was launched in 1861, the Mary Powell *was the fastest boat on the Hudson—for more than a quarter-century. A neat, comfortable steamer capable of speeds up to 25 miles an hour, the* Mary Powell *was built without the rococo frills of some of the "palaces," but she was probably the best-loved river boat of all time.*

she naturally turned in to go home and the pilot had to gently force her head back upstream. In fifty-eight years of service she never had an accident and never lost a passenger, and, said her fans, she was never late. They used to stand formations at the Military Academy by the *Mary Powell's* bell—it was more reliable than West Point clocks. West Pointers were among the *Mary's* favorite passengers; she took them up as boys and brought them back as officers and gentlemen. And she brought back the body of General Custer, wrapped in a flag, to its final resting place at the Academy.

Then or later the *Mary Powell* was the fastest boat on the river, with a top speed of 25 miles an hour. It was said that no steamboat ever passed her and it is true that no river boat ever did. She was beaten by a high-speed steam yacht in 1885, but her dedicated supporters said that "she was robbed." The Herreshoff family, famous yacht builders, brought their yacht *Stiletto* around from Rhode Island and laid for the *Mary* on the Hudson. At Sing Sing the yacht was five minutes ahead of the *Mary* when its owners quit the race and claimed a victory, but there are those who say that the yacht could never have maintained its lead to Kingston, much less Albany.

Among steamboat aficionados the *J. M. White* was the opposite number of the *Mary Powell* on the Mississippi—or, rather, the two *J. M. Whites*, the first a river queen because of her speed and the second a floating palace in magnificence. The first *White* was the fastest boat on the river, setting records in the 1840s that lasted for a quarter century. Experts claim that her speed was due to the fact that her paddle wheels were located two thirds of the way aft, where they bit into the swell that followed the bow wave. Whatever the reason, the *White* broke all records from Pittsburgh to New Orleans on her maiden trip, and her captain had posts erected on the bank to mark her 24-, 48- and 72-hour runs. They rotted away while other vessels raced against them until her record was broken by the *Natchez* (opponent of the *Robert E. Lee* in the famed race) in 1869.

While the first *White* was setting records the son of her owner was a small boy watching steamboats go past on the Ohio. More than thirty years later he was the famous river captain for whom the second famous *J. M. White*—a palatial $300,000 vessel—was named in 1878, although he never captained it. Western steamboat fans merely say that this *White* was "the finest steamboat in the world," and a St. Louis river reporter wrote, at the time:

> Aladdin built a palace,
> He built it in a night;
> And Captain Tobin bought it
> And named it *J. M. White*.

The *White* was 320 feet long and 48 feet wide, plus guards, which gave her a total width of 98 feet. Her stacks were 80 feet high and her wheels 44 feet. She could carry 7,000 bales of cotton and 350 cabin passengers. Her twin high-pressure engines were fed by ten boilers. By this time it was customary among river men to rate boats by the number of boilers rather than by length or tonnage—a "four-boiler boat," a "ten-boiler boat," etc.

But this *White*'s fame was based on luxury rather than size or capacity. Her 300-foot cabin was unusual in that it was paneled in hardwoods with a ceiling of cherry, instead of the customary white and gold. Twelve chandeliers lighted the block-long interior and the carpet was not only from Brussels, but was woven in a single piece, nineteen feet wide. On all western boats the cabin resembled a wide hall more than a room. The boiler deck did not extend over the guards and on

THE MARINERS MUSEUM, NEWPORT NEWS, VA.

Midwesterners called the J. M. White *the "finest steamboat in the world," and certainly it was one of the most magnificent. Its cabin, which was as long as a football field, featured a Belgian carpet woven in a single piece.*

each side of it there was, first, a narrow, open walk or promenade and then a line of ten- or twelve-foot staterooms that opened both onto the promenade and into the main cabin. This left a space in the center of the boat more than fifteen times as long as it was wide. Putting it another way, the cabin was as long as a football field and about as wide as four bowling alleys.

The *White*'s linen and Reed and Barton silver bore her monogram, which was also inlaid in lighter wood on her French-made walnut cabin furniture. Her specially designed china was decorated with her picture. Both her bar and her barbershop carried out her magnificence, and her final mark of distinction, other than a 2,900-pound bell and a five-toned whistle, was a mammoth, deeply engraved silver water cooler that dominated the rear end of the cabin, surrounded by eighteen heavy silver cups that were, wisely, firmly attached to the urn with chains.

During her brief life—she burned when but eight years old—the *White* was the annual "royal barge" of Rex, King of Mardi Gras at New Orleans, a role in which she replaced the beautiful but not so lush second *Robert E. Lee*. On the eve of every Shrove Tuesday she would hide against the bank above the city in the dark while the king for a day and his retinue sneaked quietly aboard. Then, with candles, lamps, and torches blazing, banners flying, bells ringing, bands playing, and whistle booming, she would sweep down to the levee to start the last day of gaiety. According to one paper she also carried "a cargo of fair freight" and, in the words of another journal, "a galaxy of beauty crowded her decks. Both these clichés caused Mark Twain to tear his graying mane but the alleged beauty of the Creole girls is one of the more solidly based legends of the Old South.

The *J. M. White* was neither the first, the last, nor the biggest of the floating palaces. Despite the existence of the railroads, the end of the war brought a rash of new or reconditioned boats to the Mississippi. Several of those that swept up the stream from St. Louis to Alton, Illinois, in September 1866 might be rightly called floating palaces. There were thirty-seven boats in this procession, each bearing the banner of one of the thirty-six states and the last that of the District of Columbia. They went to pick up President Andrew Johnson, Admiral David Farragut, and General U. S. Grant to bring them downriver in one of the mass ceremonies for which the whistles, bands, bells, smoke, and glitter of the steamboats made such a fine background.

Prominent in the procession was the new *Ruth*, which a New Orleans paper called "The Wonder of the West" that would "undoubtedly prove to be the greatest gleaner that ever harvested along the Mississippi." The *Ruth* was a four-decker; the main deck was for cargo only, 2,500 tons of it; next above was a level for 1,000 deck passengers; then the cabin deck with saloon, dining room, bar, and staterooms that were described as "two long rows of cosy white cottages with marble steps and rosewood doors." The fourth deck contained something new—a Freeman's Bureau for Negroes who could afford to travel in style, which was a smaller, less luxurious replica of the white folks' accommodations below. Here also was a nursery and room for servants, but no bar. In all, the *Ruth* could carry 1,600 persons.

Even larger was the *Great Republic*—later the *Grand Republic*—which appeared on the river in 1867. She was built at Pittsburgh and came down to her home port of St. Louis with the tops of her stacks on the deck, never to return to her natal city because she could not clear the railroad bridges over the Ohio. She was supposed to have calendar dimensions—365 feet long, 52 feet wide, 12-foot hull depths, 7 decks high—and she cost $365,000. She was also a white elephant whose owners went bankrupt in two years, selling her to an ex-river gambler who made her still larger. That the calendar dimensions were legendary is indicated by an actual measurement of her length after rebuilding—350 feet.

The saloon of the Grand Republic, *complete with Brussels carpet, oil-lamp chandeliers, and "steamboat Gothic" ceiling. The doors along the sides led to private staterooms.*

THE MARINERS MUSEUM, NEWPORT NEWS, VA.

Other early postwar floating palaces were the second *Robert E. Lee,* the sixth *Natchez,* and the *Richmond.* The last boasted both a band and a string orchestra and published a daily paper, *The Richmond Headlight,* for her passengers, who were characterized as "rich and titled people from all over the world." In truth, few of the early postwar river travelers were "rich and titled people." This was the era of the carpetbaggers; the percentage of northerners among cabin passengers had increased, and included politicians, speculators, and businessmen seeking to glean a profit from the South's distress. Prosperous farmers accompanied their produce to southern markets and mingled with the European and eastern tourists who had returned to the river after four years of war. The price of a cabin passage made all men equal on a steamboat and the saloon was a melting pot in which the diverse intercourse presumably broadened the horizons and weakened the provincialism of midwestern travelers.

If the memoirs of eastern and foreign visitors may be believed, it did not do much for their table manners, which still ran roughshod over the conventions of more polite areas. "Undisguised sensuality," "bestial feeding," and "no quarter given" were expression used by more sophisticated travelers to describe the local trenchermen. Most of the travelers were unused to the elaborate fare of a floating palace and, having paid for board and lodging, they made sure that they got their money's worth. A Cincinnati editor described the approach to dinner of his fellow travelers by writing: "At least one-half the passengers ate extravagantly—very many excessively and promiscuously, devouring everything within their reach, selecting the nearest dishes *in their order.* I saw one man commence his dinner by swallowing . . . a beautifully moulded dish of blanc mange—some began upon the tarts, pies and jellies, and others upon raisins and almonds—not perhaps as a matter of choice, but because they were too impatient and greedy to be served."

The social life of the cabin had not changed much from prewar years. There was still little to do on a trip that might last four days or more. Today no airline could hope to compete on a six-hour flight if it did not offer its passengers a choice of a movie or six soundtracks, but in those days travelers were presumably more self-reliant and steamboat owners felt no responsibility to entertain their patrons. To while away the tedious hours some men—indeed, many men—engaged in friendly games of cards, some of which did not remain so friendly.

Of all the legends of the western river boats the Mississippi steamboat gambler is among the most persistent. Always he is visualized as Gaylord Ravenal in *Show Boat:* beaver hat, jeweled studs in frilled shirt, perfectly fitting broadcloth long-tailed coat above taut Congress gaiters and shining boats, and smoking a panatella cigar. There probably were some such professional gamblers on the river boats, but the few on which there is any information are less glamorous types; in fact, the shabby carnival type of shell-game operator seems to have been more common.

It is difficult to separate fact from fiction on this subject. The legend of the ante bellum southern planter who lost his acres or his beautiful quadroon mistress on the turn of a card and then put a derringer to his temple is such a colorful dramatic story that it is a shame to deflate it, but there is nothing to authenticate it. Most of those who gambled on the postwar boats were *nouveau riche* farmers, merchants, or other businessmen who were returning with heavy money belts after a profitable trip south. After a few drinks, with time heavy on their hands, they were easy prey for such marked deck artists, three-card monte

The suave professional gambler romanticized in fiction was probably a rarity on river boats. These roustabouts, shown shooting craps, were more typical. Note pickpocket at work in foreground.

throwers, and other varieties of river sharpers as traveled the boats. Most boats carried signs warning gentlemen who played cards with strangers that they did so at their own risk, but made no effort to restrain their stewards from providing card tables in the bar or, for big games, in the texas. If a loser could prove that he had been cheated, the captain would usually put the offending player off the boat at the next stop.

There are countless stories of piles of golden double-eagles stacked before players and, between their feet, satchels bursting with currency from which they made Midas-like wagers. One such tale describes a poker game that lasted for five days from New Orleans to New Albany, Indiana, in which the biggest pot contained $8,362 and the bar bill was $791.50. Against this is the testimony of one ex-gambler who wrote, "As for tales regarding the fabulous sums bet at poker tables on our western rivers, they are all pure humbug. I have grave doubts whether a brag of two thousand dollars has ever been lost and won at a card table on the Mississippi River." Of course, some folks still think $2,000 is a lot of money.

Gamblers are usually not loquacious as to their profession, but in 1892 one Mississippi River gambler, George Devol, did write his memoirs, under the title *Forty Years a Gambler on the Mississippi*. When one strips what is obviously a varnish of drama and excitement from Devol's autobiography there remains a tale of a cheat and sharper who lived by preying on the unsophisticated. He operated on river boats because they provided a steady flow of ever-new affluent innocents away from the moral restraints of home and frequently softened for the kill by liquor. Devol carried the paraphernalia for several games—a roulette wheel, faro shoe, keno layout etc.—but his favorite game seems to have been three-card monte, a competition in which no skill is involved. This was really the shell game played with cards, or "tickets," imprinted with pictures of a man, a woman, and a baby. The sucker was required to pick the baby after the cards had been turned down and mixed up. In his memoirs Devol says he made no pretense that the hand was quicker than the eye. He usually operated with a confederate—a "shill" or "capper"—who pretended to be a player and marked a card in view of a victim but supposedly without Devol's knowledge. When the sucker bet his all on the marked card it turned out not to be the baby.

Devol claimed that the bartenders on the boats he traveled were in his pay and carried a stock of packs of "new" cards that the gambler had marked by shaving and returned to their original wrappings. No matter how often players called for a new deck of cards they always got a marked deck. Obviously such techniques could be effective only with the most gullible "yokel" type of traveler.

Deck passage on the postwar floating palaces was less rugged than in prewar years. A few boats had a separate deck for second-class passengers; others had bunks, such as they were, and tables at which travelers could buy low-cost meals. But the change was mainly in the passengers themselves. For four years New Orleans had been closed as a port of entry and it never regained its prominence in the immigrant trade. Most postwar deck passengers were Americans who could not afford the luxury of the cabin, but neither could they be treated like cattle.

A marked change on the main deck was in the roustabouts. With the decline in foreign immigration and the end of slavery, Negro labor became cheaper than white foreigners and the postwar era of river boating was the age of the colorful Negro roustabouts of song and story, particularly song. The rouster songs became an important part of the folk music of the midwestern valley, yet they are seldom found in printed collections of folk music. They do not lend themselves to formal musical interpretation, as they grew spontaneously from an inner sense of rhythm that was applied by the roustabouts to lighten their labor. Roustabout songs differ radically from the spirituals of the plantation Negro or the later jazz that came from Basin Street. Possibly they all have a common African origin, but roustabout "coonjine" was unique.

No one knows the origin of the word "coonjine." It was applied to the parade of rousters "walking coonjine" to carry cargo aboard a boat and also to the chanting that accompanied their work. There are those who say that the rhythm of coonjine is based on the bouncing of the swaying gangplank. The lyrics of a basic melody were:

> De Coonjine, jine de Coonjine,
> De Coonjine, jine de Coonjine,
> Roll dat cotton bale down de hill
> De Coonjine, jine de Coonjine.

Or coonjine might be sung in parts, as when the rousters who were ashore to lift sacks on to the shoulders of carriers sang:

> Come hyuh, you ole rouster!
> Poke out yo' neck ve'y long!
> Tell me which shoulder you wants it on!

And the carrier replied,

> Ole roustabout ain' got no home,
> Makes his livin' by his shoulder bone!

Sometimes an amusing reference to a particular boat or a personality was woven into the work chant, such as:

> Oh, I thought I heard the *Kate Adams* when she blowed,
> She blowed jes' lak she ain't goin' to blow no mo'.
> The reason that I lak the *Kate Adams* so,

[2 2 5]

She carries a chambermaid an' a watch below.
Come on boys with yo' neck out long,
Show me what shoulder you want it on.

And current events found their way into the rouster's lyrics. The following was obviously created in the later years of steamboating after "de cars" became a threat to the river boats:

Oh, roll, Nancy gal, roll, gal,
I'll meet you by and by;
We gwine to roll de cotton
Way up ten tiers high.

Oh shovel up de furnace
Till smoke put out de stars;
We's gwine along de river
Like we's bound to beat de cars.

Some of the songs grew from aspirations of the singer-composer, as this one:

I'm wukin' my way back home,
I'm wukin' my way back home,
I'm wukin' my way back home, Baby
I'm wukin' my way back home.
Timber don't get too heavy fo' me,
An' sacks too heavy to stack,
All that I crave fo' many a long day,
Is yo' lovin' when I git back.
Oh, fireman, keep her rollin' for me,
Let's make it to Memphis, Tennessee.
Fo' my back is gittin' tired,
An' my shoulder is gittin' sore.

Or this one:

I's gwine from de cotton fields,
I's gwine from de cane,
I's gwine from de o' log hut
Dat stan's down in de lane;
De boat am in de river,
Dat comes to take me off,
An' I's gwine to join de exodus,
an' strike out fo' de no'f.

What started as spontaneous singing by roustabouts gradually developed into a more formal type of entertainment with a chorus from both levee and deck added to the bell and whistle to lend color to departures. Some boats developed sextets among rousters and firemen, which performed to gain gratuities from cabin passengers or to attract customers at a landing. By the floating-palace days most boat owners took advantage of the Negro's native musical ability to form six- or eight-man orchestras from the cabin personnel—waiters, barbers, porters, etc.

Other postwar changes on the Mississippi involved the ownership of the boats. More of the larger ones were now owned by "lines" than by individuals. In most cases the line was a partnership of individual owners who had banded together to effect operating economies and to attract business by offering a regular schedule with several boats. The owner-captain who got business for his boat by his personal friendship with planters along the river was largely replaced by resident agents who secured contracts for their lines with carefully figured bids. Marking the change, captains were now uniformed in blue and gold like deep-sea skippers instead of the frock coat and beaver hat of their own choice that had been their badge of office before the war.

But there were some of the old school left, among them captains John W. Cannon and Thomas P. Leathers, two longtime steamboat men, personal friends, and business rivals, but very different in character and manners. Cannon was polite and soft-spoken, Leathers loud, aggressive, and headstrong. Both men were Kentuckians, but Cannon was a northern sympathizer, Leathers an unreconstructed southerner. Despite his Union leanings, Cannon named two successive boats *Robert E. Lee*. When the second was built at New Albany, Indiana, in 1866, he thought it prudent to take it across the river to the Kentucky side before painting on the name. Leathers made no bones of his southern preference before, during, or after the war. His seven successive steamers named *Natchez* were southern boats that flew the Stars and Bars during the war and no flag after it until a Democrat, Grover Cleveland, came to the White House in 1885. Then he declared that the war was over, fired a cannon, and hoisted the Stars and Stripes.

In 1869 Leathers brought his newest *Natchez*, the sixth, down to New Orleans and, the next spring, broke the ancient speed record of the *J. M. White*. Cannon's second *Robert E. Lee* was known as a fast boat, although it held no records. It was almost foreordained that the boats, both river queens and floating palaces and both operating out of New Orleans, would some day race, as they did, starting at 5 P.M. on June 30, 1870—a race that is perhaps the best-known sporting competition in American history.

Conflicting stories are told of the background of the race. Some say that one or the other captain challenged the other in a club in St. Louis or a bar in New Orleans, although both captains denied that they intended to race and published notices to that effect in the New Orleans papers. While the notices were running they each prepared for the race, Cannon extensively, Leathers moderately; he merely took aboard some fat pine to use as hot fuel and ordered fueling points upstream to have more on hand. Leathers carried a moderate amount of freight and a load of passengers.

Cannon refused all freight and passengers and groomed his vessel as a racing machine, removing every unnecessary pound of weight and cutting away some of her guards abaft the wheel housings to prevent dead water. Although both boats burned coal as a basic fuel, he loaded his deck with spoiled bacon, rosin, pitch, and tallow candles to use as boiler stimulants. He also sent the steamer *Frank Pargaud* upstream to pick up a coal barge to refuel the *Lee* en route, an act that would lead to much controversy among bettors when *Natchez* backers claimed that it was unfair and against the rules, although, in fact, there were no formal rules.

The two vessels were well matched, both having eight boilers and engines of equal size. The *Lee* was slightly smaller, 1,467 tons against 1,547 for the *Natchez*. On the other hand, the *Natchez* was "sharper" in design and she was the champion. In the deep south the *Natchez* was a slight favorite in the betting; she was known as a southern boat. At St. Louis, in the East, and in Europe, the *Lee* was favored. For some reason the race caught the imagination of sporting men the world over. Odds were posted in London, Paris, Berlin, and Vienna as well as New York and Chicago, and during the four days of the contest quotations on stock and produce exchanges were interrupted with bulletins of the race.

Along the 1,200-mile route people on the river bank literally went mad with excitement. The New Orleans levee was thronged with most of the city's population when the vessels left and, upstream, schools were let out and business stopped as entire communities closed down while their people lined the river bank to await the racers. This is perhaps the most incredible part of the event for, with the possible exception of the America's Cup sailing races, there was never a duller sporting event for spectators. Despite all the paintings and lithographs showing the boats racing neck and neck, they were never within sight at the same time after the first ten miles of the race and their speed was about 14 miles an hour. Public interest was amusingly described by an observer at Memphis as follows:

The population turned out *en masse* to give greeting to the racers. So great was the interest manifested that business was suspended in that city, and the Mississippi river, for miles, was alive with steamboats and every other conceivable sort of craft, conveying excursion parties to meet the rival steamers....

There was much amusement over a mistake made by the crowd in identifying the *Thompson Dean* as one of the racers, the *Dean* being given a most vociferous ovation as she came in view from a bend in the river below the city. But this misplaced greeting, as well as the embarrassment that followed, was not without its extenuating circumstances, the *Dean's* peculiar conduct in the premises having left nothing undone to invite to itself the honors that should have gone to others.

Had the *Dean* not blown her whistle in the noisiest possible manner, had she not fired her gun with incessant repetition, and otherwise demeaned herself in the most provocative way to create the impression that she was the victor, the booming of cannon, the plenteous discharge of fire rockets and Roman candles, and the shouts of the multitude would not have been hers; but would have gone first to the *Lee* and then to the *Natchez* in the order in which they arrived a little later—arrived when the Memphis magazines were exhausted, when the stock of skyrockets and Roman candles were gone, and the voice of the multitude, hoarse and weakened from a strenuous vociferation of more than an hour, could not have been heard, as one indignant citizen expressed it, further than you could throw a bull by the tail.

At the start of the race the *Lee* was moored two boats above the *Natchez* at the levee and got away first by four minutes. The whole story of the race can be capsuled in the statement that when the *Lee* reached St. Louis, approximately 1,200 miles away, her lead had increased to three hours and fifty-four minutes. Despite the wild excitement of spectators and the dramatized stories of reporters, the race was merely a case of two boats going up the river, one slightly faster than the other and gaining progressively. The *Lee* was ten minutes ahead at Baton Rouge, sixteen at Vicksburg, an hour and two minutes at Memphis, etc.

Of course dramatic incidents can be found, or created. The symbol for the fastest boat on the river, or any part thereof, was a set of deer antlers. When Leathers beat the old *White's* time he had a gilded set placed on the wharf boat at his vessel's namesake city, Natchez, with the name of his vessel and the date. As he passed Natchez, Cannon is supposed to have swerved the *Lee* toward the bank and shouted, "Take down those horns." Also, the *Lee* developed a leak in a steampipe during the race and much has been made of the young engineer who inched his way through the narrow space below the fiery furnace to repair it.

Toward the end of the race the *Natchez* developed engine trouble and was delayed by fog, which caused Leathers to claim that but for these misfortunes he would have beat the *Lee* by twenty minutes, a computation that is difficult to follow since he was seventy minutes behind when he ran into difficulties. This, and the help of the *Paragoud* in coaling, led to controversy that lasted for the rest of the lives of those involved. The *Lee's* time to St. Louis was three days, eighteen hours and fourteen minutes, which was never equaled by another paddle-wheeler. But there are those who say that the famed *J. M. White* could have bested it with ease. Captain Tobin of the *White* was a good friend of Cannon's who, by the time the *White* came along, was an old man to whom the antlers were a most prized possession. Supposedly, when Tobin was not looking, the engineer and pilot connived to run the *White* much faster than the *Lee*'s best time, but Tobin would never permit her to set a record that would take the horns away from the old man while he lived—and the *White* burned before Cannon died.

To complete the story of the floating palaces we must go back to the Hudson River, the year 1862, and "Deacon" Daniel Drew, who was still piously operating under the banner of the People's Line. By the end of the war Commodore Vanderbilt had turned from steamboats and steamships to railroads and was no longer a factor on the river. The war gave him an opportunity to dispose of his watercraft at vastly inflated prices, but not before he had rented his principal river boat, the *C. Vanderbilt*, to the government as a transport for a lengthy period at $2,000 per day.

Drew's first palatial Hudson steamer was the *St. John*, which made its appearance on the stream in 1862. This was the largest steamboat in the world to that time—larger, in fact, than anything afloat except the English ocean steamship *Great Eastern*. The *St. John* measured 420 feet in

BOATMAN'S NATIONAL BANK, ST. LOUIS, MO.

One of the most famous races in American history began at 5 P.M. on June 30, 1870, when the river queens Natchez *and* Robert E. Lee *set out from New Orleans for St. Louis, approximately 1,200 miles upstream. In most paintings of the race, as in this one by Dean Cornwall, the boats are shown close together. Actually, they seldom saw each other after the first few hours, and the* Lee *reached her destination almost four hours ahead of her opponent.*

length with a beam of 84 feet. Its massive engine had a cylinder 76 inches in diameter with a 15-foot stroke. Tiers of staterooms opened into a domed duplex saloon through which rose a staircase of carved San Domingo mahogany inlaid with white holly which accounted for $25,000 of the *St. John's* total cost of $600,000. Drew soon followed this floating palace with another, only slightly smaller, which he named after himself. By this time the *Francis Skiddy*, pride of the 1850s, was gone; she struck a ledge and sank in 1864. Drew's boats became the principal carriers from New York to Albany for those who sought status in their steamboat travels. On only one occasion was the *Drew* humbled through a piece of chicanery that was worthy of Daniel himself.

There was an annoying little independent boat called the *J. B. Schuyler* owned by Commodore J. W. Hancox and his son. One misty night the *Drew* pulled up to the end of the railroad pier at Albany ready to receive her cargo of travelers from the west for the last stage of their journey to New York—the overnight trip on the floating palace would

The only known photograph of the race is this grainy, out-of-focus picture of the Robert E. Lee *as she passed Carondelet Bluffs. The* Natchez *is far behind.*

FREDERICK WAY, JR.

be a fine climax to their trip. Quietly, through the mist, Hancox brought the *Schuyler* to the pier ahead of the *Drew*, and when the train started to back down, his son flagged it to a stop beside the *Schuyler* with a red lantern and loudly called, "This way to the New York boat." Unsuspecting passengers, looking forward to a good night's sleep aboard the luxurious *Drew*, stumbled aboard through the dark and did not learn that they had been herded aboard a day boat with no berths until the gangplank had been pulled in and the *Schuyler* was standing out in the river, leaving "Deacon" Daniel cursing from the pilothouse of his empty luxury packet.

The floating palaces of this era brought to full flower the watering places of the East. Saratoga—"the Medicine Spring of the Great Spirit" of the Indians—antedated the steamboat; George Washington and Alexander Hamilton had traveled by coach to partake of its curative waters. But the river boats, with an assist first from stagecoaches and then from railroads, made the resort the favored haunt of "the rich merchant from New Orleans, the planter from Arkansas and Alabama . . . the polished landowner from the Carolinas and Virginia, the successful speculator in real estate from the West, the rich capitalist from Boston & New York, the official functionary from Washington, the learned professor from New Haven or Cambridge."

Presidents Tyler, Harrison, and Arthur journeyed to the spa on steamboats. Commodore Vanderbilt kept a suite at the United States Hotel and at the age of seventy-five spent a honeymoon there with his second wife. "Deacon" Drew clasped his prayer book as he paced the sweeping porch of the mammoth caravansary, and a story is told of "Liveoak" George Law strolling along the piazza with a tray of gems from the Grand Union jewelry shop, pausing beside the rocking chair of each lady of his acquaintance to have her select a jewel as a slight token of something. In later years, after the railroads were running through from New York, the river boat and railroad combination was still the approved way for the better people to reach the resort.

Long Branch, New Jersey, flourished for a while as a somewhat more garish and promiscuous playground served by the river boats. This New Jersey resort had come into being in the early 1800s as a haven for Quakers until "the new steamship line from New York brought about a swift change, like a slapping gust of wind that fills out a flaccid sail, the impact of the brisk city on the Hudson startled the resort out of its becalmed lethargy." Although not as socially distinguished as Saratoga, Long Branch had its share of dignitaries. General Grant spent some time on its beach in his declining years; President Garfield died there; and it was at Long Branch that a little boy named Theodore

Roosevelt threw a stone that knocked out one of Mrs. John King Van Rensselaer's front teeth.

In 1870 the *Plymouth Rock* was refurbished as a floating palace solely to cruise to Long Branch. It left New York in the afternoon, when its white-marble-finished barroom did a brisk business before its patrons retired to the vessel's thirty-two ducal suites with their mirrors, gilt furniture, plush, velvet, and silk in order to dress for dinner. After dining on delicacies on board the passengers went ashore for an evening at Long Branch, returning to the boat in time to get back to New York in the morning.

Far removed from the regal giants of the river was a group of fast, jaunty little paddlers that served as Manhattan Island's elite rapid-transit service—"commuting boats" which, during the 1870s, took workers and shoppers from the business section of Manhattan to "suburbs" above 125th Street on the East River and to Mott Haven in the Bronx. Express boats made the trip to Spuyten Duyvil, at the upper end

THE MARINERS MUSEUM, NEWPORT NEWS, VA.

A Currier & Ives impression of the duplex grand saloon of the Drew. *Elaborate stairways, chandeliers, balconies, and Corinthian columns were common to the eastern "floating palaces." There is no explanation of why the men kept their hats on.*

In 1862 when she went into service on the Hudson, the St.

John, *420 feet long, was the largest steamboat in the world.*

of Manhattan, in thirty minutes, far better time than horsecars or stages. The principal commuting boats were the Sylvan steamboats—the *Sylvan Shore, Sylvan Stream, Sylvan Grove, Sylvan Glen,* and *Sylvan Dell*— which were close to being sister ships. The gay little craft enlivened the scene on the rivers until, sadly, the dirty, noisy, steam-powered elevated trains reached the farthest limits of Harlem in about 1885.

Floating palaces in the East came to full flower on Long Island Sound. In this area the entrepreneur was colorful and expansive Jim Fisk. It must be sadly admitted that Jim Fisk was not entirely honest, but he was a most engaging rogue. By the code of the day Vanderbilt was merely shrewd, although his methods would be beyond the pale today. "Deacon" Drew was a wily, slimy rascal in spite of his endowment of the theological seminary that bears his name. Fisk's partner, Jay Gould, was unscrupulous to the point that he did not even respect the code of "honor among thieves." Fisk was of a piece with these, but he gave the impression of being in bad company rather than being basically bad, and his extravagant generosity and exuberance at least partially compensated for his delinquencies. Although he was involved in the Black Friday gold panic and the watering of the Erie Railroad stock, his extracurricular escapades were more characteristic. He maintained, virtually at his own expense, a New York national guard regiment so that he could march at its head in parades and take it on outings to Long Branch on his steamboats, with cannon booming happily from the decks. He supported entirely at his own expense an opera house because he was partial to girls who danced in ballet; he told one French dancer that Central Park was part of his New York estate. But his company did give good performances which the public enjoyed.

Fisk liked to call himself a "Green Mountain Boy" because he had started as a peddler in Vermont. Later, representing a group of Boston capitalists in New York, he announced from his lavish quarters in the Fifth Avenue Hotel that the Boston interests were going to start a new steamboat line between New York and Bristol, Rhode Island. Daniel Drew already had boats on the route and, frightened by the potential competition, he hastened to sell out to Fisk at a sacrifice price. Through further machinations, in 1869 Fisk became president of the Fall River Line, which had been partly owned by the Borden family, one of whose females gained immortality by giving her parents forty and forty-one whacks, respectively, with a hatchet.

The new steamboat tycoon now controlled seven vessels and promptly selected two of them, the *Bristol* and the *Providence,* for conversion to floating palaces. Their paddle boxes were painted lavender and their smokestacks deep yellow, and their outside decks were replaced with alternating strips of black walnut and yellow pine. Grand staircases of mahogany swept up to their 300-foot saloons, from which rosewood doors opened into staterooms. Brilliant light from gas chandeliers flooded the white and gold trimmings and the acres of velvet-pile carpeting. A concert orchestra played on each vessel, joined by the trilling of 200 canaries in gilded cages, each bird personally named by Fisk. Life-sized portraits of Fisk and his partner Jay Gould flanked the mirror at the turn of the staircase of one of the boats, a decoration that caused one wit to quip: "I see the two thieves, all right, but where is Jesus Christ?"

The officers of Fisk's boats had more gold braid and buttons than any other steamboat men, but not so much as their master. Fisk said, "If Vanderbilt can be a Commodore, I can be an Admiral," and had a gaudy and glorious admiral's uniform designed for himself. Jim Fisk also had a mistress, buxom Josie Mansfield, for whom he created a female admiral's suit. As passengers came aboard the *Bristol* or the *Providence* at their Hudson River pier, Jim and Josie graciously received them at the head of the gangplank and then democratically mingled with the crowd while the boat rounded the Battery, leaving it in a launch as it plowed up the East River.

The *Providence* played a minor role in the planning of the corner on gold that led to Black Friday. Gould had an inside track to the White House through President Grant's brother-in-law, Abel Corbin. When he

THE MARINERS MUSEUM, NEWPORT NEWS, VA.

In the 1870s the fastest and most pleasant way to get from the "suburbs" of upper Manhattan or the Bronx was by steamboat. The little Water Lily, *left foreground, was a commuting boat.*

conceived the idea of the gold coup he wanted to further assure its success by influencing the government to support the price of gold at a high level. For this purpose Corbin brought the President aboard the *Providence* during his trip to the Boston Peace Jubilee in 1869 and the three conspirators—Gould, Fisk, and Corbin—worked on the old general in the plush bridal suite of the vessel to convince him that the sale of farm commodities in Europe would be benefiited by supporting the price of gold. Grant puffed on his cigar and, so far as is known, was not taken in. He was escorted to the Jubilee by Fisk, and as the latter bowed and waved to the crowds many undoubtedly thought he was the President; in any event, it was there that he earned the nickname "Jubilee Jim" by which he was known thereafter.

The era that Jim Fisk started was "the gilded age" of steamboating in the East. The postwar decades were affluent years for a mushrooming privileged class. Travel on the floating palaces was something of a status symbol, and on the Long Island Sound vessels social climbers might rub shoulders with the true elite, as the Vanderbilts, Astors, Belmonts, and Rockefellers used the palatial boats regularly to journey to their estates in Newport.

Fisk's tenure as a steamboat tycoon did not last long. In 1872 he had a tiff with Josie Mansfield, who then took up with a man named Edward Stokes. Fisk was naturally resentful when Stokes moved into the house for which Fisk had paid and when, to add insult to injury, Stokes tried to blackmail his predecessor by threatening to publish the admiral's love letters to his paramour. Fisk made one payment, published the letters himself, and had Stokes arrested for blackmail, whereupon Stokes shot Fisk to death on the stairs of the Grand Hotel. When Fisk's canaries from the *Bristol* and the *Providence* were auctioned off, such birds as Jeff Davis, Robinson Crusoe, Commodore Vanderbilt, and August Belmont went for between $6.00 and $7.00, but Col. Fisk, Jr., brought the premium price of $16.25.

After Fisk's death the Fall River Line went on to become a generic name for all steamboats on the Sound. Just as all phonographs were once called Victrolas and all electric refrigerators Frigidaires, most people called all Sound steamers Fall River boats. The line itself had originally been the Bay State Steamboat Company and, after Fisk's death, became the Old Colony Steamboat Company. But the Fall River Line was the name that lived in memory and that inspired one of the popular songs of the early twentieth century. Ultimately, the "Admiral" of all Sound steamers was a most unlikely steamboat man—J. P. Morgan. It was Morgan who combined a lot of little railroads to form the New York, New Haven and Hartford in 1872, and this railroad finally acquired control of all the Sound steamboat lines.

One of the competing companies in the 1870s was the Stonington Line, which promoted its accident-free record by caling itself the Old Reliable Line. No sooner did it adopt this slogan, after a long accident-free operation, than two of its vessels, the *Massachusetts* and the *Rhode Island*, ran aground in close succession. Shortly after, Old Reliable's *Stonington* and *Narragansett* were proceeding in opposite directions in a fog at full speed, to maintain their schedule and "lick" the rival Fall River Line boats, when they crashed head-on. The *Narragansett* caught fire and sank as the wounded *Stonington* probed the fog for survivors. At least thirty lives were lost, and the press lashed out at the evil steamboat barons who wantonly risked the lives of travelers in their lust for profits. In Jersey City a minister preached a sermon on the subject in a service attended by the captain of the *Narragansett*. When the reverend branded the officers of that vessel as "the biggest set of cowards in existence," the captain rose in his pew and shouted, "Sir, you're a liar." His trial for breach of the peace brought about an interesting judicial decision. The judge ruled that, since those who agreed with the preacher traditionally shouted "amen," the captain of the *Narragansett* had the right to express his disagreement vocally.

In the decade starting in 1883 the Fall River Line produced three successive "queens of the Sound" with names from Massachusetts history—the *Pilgrim* in 1883, the *Puritan* in 1889, and the *Priscilla* in 1893. Each was bigger and better than its predecessor; the *Pilgrim* was 390 feet, the *Priscilla* 440. Each called for new adjectives to describe its magnificence until, when the *Priscilla* came along, one writer could do no better than dredge up from Shakespeare: " 'Tis truly beauty bent."

Of the first boat, the *Pilgrim*, it was said: "Her grand saloons, cabins, staterooms, social halls, dining saloons, offices, every provision in fact, are equal to anything found in the fittings of the most elegant caravansary on land . . . . A thousand persons present in her grand saloons at one time serve only to animate the scene without the least appearance of crowding, and two or three times that number might be 'stowed away' within her depths . . . . Here one meets the elite of every land. In the grand saloons of an evening the recherche orchestral performances attract audiences representing the wealth and culture and fame of every nation and people." Here one could also meet some of the finest horses—the *Pilgrim* had box stalls for forty-two of them.

The *Pilgrim* was also extolled as the first steamboat to be lighted by electricity, although in fact that honor belongs to the *City of Worcester* launched two years earlier, which had electric lights nine years before the White House did. But the *Pilgrim*'s blurb proclaimed that she was "lighted with 1,000 incandescent electric lights, aggregating 12,000 candles, and Mr. Edison has exhausted his inventive faculties in fitting up this magnificent vessel." The new Sound queen, which could comfortably accommodate 1,200 passengers, also had a double-bottomed iron hull—another innovation—and was the first vessel in which a serious effort at fireproofing was made.

The *Puritan*, which came four years later, could claim no such firsts, although it was bigger, faster, and somewhat more luxurious, with a walking beam that weighed forty-six tons, thirteen more than the *Pilgrim*'s. A contemporary described it by writing: "The boat itself is of grand proportions, and while it follows the general plan of the four-deck boats, it varies sufficiently to give it a character of its own. The most noticeable feature is the absence of the conventional paddle boxes, the wheels being inclosed in the house. Another feature is the covering of the walking beam by a dome above the hurricane deck. All the decks except the first give a free promenade by means of galleries outside or over the wheels the entire length of the boat. The decoration of the boat is in the style of the Italian Renaissance, the ornamentation being brought out by judicious gilding on an ivory-white ground."

Superlatives were again rained on the *Priscilla* when she made her bow four years later; at 440 feet she was the largest steamboat of the nineteenth century. She was simply described as "pre-eminently the world's greatest

THE MARINERS MUSEUM, NEWPORT NEWS, VA.

The largest steamboat of the nineteenth century, the Priscilla *was 440 feet long and ran between New York and Boston. She is shown above at the Fall River Line piers on the Hudson in lower Manhattan. At right, the saloon of the* Priscilla.

steamboat, a mighty contrast in size, speed and splendor to the *Clermont* of Fulton. The advent of this wonderful example of marine architecture marked an epoch in American steamboat annals. She cost $1,500,000, being capable of accommodating 1500 passengers with berths for sleeping." A visiting Scottish author, David Murray, had this to say about her: "The *Priscilla* is a boat, or so they all tell me. It is a thing built in stories, about as high as the Pyramids, more or less . . . . You walk from the dock into an entrance hall. There is room here for a pair of tennis courts. You don't believe it but you are 'on board.' You go up a huge, great staircase and find yourself in a concert hall in which there is ample room to seat a thousand people . . . . You go up another magnificent staircase, and lose yourself in hundreds of yards of lordly corridor . . . . There is plush velvet enough to upholster several theaters . . . . There are more staircases and more stories and a restaurant like a football field in its dimensions, and you laugh at the ridiculous Aladdin who made his genii build such a city of a vessel under the impression that it is in the power of any machinery made by man to make the 'derned' thing move. And while you are sniggering and wondering when the skipper and his officers are going to apologize for the whole gigantic hoax, bells begin to ring, machinery begins to

THE MARINERS MUSEUM, NEWPORT NEWS, VA.

The $2,000,000 Commonwealth—at 456 feet—was the world's longest and costliest river boat. It was built by the New Haven Railroad in 1908 and named "Charley Mellen's apartment house," after the New Haven's president.

move, and away you glide, majestic, impossible . . . . and before you know it you are doing three and twenty miles an hour."

The final floating palace, the $2,000,000 *Commonwealth*, appeared on the Sound in 1908; 456 feet long, she was known as "Charley Mellen's apartment house"—Mellen was president of the New Haven Railroad. Perhaps with a subconscious sense that this would be their last opportunity to astound the world, her designers did not limit themselves to one decorative theme. Her various decks and several public rooms represented seven distinct architectural styles—her grand saloon was done in Venetian Gothic, her dining room in Louis XVI, her cafe in sixteenth-century

THE MARINERS MUSEUM, NEWPORT NEWS, VA.

Owning a steamboat was an industrial status symbol. There never was an Elias Howe Jr. The artist who drew the sewing-machine company's catalogue cover added it, along with the fountain and the barouche with a matched pair. The steamboat indicated the affluence of the company and attested that it was ready to rush sewing machines to customers by the fastest means possible.

Italian. Superimposed on the period design was a motif involving gro-
tesquely carved mariners' heads and mermaids snared in fishing lines.

The *Commonwealth*'s main claim to fame was her dining room fifty
feet above the water, with outer walls almost entirely of glass supporting
a ceiling of three great domes. One writer declaimed: "What a brilliant
and animated place it was to enjoy caviar, New England clam chowder,
or the other delicacies always found on Fall River menus." After partak-
ing of caviar and clam chowder, a combination that marked true New
England provincialism, a voyager might pass through "an inviting door-
way" to dance in the grill under "an illuminated painting of a Spanish
galleon outlined against a setting sun," or stop for a drink in the garden
café on the main deck, which was "a glimpse of a Parisian sidewalk café
afloat," or he might elect to loaf in the "vastness of the grand saloon, done
in Gothic style, with its palms, Oriental rugs, deep comfortable chairs,
attractive table lamps, and its vaulted ceiling." In connection with all this
it should be borne in mind that this was not a crack ocean liner that was
being described; it was simply a paddle-wheel steamboat that made a
nightly trip of about nine hours between New York City and Fall River,
Massachusetts.

It is hard to understand why the New Haven Railroad built the *Commonwealth* in 1908, for nineteen years earlier it had built something else
that ultimately undermined all the Sound steamers. This was a drawbridge
across the Thames River at New London, Connecticut, which, in 1889,
completed the first through shore railroad line betwen New York and
Boston. Prior to that time cars were floated across the Thames on barges
and the only all-rail route was a rather roundabout inland course. The Fall
River Line's boats were still the elegant and interesting way to travel,
despite the need for proceeding on from Fall River by rail. But with fast
through trains running along the coast, the handwriting was on the wall.

Drama and

Glamour Afloat

Riverboats brought the settlers to the lush lands of the Mississippi Valley. Succeeding watercraft brought them calico and cooking utensils and other of life's necessities. After shelter and food and security from the Indians, the pioneers wanted something more to relieve the lonely rigors of their isolated existence: entertainment. Since they lived by the rivers it was natural that this need, too, would be filled by river boats, and the showboat was born.

Water-borne entertainment started long before the first actual showboat. Medicine boats and whiskey boats lured customers with fiddles and banjos, singing and dancing, mimics and acrobats. Some crews of flatboats raised money for drinks at way stops by performances of fiddle playing and dancing. And in 1817 a young actor named Noah Ludlow brought the first floating company of professional actors to the western river valleys.

While playing in his native Albany, New York, Ludlow, aged nineteen, heard that frontier Kentucky was starved for "theater." With a troupe of eleven fellow thespians he set out for the western outpost. They reached the Allegheny River at Olean, bought a little broadhorn, and floated the 260 miles to Pittsburgh. Some nights they slept in taverns, on one such occasion securing accommodations in a crowded inn by frightening away some of its earlier occupants with a boisterous representation of the ghost from *Hamlet*. When they slept on the boat one of the company woke the group each morn "with a touch of Shakespeare" delivered in stentorian tones at sunrise.

At Pittsburgh they bought a wagon and set off overland for Frankfort, Kentucky, to entertain while the legislature was in session. When it developed that the Kentucky capital was not as good a show town as rumored, they barnstormed through Tennessee until they reached the river at Nashville. Here Ludlow adopted the resounding title of American Theatrical Commonwealth Company for his enterprise and purchased a 100-foot keelboat to travel to New Orleans. After one day's instruction from an experienced river man the troupe set out on their journey, probably unaware of the perils of snags, bars, and eddies ahead. They did know about river pirates and when they passed the supposed lairs of these ruffians the entire compatny, male and female, armed themselevs with sabers, cutlasses, rapiers, poniards, and dirks from the property stores to repel boarders. The same deity that protects fools and drunkards must have guided these innocents, for they reached Natchez without incident.

At Natchez they performed "that amusing comedy, the *Honeymoon*" in a building in the upper town. In Ludlow's memoirs, written many years later when showboats were in disrepute, he does not mention performing on the boat, but newspaper accounts refer to at least two performances at way stops where there probably were no other facilities, and it is possible that these, and perhaps other performances, were held on the keelboat. If so, this craft, which Ludlow had named *Noah's Ark*, was the first showboat.

The first unquestioned—and unnamed—floating theater was launched at Pittsburgh in 1831 by an engaging, capable, and industrious English theatrical family named Chapman. There was papa Chapman, William; mamma Chapman, Sarah; grandma Chapman, name unknown; sons William, Jr., and George; daughters Carolina and Therese Sarah; daughter-in-law Phoebe; and grandson Harry, aged 9. They all got into the act both on stage and in handling the boat, which carried only one river man.

The theater boat came into existence because of the strong family affection among the Chapmans. When no New York manager would hire them as a unit they decided to go to the drama-starved West with their own repertoire. Their first stop, Pittsburgh, was a great disappointment. The only theater had been turned into a machine shop—everybody was building steamboats. The manager of the Old Red Lion Hotel reluctantly permitted them to use the hostelry's dining room as a stage only after Chapman assured him that the dramatic fare offered would be plays by Shakespeare. For some unexplained reason the Immortal Bard seemed to compensate for the supposed immorality of actors. This was true throughout the West, and in towns where there was a vocal church element showboats could secure a license only by promising to play *Catherine and Petruccio*—an adaptation of *The Taming of the Shrew*—or a frontier version of *Hamlet* in which Ophelia was the principal character; valley people preferred the emotional maiden to the intellectual Prince of Denmark.

No record exists of the discussions among the Chapmans that led them to take to the water. In hindsight the idea of a theater on a boat seems obvious in an area where entertainment-hungry audiences could best be reached by water. In any event, with or without discussion, papa Chapman bought a barge 100 feet long and 16 feet wide and had constructed atop it a rather crude barn. A shallow stage, with muslin draw curtains and candle footlights stretched across the stern, and board benches, securely fastened down and without cushions or backs, filled the center of the barge deck. Audiences testified that the only undesirable seats in the house were directly in the center, under the tallow-dripping candles in the hogshead-hoop chandelier. A small gallery for Negroes and the family's living quarters occupied the bow. Mamma Chapman's contribution to the enterprise was a mammoth banner on which she appliquéd the words Floating Theatre.

The plan was to drift down the Ohio and Mississippi to New Orleans, stopping for one-night performances wherever an audience might be obtained. Since they moved at the mercy of the current they had no schedule and no advance man to proclaim their coming. When they reached a settlement they hired a local "town crier" to parade the street blowing a trumpet and tacking up posters hand-lettered by daughter-in-law Phoebe. Admission was 50¢ for adults, half price for children and Negroes, but a peck of potatoes, a bushel of fruit, or a side of bacon was more common currency.

The program stressed drama. A full-length play was followed by a monologue, sketches, impersonations, and music and singing. One of Phoebe's posters read:

> This Evening, Saturday, 1st Oct., will be
> performed Kotzebue's play of the
>
> ### STRANGER
>
> With a variety of Singing. To conclude
> with the farce of
>
> ### PERFECTION
>
> Great care has been taken to render the
> Wharf commodious for ladies.
> Memphis, Oct. 1.

In addition to the *Stranger* a favorite was a dramatized version of *Cinderella*—the family had to find parts for all its females—and the western version of *Hamlet*, which was performed in those settlements that demanded culture.

It was an ideal life for the Chapmans, living, playing, and working together. The male members of the family fished for fun and food while awaiting their cues. An anecdote is told of one performance in which papa Chapman was playing the Stranger and William his son Francis. When papa reached William's cue—"Francis, come here"—the son failed to make his entrance. When Chapman repeated the cue sternly, as the father rather than the actor, a distant voice answered, "Coming, sir." After another wait the following dialogue ensued:

FRANCIS (entering). Here I am, sir.
THE STRANGER.   Why did you not come when I called?
FRANCIS.   Why, sir, I was just hauling in one of the damnedest
                  big catfish you ever saw.

Obviously, with a river audience, this line brought down the house, and one is tempted to doubt that it was entirely extempore. At New Orleans the Chapmans sold their boat and took a steamer to Pittsburgh, and for each of the next four years built another Floating Theatre in the spring.

The British actor Tyrone Power heard of the Chapmans' showboat when he was playing New Orleans in 1835 and wrote this summary of their venture:

"This floating theatre, about which I make constant inquiry, and which I yet hope to fall in with, is not the least original or singular speculation ventured on these waters. It was projected and is carried on by the Elder Chapman, well known for many years as a Covent Garden actor; his practice is to have a building erected upon a raft at some point high up the Mississippi, or one of its tributaries. Whence he takes his departure early in the fall, with scenery, dresses, and decorations, all prepared for representation. At each village or large plantation he hoists banner and blows trumpet and few who love a play suffer his ark to pass the door, since they know it is to return no more until the next year; for, however easy may prove the downward course of the drama's temple, to retrograde, upwards, is quite beyond its power. Sometimes a large steamer from Louisville, with a thousand souls on board, will command a play whilst taking in fuel, when the profit must be famous. The *corps dramatique* is, I believe, principally composed of members of his own family, which is numerous, and, despite of alligators and yellow fever, likely to increase and flourish.

By 1836 the Chapmans had prospered sufficiently to substitute a steamboat for the flatboats, and could thus expand their territory by pushing up such tributaries as the Wabash, the Yazoo, the Tennessee, and the Green and into the bayou back country of Louisiana, where nobody had ever seen a theatrical performance. Although the Mississippi River showboat is usually envisioned as a palatial steamer like the ornate craft that M-G-M built as the *Cotton Blossom* for the picture *Show Boat*, the Chapmans' use of a steamboat as a showboat was a rare exception; they virtually all were barges pushed by small steamers.

The Chapmans made a grievous error on their steam-powered craft. By this time they could afford a velvet curtain, on which they had painted a picture of a lady dipping her foot in a pool of water. Her leg was bare to *midcalf*, and when husbands lasciviously eyed this shocking nudity many wives led them from the pit and demanded their money back before the show started. The curtain decoration was soon changed.

The success of the Chapmans brought many more showboats to the western rivers but, sadly, few measured up to the original. It cost little to put a crude barge on the river, and many of the performers who took to the water were amateurs or the least capable of professionals whose offerings were unacceptable even by tolerant frontier standards. Crooks, mountebanks, and gamblers used the showboat to disguise their operations, as did quacks selling flavored river water as a magic medical cure-all. As a result, showboats were in such bad repute by the 1850s that the few good ones were frequently met at the river bank by an armed posse of citizens who ordered them to move on.

One medicine boat is worthy of mention, although it is hoped that it will not attract the attention of the moguls of Madison Avenue who desperately seek to integrate commercials into television shows. This boat's entire performance was a commercial built around a wan and wistful heroine in ill health who wandered in search of a remedy for her sad condition. The villain sought to lead her from the real cure, hoping that he could more easily have his evil way with the damsel in her run-down condition. But the hero foiled him by giving her a magic potion that restored her to wonderful health and marvelous beauty. At this point the curtains closed and the Professor offered this very same restorative to the audience at fifty cents a bottle—three for a dollar.

One type of showboat that did not fall under the ban of the 1850s was the circus boat. These were substantial enterprises involving sizable investments and many people. While other showboats found business best in small settlements that had no other theatrical entertainment, the circus boats played only the larger towns where an annual visit by a circus, ashore or afloat, was the custom.

The first big circus boat was Spaulding and Rogers' *Floating Circus Palace*, which was built in Cincinnati in 1851. This floating amphitheater was a huge box on a barge, twice the size of the largest western theater, the St. Charles in New Orleans. She was 200 feet long and 35 feet wide. The arena was forward on the main deck, which also contained 1,000 cane-bottomed armchairs in the Dress Circle. The Family Circle in the first gallery seated 1,500 on cushioned seats, and the second gallery provided space for 900 Negroes on benches—a total capacity of 3,400, not counting the standees who looked through the windows that lined both decks. At the stern of the main deck was a museum of "curiosities and wonders" plus dressing rooms and stalls for the horses, with cabins, kitchen, and dining room above. The vessel carried over a hundred people and forty performing horses, not to mention wax effigies of George Washington, Captain Kidd, and the Twelve Apsotles in the museum.

The *Floating Circus Palace* was pushed from city to city by the steamboat *James Raymond,* which was also a showboat with a "concert saloon" in which dramatic performances, vaudeville, and minstrel acts were put on, for an added fee, after the show in the floating big top. Both boats were brilliantly lighted by that new illuminant, gas, and the Natchez *Courier* averred that it was worth the price of admission just to see the lights. The audio part of the spectacle included a pipe organ, a set of chimes, a twelve-piece band, and a calliope.

The boat played the principal cities on the Ohio, Wabash, Allegheny, and upper and lower Mississippi, and it even, on one occasion, went around to Mobile through the Gulf of Mexico. The show was little different than those of land-based circuses; clowns, acrobats, trained horses, and other animals were the mainstays, and the stellar act was Polish Madame Olinza, who made audiences gasp with her performance on a tightrope stretched from the gallery to the top of the museum—wire walking was a novelty

Beginning in 1851 the first big circus boat, the Floating Palace, *played the major cities on the Ohio, Wabash, Allegheny, and Mississippi rivers. On board audiences watched clowns, acrobats, trained animals, and a Polish tightrope walker named Madame Olinza. This picture shows the boat in rough water in the Gulf of Mexico on the one trip she made to Mobile.*

to western audiences at the time. The museum featured "Professor and Madame Lowe's Invisible Lady Act," of interest because Professor Lowe later became a balloonist and served as the first head of the American air force when he commanded the Union Army's balloons during the Civil War.

The *Floating Circus Palace* brought pleasure to the river folk and profit to Spaulding and Rogers until 1862, when the Confederates confiscated the mammoth craft and converted it into a floating hospital at New Orleans.

Although the showboat was primarily a western river institution, the East saw a few. The first made its appearance on the Erie Canal in 1836 when entrepreneur Henry Butler converted a canal boat to serve as both living quarters and theater and played the towns of the Mohawk Valley. His vessel also carried a museum with stuffed birds and tigers, the usual wax figures, and phrenological charts. The museum functioned during the day; in the evening a blood-red melodrama was presented on the stage. Butler continued to ply the canal until advanced age forced him to retire, but even blindness late in life did not deter him. He continued to operate the museum portion of his show, and sold tickets himself to adults for thirty cents and children for ten cents, determining which was which by placing his hand on the head of the buyer.

A more pretentious showboat made its bow in New York City in 1845 when, with much fanfare, the *Temple of the Muses* appeared. This was the ninety-foot Mississippi packet *Virginia*, which the producers had brought up the coast and, after sinking a pit in her main deck, building a stage at her stern, and raising a tier of boxes above her boiler deck, advertised in the New York *Courier and Enquirer* as follows:

TEMPLE OF THE MUSES

The public is most respectfully informed that this Novel and Splendid Establishment, erected in the form of a Theatre, on a large Man-of-War built Steamship, at an enormous expense, and large enough to accommodate an audience of 200 persons, will open for a few evenings before leaving New York, near the foot of Canal Street . . . . Admission to the Dress Circle, 50 cents—Parquett, 25 cents—Private Boxes, \$3.

The *Temple of the Muses* specialized in melodrama. It opened at the foot of Canal Street with *Our Flag, or Nailed to the Mast, An Original National Drama*, following which, based on the show-business edict "always leave them laughing," the audience was coaxed into a lighter mood by "the laughable farce, *A Lady and a Gentleman in a Peculiarly Perplexing Predicament*." The next week, at a new location at the foot of Chambers Street, the boat presented *Jack's the Lad, or the Pride of the Ocean* with such success that the New York *Herald* reported that "the old playgoers, the could be *cognescenti* who sneered at the undertaking and predicted for it certain failure now admit their mistake." Other numbers in the repertoire included *Black Eyed Susan*, *Jackets of Blue*, and *The Cherokee Chief*, which thrilled audiences at Delancey Street and the East River piers. But no production was so successful, nor so appropriate to a floating theater, as the *The Floating Beacon, or the Wild Woman of the Wreck*.

In this opus the curtain rises on the deck of a rocking lightship during a thunderstorm—in those non-union days a producer could afford an ocean, a thunderstorm, and a rocking ship. A mad woman staggers about the deck complaining about the weather: "Another and another dreadful flash succeeds, the breakers beat fearfully against these rocks as if to usher in new victims to the sanguinary assassins of the desolate beacon—the beacon of death, the abode of horror and despair!" The hero climbs aboard, panting, "I am exhausted; the rugged edges of these rocks have lacerated my brow. I bleed—I am strengthless—pity!" The woman tells the youth that she lives on the floating beacon as the slave to a human monster: "Oh God! how often have I prayed for death that my blood, mine—could be shed upon the ebbing tide and bear to yon distant shore a crimson testimony of wrongs never to be effaced."

The villain keeps things so stirred up with his efforts to "dye the yelling waves" with the blood of the virtuous pair that it is act two before the hero learns that "to avert a dreadful fate" the woman has consented "to become the human monster's wife"; she then makes this revelation to the hero: "My child, my child. I am thy wretched mother!" And so it goes until the villain is finally thwarted at the end of act three when a boat load of United States Marines sails onstage, rescues the mother and child, and sinks the vile villain and the foundering lightship with a well-placed cannon shot. The unsophisticated audiences of the mid-nineteenth century loved such corny fare, and one is inclined to wonder whether it might not have been more fun than Tennessee Williams.

The *Temple of the Muses* had grandiose plans for bringing theater to the towns of Long Island Sound, the Hudson Valley, and the Great Lakes via the Erie Canal, but history knows her not after she closed in New York in the late spring of 1845. Another showboat, however, did bring both drama and a demand for political action to the banks of the Hudson that summer.

In 1844 the tenant farmers of the upper valley had risen in revolt against their landlords—the Livingstons were one of their principal targets. Dressed as "Calico Indians," the farmers had mistreated rent collectors and terrorized villages to the point where the militia had to be mobilized. Their leader, Big Thunder (Dr. Smith Broughton in private life), was awaiting trial when a New York promoter conceived the idea of capitalizing on the farmers' unrest by taking to them a three-year-old English play entitled *The Rent Day*. For this purpose the producer refurbished a large barn of a showboat that had been built on a safety barge at Jersey City but never successfully operated, and set off upstream behind a hired steamer. (On the Hudson towboats towed instead of pushing.)

The Rent Day told of the woes of English tenant farmers under the cruel lords of the manor, whose agents wrung the master's gambling losses from the poor tenants. Said Toby, the play's hero: "If the landlord lose at gaming his tenants must suffer for 't. The Squire plays a low card—issue a distress warrant! He throws a deuce-ace—turn a family into the fields! 'Tis only awkward to lose hundreds on a card; but very rascally to be behind with one's rent!"

The play was enlivened by the villainous rent collector who offered the hero's wife, Rachel, amnesty in return for her person, which precipitated the following dialogue:

RACHEL. He who would destroy a happy fireside is vile and infamous, but he who would insult its wretchedness is base indeed.

JACK. Base! Look you! Zounds! To be whipped by a woman's tongue!

RACHEL. Let me pass. I must, will to my children.

JACK. And they may want breakfast.

RACHEL. Villain, though you insult the wife, have pity on the mother. Let me go.

JACK. Not now—I have gone too far.

Although there is no evidence that the agents of the Livingstons, Van Rensselaers, and their kind ever tried to take the rent in trade, so to speak, from the wives of the Hudson Valley farmers, the latter saw in the performance a presentation of their grievances against the American manor lords and loudly cheered the play's denouement, in which it was disclosed that the noble English landlord knew nought of the villainy of his hirelings. When this was disclosed to him in the last act he generously said, "This farm has, I hear, been in your family for sixty years. May it remain so while the country stands! To-morrow shall give you a freeholder's right to it." This was greeted with loud huzzas by the valley farmers, who hoped—unrealistically—that the local lords of the manor might take a lesson from the noble Englishman.

The converted safety barge played two smash seasons on the Hudson, operating, her owner proclaimed, for the benefit of the poor. No patron ever learned what charities benefited from his admission fee; it is possible that the owner was poor when he started. The vessel's success was marred on only one occasion, when someone—perhaps a Livingston—induced a sheriff to arrest the owner for operating without a license, for which he was fined fifty dollars. This second New York showboat ended its days as a floating restaurant at Coney Island.

A third New York showboat in that same season of 1845 is scarcely worthy of mention because it was, in show-business parlance, a flop. Palmo's Burlesque Opera Company gave only thirteen performances in a floating theater anchored in Brooklyn before the venture folded, possibly because it advertised that only "temperance beverages" were served at its bar.

But showboats, as a distinct form of entertainment, never really caught on in the East. The Mississippi system was their true home, and their great era was the half century from the 1870s to the 1920s. The Civil War swept them from the western waters, and it was some years after the war before they returned. The man largely responsible for the reacceptance of show-boats by the western valley folk was Augustus Byron French, who, over more than a quarter of a century, owned five such craft, each named *French's New Sensation*.

At the age of sixteen French ran away from his Missouri river-bank home to become a cabin boy of a New Orleans-bound steamer. At a way stop he visited a shanty boat from which a Mr. Church and his teen-age daughter Celeste made a precarious living by performing in wharf sheds or taverns. This seemed like more fun than steamboating to French, and the Churches were happy to receive the youth and his banjo aboard the shanty boat and into the act. For two years he strummed his instrument while Celeste sang and danced and papa Church performed a magic act which he taught to French.

For the next twenty-seven years French wandered through western show business. He was working as a magician, doubling in the band, on the *Floating Circus Palace* when the circus boat joined the Confederacy. During the war he traveled with wagon shows and then set up a one-wagon show of his own that developed into a six-wagon circus called *French's New Sensation*. At Waterloo, Ohio, in 1878 a town belle named Miss Callie Leach was smitten with the glamorous showman, and forty-five-year-old French married sixteen-year-old Callie.

Shortly after the marriage the wagon show was bogged down by floods, and French decided that if he had to float he was going to do it on a boat. At Cincinnati he bought a barge and built a floating theater very similar to that of the Chapmans almost fifty years earlier. It was a single-deck affair with broadhorn sweeps and a steering oar and could seat, crowded, only a hundred. The first six rows of benches were reserved seats covered with red and white ticking, which sold for thirty-five cents instead of the usual quarter, thus starting the expression "a bench with a rag on it for a dime."

French's show differed from the Chapmans' in that it was, then and later, strictly a vaudeville show. The original acts included French's banjo and magic, a cousin who performed as a blackface minstrel, a cousin of

Callie's who was a comic singer, a married couple of globe-rollers, and a male comic singer. Callie was houskeeper and cook. With this fare they floated from Cincinnati to New Orleans, playing wherever they might hope to attract more than twenty-five people. They had the usual adventures of flatboat travel—a near wreck at the Falls of the Ohio, a bout with the ice at the mouth of the Ohio, stranding on bars, swirling in eddies, etc.—but they reached the mouth of the Mississippi only slightly battered and with enough cash to pay twenty-five dollars for a tow upstream.

Only Callie was unhappy with her role on the showboat; she wanted to be part of the act. During the winter layover, while French and the cousins repaired and repainted the boat, she practiced wire walking on a rope stretched between two trees, made herself a fetching costume, and learned two sentimental songs and how to play the dulcimer. On the second downriver cruise she sang "The Blue Alsatian Mountains" and "By Killarney's Lakes and Hills" while daintily balanced on the wire, accompanied her husband's banjo on the dulcimer and assisted him in the magic act. Later this unusual girl would secure a pilot's license for the Mississippi from New Orleans to St. Louis and for the Ohio, as well as a steamboat captain's license.

As nine years passed the French show got bigger and better, finally including eighteen acts. In a reminiscent mood, French described the problems they had in gaining acceptance: "In the old days at many a landing the sheriff and half the men of the town met us at the bank, shaking their fists and their guns at us, and pointing downstream. You see, too many whiskey boats, and medicine boats, and gambling dives had come by, all pretending to be a show, and they naturally thought we were one of them. People didn't know the difference and you couldn't blame 'em. It was mighty hard to cure them of that idea, but they know us now."

Callie took up the story to tell how her husband was responsible for the change. One night in Arkansas, she recalled, "I was selling tickets and I noticed that not a single woman had passed in. Too many of the men had winked at me as they paid their money. Curtain time came, and a good crowd was in, but still not a single woman. I knew Mr. French was getting madder and madder, because he was red clear down to his collar. Instead of pulling the curtain, he walked out in front of it, and said something like this:

"'Men, there is not a woman in the audience. Not a wife, mother, daughter, or sweetheart. This is not a show for men only. If you thought it was, you never made a bigger mistake in your life. My wife is a member of our troupe, and I respect her as much as any of you respect your wife. Now go, and as you pass out, get your money at the ticket office.'"

The story, as Callie told it, ended happily. The male audience left the boat, too shamefaced to ask for their money. The troupe went to bed.

LARGEST FLOATING THEATRE IN THE WORLD
$50,000 ACTUALLY INVESTED.

A Select Company of Players, presenting the latest successes in High-class Musical Comedies

SAFE COMFORTABLE SEATS.

THE KEY TO MIRTH AND MUSIC

ONE LONG LAUGH

MORAL and REFINED

THE HIGH-WATER MARK OF

MIRTH, MELODY AND MINSTRELSY
━ ALL NEW. ━

Up-to-date Comedians, Wonderful Dancers, Cultivated Singers, Brand-New Specialties.

GRAND DOUBLE ORCHESTRA

LIGHTED BY ELECTRICITY. COOLED BY ELECTRIC FANS

Nothing like it ever seen before. Sweet Singers, Pretty Girls, Elegant Costumes and Gorgeous New Scenery.

Don't be misled, wait and see the Largest, Cleanest, Safest Floating Theatre ever presented to the American public. You are cordially invited to inspect the Floating Palace during the day.

Showboats that played to small towns had to offer "family" entertainment suitable for women and children. A typical poster advertised a "moral and refined" show.

Later there was a commotion on the bank where the erstwhile stags, now accompanied by wives, were demanding a show. The Frenches put on a midnight performance. According to Callie, word of this incident traveled through the valley and did much to break down the resistance to show-boats.

The *New Sensation* drifted until 1885, when French traded his gold watch and $10 for the little steamer *Martin P. Murphy*, which was not strong enough to push the showboat up the Mississippi but could land it and take it up the backwaters. Next year he traded the *Murphy* and $350 for the *Sentinel* and became completely independent of the current. Then, in 1886, the first battered old *New Sensation* was retired and a second, somewhat larger *New Sensation* was built, with elegant stained-glass windows and a steam calliope—or *cal*-li-ope as it was always pronounced on the river. Of course, Callie played the calliope—with asbestos gloves.

The calliope became a symbol of postwar showboats; because its screams could be heard for eight miles, it was a great crowd attractor. Some showboat owners kept their calliopes when they retired as mementos of the river. There is a story of one who refused an offer from a movie company for three times the cost of a corroded calliope that he had stored in his garage—the memories were worth more.

The Frenches inspired many of the successful showboat owners of the era. Sometime French partners, associates, and performers branched out to start their own floating theaters, in some cases even unto the second generation. One such French alumnus was John McNair. French first saw John in a circus in Natchez performing as an acrobat and doubling on the tuba. He offered him a job on the *New Sensation* where John soon became, in addition to a performer and musician, the engineer of the tug. Shortly after, a thirteen-year-old friend of Callie's, Ida Fitch, visited the *New Sensation*. The next year she returned and married John on the stage. Later their daughters, Frenchie and Clarkie, were born on the showboat.

Ida followed in Callie's footsteps, taking minor roles in the skits and minstrel turns and developing a juggling act of her own. Later she took over designing costumes, directing, stage managing, and planning the show. After French built his third and fourth *New Sensations*, which operated simultaneously, an interesting *ménage à seize* developed between the two families. Captain Augustus French operated and piloted *Sensation* #*1* and worked in the show. Ida McNair managed, and worked in, the show on this boat. Captain Callie French piloted *Sensation* #*2* and worked in the show. John McNair was engineer and business manager on this boat, and worked in the show. To even things out, Clarkie McNair traveled on #*1* and Frenchie on #*2*, and both worked in the shows.

The McNairs finally left the Frenches and acquired the *New Era* in which, during the ten next years, they traveled over 80,000 miles, gave 2,500 performances, and entertained more than 500,000 people, to most of whom this was the only type of entertainment available.

Many of the most successful showboats were family institutions, both as to ownership and patronage. The Frenches operated the *New Sensations*; the McNairs, the *New Era*; the Hyatts toured in the *Water Queen*; the Thomses, in the *Princess*; the Reynoldses, in the *America*; the Kruses, in the *Twentieth Century*; the Bryants in the *New Showboat*; and there were more. All these operators were successful because they understood the basic axiom of showboating: it was an entertainment medium for rural and small-town families, and it was best when run by families for families.

When a showboat reached a town far up one of the tributaries, the screeching calliope and the parading band on the main street were often the signal for a holiday. The town closed down, and everybody went to see the show. There were no such things as babysitters, so the kids came too. One problem with melodramas with much gunplay was that the shots woke the babies in the audience, who then might make more noise than the actors. A show for such audiences should be entertaining, but it *must* be clean. Whether it played vaudeville or drama, no dirty joke or double entendre was ever heard from a showboat stage, and sex was confined to those melodramas whose story lines evolved around the efforts of the hero to protect the virtuous heroine from the evil designs of the villain on her person.

Norman Thoms' *Princess* was typical of a family boat. Norman was captain, director, and leading man; his wife Grace was leading lady; their daughter Norma was ingénue; and Grace's mother was cook. When they reached a town Norm called on the postmaster with two tickets—there were no newspapers in most of the places they played—and then toured the countryside in a hired buggy to advise all he met that there was a "show at the river tonight." Before dark farm wagons started to arrive at the river bank. Thoms recorded one family of fourteen—"Pa Kinney, Ma Kinney and twelve young 'uns"—who walked eleven miles to see their first show and offered seven gallons of blueberries for their tickets. For weeks the Thomses and their company had fresh blueberries for breakfast, blueberry cobbler for lunch, and blueberry pie for dinner.

Showboat females were far from the "painted Jezebels" about whom many ministers thundered. John McNair's brother joined the *New Era* and married one of the girls in the chorus, who maintained that she "had never smoked a cigarette, never had a drink, never heard a dirty story, and had never been accosted by a stage door Johnny." Such extreme righteousness may not have been the rule, but it was far more typical than the "loose woman" concept of popular imagery. When the colorful pennants came down at the close of a performance the family wash usually went up while the vessel moved on. John McNair told of one time when they played a town for three days and Ida gave the wash to a local laundress, not knowing that her husband had forgotten to remove the $100 bill that he carried in a pocket of his long underwear for emergencies. John toured the town seeking the cabin where his wash was being done. He finally found a pickaninny playing on the floor with his $100—his mammy thought that the big bill was some kind of an advertisement.

The family boats overcame church resistance by various means. One owner made his craft available for Sunday School picnics on Sunday afternoons; another gave a free concert of religious music after the church service. The most successful technique was to offer a minister a quarter of the receipts of a special performance to which the grateful pastor led his entire flock.

Melodramas vied with vaudeville as the principal fare of showboats. Some vessels played one, some the other, some both. John McNair's *New Era* played *Uncle Tom's Cabin* in the North and vaudeville in the South, emphasizing acts with few spoken lines because his most lucrative territory was back in the Louisiana bayous where the Cajuns spoke only French patois. *Ten Nights in a Bar Room* was a popular piece. Of one boat that offered nothing else, a wit quipped that its owner played "Ten Nights for ten months with ten actors and made ten mints." Other favorites of fond memory to oldsters were *East Lynne, Bertha the Sewing Machine Girl, Way Down East, The Old Homestead, The Drunkard*, and many, many more.

These unsubtle stories presented life in sharp, simple terms of good and evil—there were blacks and whites, no grays. They showed the evil of drink, the evil of the Big City, the evil of men in their designs on innocent women. In each there were one or more villains who fostered such evils, a virtuous heroine who was their prospective victim, and a shining hero who *always* made virtue triumph. For showboat audiences the melodramas were played absolutely straight, and the unsophisticated playgoers accepted it as a representation of life in the outside world. Come to think of it, there are a few western television shows with exactly the same format that have been doing very well in recent seasons.

The total identification of the audience with the play onstage caused some troublesome and many amusing incidents. Villains were sometimes held off at gunpoint by members of the audience, and one brawny West Virginia miner climbed onstage and threw the dastardly cur into the river as he was about to force himself on the helpless heroine. In one play there was a line that referred to the eagles overhead. One night a solemn youth in the audience arose to inform the actor, "Them must have been buzzards, mister, there ain't no eagles around here." Another anecdote tells of a hero who lay dying under a leak in the roof from which the water dripped on his face. A colored lady clambered over the footlights and held an umbrella over him, saying, " 'Tain't right this poor boy should die with his face all wet."

Space and economy restricted the cast of these small boats, and everybody doubled—or tripled or quadrupled. Cast, crew, and cook all marched in the band in the morning parade, those who could not play carrying a horn with a cork. In the play itself each actor usually handled two or more parts, did a vaudeville turn between acts, and sang and danced in the afterpiece. It was rather confusing when the villain and the ingénue ended the second act in a struggle over her honor and immediately came back between acts as smiling partners in a dance. Cathy Reynolds—who, incidentally, raised nine children on the *Majestic*—told of handling three parts

Robinson's Floating Palaces *was a double barge with a wide variety of attractions. The first section included a museum, a menagerie, and an aquarium. Connected to it was the "Grand Opera House," a scarlet-carpeted theater with 1,000 cushioned arm chairs.*

in the melodrama, playing the calliope and piano, singing two songs, selling candy, and ushering, all in the same evening.

Immediately after the turn of the twentieth century a new type of showboat appeared on the Mississippi, introduced by one "Double R" Markle, a promoter rather than a showman or a river man. Markle reasoned that if little showboats were doing well, a big floating theater would do better, and he ordered the king of showboats from the Pope Dock Company in Pittsburgh. His *Grand Floating Palace*, launched in 1901, was over 150 feet long and 45 feet wide, seating over a thousand in cushioned armchairs in a white and gold auditorium carpeted in scarlet. Other mammoth floating theaters quickly followed; Pope Dock built nothing else for several years. In 1909 Markle achieved his ambition of building the all-time world's largest showboat other than a circus boat. His *Goldenrod* was over 200 feet long and seated 1,400.

The basic fallacy of these big boats was that they could not play the small towns where the real showboat audiences lived. Communities of 200 souls might supply audiences of up to 500 from the surrounding country-side, but they could not fill a boat seating 1,000 or more. The big boats had to play cities, where they faced more sophisticated audiences and the competition of shore-based theaters. To appeal to urban audiences owners of the big boats scouted the Keith vaudeville circuit for big-time acts and advertised glowingly in *Billboard*, the show-business bible.

Most of the acts on the small boats were either youngsters or old-timers if they were not in the family of the owner, but many more competent acts played the boats, at least for one season, as a combined vacation and financial retrenchment. Ashore they played up to six shows a day, traveled in hot, sooty trains, carried luggage and costumes from station to hotel to theater, and spent their money in restaurants. Afloat they marched in the parade and played one show a day. They were well fed and comfortably if snugly quartered, and, after they did their daily stint, the rest of the time was their own in which to fish, sew, gossip, swim, or simply laze in the sun. On the smaller boats the pay was not much, perhaps $15 a week for a single and $20 for a team, usually a man and wife or a sister act. But it was found money, as there was no place to spend it. Showboating offered an opportunity to pay off shore debts and, for some, to sober up. There were few rules on showboats but an invariable one was no drinking.

The unique advantages of showboating attracted some good acts to the bigger vessels; Harry Blackstone, second only to Houdini as a magician, played the boats for a couple of seasons, as did many near headliners. And the boats developed some talent on their own to the point that, during the teen years and early 1920s, Keith and Albee were scouting the boats as well as vice versa.

The big boats that offered straight plays switched from melodrama to current, or year-old, Broadway hits that were more appealing to city audiences. *Peg o' My Heart, Brewster's Million's, East Is West, Johnny Get Your Gun,* and *The Cat and the Canary* were but a few New York successes that justified one showboat owner's boast: "We Show You the Present, Others Only the Past."

Showboating started to decline gradually but surely about 1910 although, as with steamboats, the biggest floating theaters arrived on the scene around or after the turning point. Motion pictures were largely to blame for the showboats' difficulties—the boat owner's ingénue daughter could not compete with Mary Pickford nor could his wife vie with Theda Bara. Showboat comics could not match the Keystone Cops, and there were no leading men like Francis X. Bushman afloat. Many of the big boats devoted half their show to motion pictures but, with flickers running every night in town, there was little appeal in an annual visit from a floating movie. Sharing honors with the movies in the demise of show-boating was the Model T Ford. Families who could pile into the flivver every Saturday night for a trip to the cinema at the county seat were no longer dependent on an annual visit from a floating theater for escapism. There were about forty authentic showboats on the western rivers at the turn of the century. By 1910 there were but twenty-six, and, by 1928 these were reduced to fourteen, of which the depression that started in the next year killed most that did not anchor at a big-city pier and try to do business as permanent theaters.

Surely the best-known showboat of all time is the *Cotton Blossom,* thanks to Edna Ferber, the *Woman's Home Companion,* the Book-of-the-Month Club, Florenz Ziegfeld, Jerome Kern and Oscar Hammerstein, Universal Pictures, and Metro-Goldwyn-Mayer, all of whom publicized a vessel of this name in a novel, a serial, a musical play, and two movies. There really was a *Cotton Blossom*—in fact there was a whole bouquet of *Cotton Blossoms.* There was the *Cotton Blossom #1,* which was the third *Cotton Blossom,* and the *Cotton Blossom #2,* which was the fourth *Cotton Blossom.* The second *Cotton Blossom* was really the *Cotton Blossom Pavilion,* and the original *Cotton Blossom* was originally the *Eisenbarth Henderson Floating Theatre—The New Great Modern Temple of Amusement.* In addition, there were at least four other vessels that bore the name *Cotton Blossom* for shorter or longer periods after Miss Ferber made it famous.

The original *Cotton Blossom* needed no novelist to enhance its name on the rivers; its owner, Ralph Waldo Emerson, was quite capable of doing that himself. Emerson had a partial claim to his own famous name. These three given names had originally preceded his real surname, Gaches, which he dropped when he entered show businss. Gaches, or Emerson, started as an advance man for the *Water Queen* and was one of the best. He later owned, in all, nine different showboats. The original *Cotton Blossom* had already received that name when he bought her in 1910.

Emerson put a good show on the *Cotton Blossom*—Broadway plays and spectacular entre'acts—and plastered each stop with the vessel's slogan, "After the Minnow Comes the Whale." On each trip he had a publicity-getting advance act like "Gay the Handcuff King," who broke out of town jails in the presence of the press. He also carried a baseball team, recruited from cast and crew but smartly uniformed. The showboat team played the local team before the show, and when the evening performance started the audience had fine fun identifying the villain as the third baseman and the hero as the shortstop.

Emerson sold the first *Cotton Blossom* to Daniel Hintner and his wife shortly before the vessel was crushed in the ice during a performance of *Uncle Tom's Cabin* in 1917. The name was too good to rest on the bottom of the river so the Hintners called their next boat the *Cotton Blossom Pavilion* and subsequently acquired vessels that they dubbed *Cotton Blossom #1* and *Cotton Blossom #2*. These were unique crosses between big boats and family boats. Mrs. Hintner was the show's comedienne and daughter Hope the ingénue. To take advantage of current best-sellers without paying copyright fees for Broadway plays, Mrs. Hintner adapted popular novels such as *The Little Shepherd of Kingdom Come* and *Mrs. Wiggs of the Cabbage Patch* to the stage, presumably without paying royalties.

The last big *Cotton Blossom* was sold for debt in 1931. Some of the little ones lasted longer; the last burned in 1942. When Ralph Waldo Emerson retired in 1931 he built, out of sentiment, a little *Cotton Blossom* that operated on the Chicago River until she burned in 1933.

Edna Ferber had no part in the saga of the vessels that she made famous; in fact, she never set foot on a Mississippi River showboat. She did her showboating on the *John Adams Floating Theatre* in Chesapeake Bay. This, the leading salt-water showboat, played the Chesapeake and Albemarle Sound regions for thirty years until she sank in 1939. It was a family boat or, rather, a two-family boat. Mr. and Mrs. John Adams, who had been circus performers, managed it, and Mr. and Mrs. Charles Hunter staged the shows and acted in them, Mr. Hunter as director and leading man and Mrs. Hunter as a leading lady who was known, for seventeen years, as "the Mary Pickford of the Chesapeake."

Edna Ferber spent a week on the *Adams* in 1924, absorbing background material for her novel, which, despite its great success, is viewed with disdain by most showboat aficionados because in *Show Boat* more melodrama takes place backstage than onstage. Her fictional showboat-owning

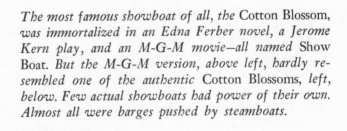

The most famous showboat of all, the Cotton Blossom, *was immortalized in an Edna Ferber novel, a Jerome Kern play, and an M-G-M movie—all named* Show Boat. *But the M-G-M version, above left, hardly resembled one of the authentic* Cotton Blossoms, *left, below. Few actual showboats had power of their own. Almost all were barges pushed by steamboats.*

family—Captain Andy Hawks, his wife Parthenia, and daughter Magnolia —bore little relation to any real-life showboat owners, most of whom were typical midwestern families who happened to be in show business on the rivers.

Showboating had one final, brief upsurge in the early 1930s, thanks to the alcohol-inspired risibilities of a yachtload of merrymakers. Sam and Vivian Bryant, with their two sons and daughters-in-law, had been playing the rivers for thirty years, first owning the *Princess* and then *Bryant's New Showboat*. Their claim to fame, if any, was that George M. Cohan had given them the rights to his plays for presentation on the river, apparently because Bryant admired Cohan to the point of adulation. They played their own adaptations of *Broadway Jones, Rosie O'Grady, The Song and Dance Man,* and other Cohan successes for years, but by the time the depression struck in 1929 they had gone back to *Ten Nights in a Bar Room.* Business was so bad that they could not afford to tour, so they moored the *New Showboat* at the Cincinnati water front, hoping to make "eating money" with the old melodrama.

The first two nights they played to almost empty houses. On the third day a yacht anchored alongside, the owner of which gave a large party. As a novelty to entertain his guests he offered Bryant $25 to put on a special performance. Up to this time melodrama had always been played straight on showboats—these plays were deadly serious. The Bryants started *Ten Nights in a Bar Room* in this vein, but the gay yachtsmen would not have it so. To these sophisticates the only merit in the hoary old play was the opportunity it offered for audience participation —hissing the villain, encouraging the hero, and shouting witty advice and warnings to the heroine. The melodrama was so foreign to their experience that perhaps they quite genuinely thought it was supposed to be funny.

At first the cast was resentful, until the quick-witted Bryant, who had not heard such laughter and applause for many years, realized that this audience wanted burlesque, and tipped off his cast to "ham it up." They were not very good actors to begin with, and when they deliberately tried to be bad actors the results were screamingly funny. A newspaperman in the audience wrote a feature article on this hilarious spoof, and a new "art form" was born—burlesque melodrama. The *New Sensation* played the season at Cincinnati to standing room only.

Most of the few remaining showboats adopted the new technique with temporary success, although those that stopped at some smaller communities had a novel problem. Here the part of the audience that wanted the play in the old tradition resented the other part that kidded it, sometimes to the point of fisticuffs.

But burlesque melodrama could not save the showboats. By 1938 only five remained on the rivers and in 1943 only the biggest of them, the *Goldenrod*, was still operating, moored permanently at St. Louis until she burned in 1962. Motion pictures, automobiles, and the depression all contributed to their demise, but the basic cause was the disappearance of the American frontier. The showboat was born to carry entertainment to frontier families that could be reached in no other way. When the frontier passed away, the showboat soon followed.

The Decline

of the River Boats

In 1882, some thirty years after his conversion from pilot to author, Mark Twain returned to the Mississippi as a visitor. His account of the trip is a mournful dirge of decline and decay—a sad eulogy on the great and glamorous days of steamboating. He drove through St. Louis in a horse and buggy and commented on the growth of the busy city since he had last been there—until he reached the levee. Here, he said, "the ancient armies of drays and struggling throngs of men, and mountains of freight, were gone; and Sabbath reigned in their stead. The immemorial mile of cheap, foul doggeries remained, but business was dull with them; the multitude of poison-swilling Irishmen had departed, and in their places were a few scattering handfuls of ragged negroes, some drinking, some drunk, some nodding, others asleep. St. Louis is a great and prosperous and advancing city; but the river-edge of it seems dead past resurrection."

There were, said Twain, "half a dozen sound-asleep steamboats where I used to see a solid mile of wide-awake ones . . . . Mississippi steamboating was born about 1812; at the end of thirty years it had grown to mighty proportions; and in less than thirty more it was dead! A strangely short life for so majestic a creature. Of course it is not absolutely dead; neither is a crippled octogenarian who could once jump twenty-two feet on level ground; but as contrasted with what it was in its prime vigor, Mississippi steamboating may be called dead."

The humorist took passage on a boat south from St. Louis. A once-grand packet that was the only vessel advertised for that route at the time, Twain amusingly described it as follows:

She was a venerable rack-heap, and a fraud to boot; for she was playing herself for personal property, whereas the good honest dirt was so thickly caked all over her that she was righteously taxable as real estate. There are places in New England where her hurricane-deck would be worth a hundred and fifty dollars an acre. The soil on her forecastle was quite good—the new crop of wheat was already springing from the cracks in protected places. The companionway was of a dry sandy character, and would have been well suited for grapes, with a southern exposure and a little subsoiling. The soil of the boiler-deck was thin and rocky, but good enough for grazing purposes. A colored boy was on watch here—nobody else visible. We gathered from him that this calm craft would go as advertised, 'if she got her trip'; if she didn't get it, she would wait for it.

The main reason for the decline was, of course, the railroad. Quoting Twain again, "There is a locomotive in sight from the deck of the steamboat almost the whole way from St. Louis to St. Paul." And, sixty years later, William Faulkner would look back and write, "There were railroads in the wilderness now. People who used to go overland by carriage or on horseback to the river landings for the Memphis and New Orleans steamboats could take the train from almost anywhere now. And presently Pullmans too, all the way from Chicago and the Northern cities."

It may be that Mark Twain exaggerated a little in 1882. Steamboating in the midwestern valleys was declining, but it was not yet moribund. The greatest river boat of all, the *J. M. White*, was still plowing the Mississippi and would not burn for another four years. Other of the floating palaces built in the later 1860s and '70s were still afloat, although few, if any, were making money. In 1884 the levee at New Orelans was thronged with tall smokestacks as river boats carried crowds to the Centennial Cotton Exposition, including a vessel that was new that year, "the World-Renowned Electric Light Steamer *Guiding Star*." Electricity had come to the Mississippi in the last of the floating palaces. In a sense, the river boats were like dinosaurs—the biggest and most impressive came into existence shortly before the breed became extinct.

The flurry in 1884 marked the last time the New Orleans levee would be congested with the high-stacked packets. There were 2,000 landings at the Creole city in 1860. By the 1890s there were but a handful of tall steamers in operation, and the Ohio River yards that had produced most of them were building boats for the Nile, the Orinoco, the Yangtze, the Ganges, and other streams whose commerce had not yet been usurped by the iron horse.

Still, in 1911, it was possible to assemble forty-seven old-time river boats at Pittsburgh for the centennial celebration of the coming of the steamboat to the Mississippi. Portly President Taft stood on the hurricane deck of the *Virginia* to watch a replica of the original *New Orleans* steam past through a snowstorm. Then the re-created first Mississippi steamboat went down the Ohio and the Mississippi to New Orleans in what was to be a western version of the Hudson-Fulton celebration. Strangely, there was not much interest in the valley. At that time steamboats were merely old-fashioned, as the horse and buggy soon would be— they were not yet glamorous relics of dramatic history. The *New Orleans*

"The river-edge . . . seems dead past resurrection."—MARK TWAIN

puffed down a virtually empty river, deserted but for an occasional grimy coal-barge tow. At the city for which she was named a few harbor tugs whistled at the symbol of the glorious past, but when the replica was offered for sale there were no takers. She was abandoned at the little Louisiana river town of Brashear.

The river boat lasted longer on the upper river, where the railroad exerted its domination somewhat later. The immediate pre- and postwar years were the most prosperous for the lower-river boats. Above St. Louis the banner year in terms of volume was 1880, when over 1,300,000 tons of merchandise came down the river to that city. True, by this time most of it was pushed in barges rather than carried on deck, but it was pushed by steamboats. By 1900 this trade had declined to about 350,000 tons; by 1910 it was 43,000 tons.

It might be said that the western river boats did not die but, like General MacArthur's old soldiers, simply faded away. Some ended their days as towboats pushing barges or showboats. Others did business for many

KNOX COLLEGE, GALESBURG, ILL.

The Centennial Cotton Exposition in 1884 marked the last time the New Orleans levee was thronged with tall-stacked river boats.

years as excursion steamers. Mortality from accidents was still high and wrecked boats were not replaced. Few of the western boats were sufficiently well built to warrant salvaging much of their material. Most, when there were no longer cargoes for them, were merely tied up and left to rot away, or succumbed to fire or the ravages of the ice. In 1918 a fleet of idle boats was moored at Cincinnati. When the river ice broke it crumpled the large sister ships *City of Cincinnati* and *City of Louisville* and four lesser packets. On one of these, the *Peoria*, the engineer tried to fight the ice by keeping the paddle wheels revolving slowly, but when the ice broke the *Peoria*'s mooring snapped and she drifted off downstream like a ghost ship, her lights burning and her paddles slowly turning. Far below, her wreckage drifted ashore.

A most amusing yet definitive description of the riverboat, its purpose, and its end was written by a young newspaper reporter, Clyde Fitch, who said:

The Steamboat is an engine on a raft, with $11,000 worth of jig-saw work around it.

Steamships are built of steel and are severely plain except on the inside where the millionaire tourist is confined. Steamboats are built of wood, tin, shingles, canvas and twine, and look like a bride of Babylon. If a steamboat should go to sea, the ocean would take one playful slap at it and people would be picking up kindling on the beach for the next eleven years.

However, the steamboat does not go to sea. Its home is on the river, which does not rise up and stand on end in a storm. It is necessary that a steamboat shall be light and airy because if it were heavy it would stick into the bottom of the river several feet and become an island instead of a means of transportation.

The steamboat is from a hundred to three hundred feet long and from thirty to fifty feet wide. It is from forty to seventy feet high above water, but does not extend more than three feet into the water. This is because that is all the water there is. A steamboat must be so built that when the river is low and the sandbars come out for air, the first mate can tap a keg of beer and run the boat four miles on the suds.

Steamboats were once the beasts of burden for the great middle-west and the city which could not be reached at low water by a steamboat with two large, hot stacks, twenty-five negro roustabouts on the bow end and a gambler in the cabin, withered away in infancy. But the railroad, which runs in high water or low and does not stab itself in a vital spot with a snag, came along and cleared the steamboat out of business.

Paradoxically, at about the time the steamboat era was ending, the government at long last decided to improve the rivers to make them safe for steamboats. In 1874 Congress authorized the erection of beacon lights, day boards, and buoys on the western rivers as aids to navigation. During the next decade the Federal Government started a system of channel improvements with dikes, wing dams, and other devices to keep the rivers within their bounds and provide deeper, snag-free channels. All this was viewed with derision by Mark Twain during his visit in 1882. He quoted the mate of the *Gold Dust* as saying:

Government is doing a deal for the Mississippi now, spending loads of money on her. When there used to be four thousand steamboats and ten thousand acres of coal barges, and rafts, and trading-scows, there wasn't a lantern from St. Paul to New Orleans, and the snags were thicker than bristles on a hog's back; and now, when there's three dozen steamboats and nary a barge or raft, government has snatched out all the snags, and lit up the shores like Broadway, and a boat's as safe on the river as she'd be in heaven. And I reckon that by the time there ain't any boats left at all, the Commission will have the old thing all reorganized, and dredged out, and fenced in, and tidied up, to a degree that will make navigation just simply perfect, and absolutely safe and profitable.

At the time Twain was writing this an item appeared in a Cincinnati paper reporting that the steamer *Joseph B. Williams* was en route to New Orleans with a string of thirty-two coal barges, "the largest tow ever taken to New Orleans or anywhere else in the world," a total of 30,000 tons which, some river man figured, would require a train twelve miles long with 2,000 railroad cars and sixty-six locomotives. The first coal had been barged down the Ohio by the *Walter Forward* in 1845, in two flats lashed alongside and one pulled behind. During the 1880s and '90s moving coal from the mines of Pennsylvania, West Virginia, and western Kentucky to the south became big business; a ton of coal could be moved 2,000 miles by barge for $1.30, a price with which the railroad could not compete.

But the coal tows could not support a river-boat industry, and commerce on the western rivers languished until 1918, when the railroads were unable to cope with the staggering demands for transportation imposed by World War I. At this juncture a group of midwestern industrialists waited on Washington to propose that the government go into the steamboat business to break the railroad bottleneck. The result was the Federal Barge Line operated under the War Department, starting with twenty-five barges—mostly from the Army Engineers—and five towboats. This small fleet proved what river men had long maintained, that bulk freight could be moved cheaper by water than by rail. After the war the rivers were back in business again and river transport continued to grow until it far outstripped, in volume, the best years of the steamboats.

Soon a new type of vessel made its appearance on the rivers. a boat specifically designed for pushing barges. Steel-hulled, screw-propelled, and diesel-powered, these craft are sorry substitutes, in terms of glamour and romance, for the tall steamboats. Of course, they are far more powerful, efficient, and economical than the vessels of yore, but they are not really river boats. True, they run on the rivers, but they would run equally well on deep water, salt or fresh. They have no great wheels of varnished mahogany in their pilothouses nor mustachioed pilots to spin them or pit their skill and lore against Old Al, the underwater king of the river. The

AMERICAN WATERWAYS OPERATORS, INC.

River boats returned to commerce when it was discovered that they could tow bulk freight more economically than the railroads could move it. But the steamboat gave way to the diesel towboat, and the shallow, snag-infested river was dredged into deeper, man-made waterways. Here a modern diesel pushes 18 barges on a lake created by a TVA dam.

new breed of pilots relaxes in padded chairs watching radar or chatting on the ship-to-ship or ship-to-shore telephone while they maneuver the vessel with two trifling little levers. There are no colorful roustabouts to man-handle the freight the diesels move. Barges are loaded by automatic machinery at the point of origin of the coal, sulphur, limestone, oil, grain, automobiles, and other manufactured goods and agricultural products they carry down the river. The tug lines up a tow of loaded barges and impersonally pushes it down the river. When an upriver tow approaches, the two captains talk to each other by phone as to how they will pass, and then blow the traditional signal on their horns. Perhaps the most distinctive difference between a diesel towboat and a true river boat is that blaring, raucous, annoying horn that has replaced the mellow, many-toned steam whistle that drew valley folk to the river bank with stars in their eyes and dreams in their hearts to watch the boats go by to far places, smoke-belching juggernauts by day and lighted fairy palaces by night.

The midwestern rivers on which the new breed of watercraft travel today are in large part man-made. When World War I proved that this form of transportation still had a place in the economic scheme of things, the government intensified the river-improvement campaign, which had languished during the first two decades of the century. Deep snag-free channels were dredged and maintained on all the principal streams, with locks to lift the boats around the old falls and rapids. Originally most of these were 600 feet long, and the new diesels that could handle 1,200-foot tows had to double-trip. Today the early locks are being replaced with improvements that can raise or lower a 1,200-foot tow—almost a quarter mile of boats—in one piece.

By 1929 the Ohio River had a 9-foot channel rising, through locks, in forty-nine steps from Cairo to Pittsburgh. By 1970 it will have a 12-foot channel with the number of steps reduced to nineteen. When the 1,200-foot McAlpine Lock at Louisville was opened in 1961 the towboat *Philip Stern* was the first to take a string of barges 1,210 feet long past the falls of the Ohio that had held up the *Washington* 145 years before. In the early 1960s the Ohio River carried twice the traffic of the Panama Canal and three times that of the St. Lawrence Seaway.

By 1939 there was a nine-foot channel to St. Paul on the upper Mississippi, with locks around the falls that had been the nemesis of so many of the boats carrying lead from Galena. The channel has now become inadequate for the upper-river traffic and, by 1975, it will be deepened to twelve feet. The Missouri has a six-foot channel to Omaha and a four-foot depth to Sioux City, although traffic justifies a nine-foot channel all the way to Yankton, South Dakota. On this river system there is a continuing dispute over the prior rights of irrigation, power, and navigation, and there is a difference of opinion as to whether the water in the vast reservoirs behind the forty-odd dams that have been or are being built should be used to make electricity, grow crops, or provide a stable channel in the river.

TVA has made the Tennessee a series of deep-water lakes connected by locks and a nine-foot channel all the way to Knoxville, where a purse was once offered for the daring boat that could pass Muscle Shoals. That obstacle is now hundreds of feet below the water impounded by Wilson Dam. Plans are under way to open the Arkansas River to modern navigation with a nine-foot channel from the Mississippi to Tulsa, Oklahoma.

AMERICAN WATERWAYS OPERATORS, INC.

The world's highest single lift, the Wilson Dam lock, rises 100 feet over a formerly treacherous stretch of the Tennessee River in northern Alabama. It was built by the TVA and opened in 1959.

Instead of 4,000 steamboats on the western rivers there are now over 2,000 towboats pushing barges, each of which holds three or four times as much freight as an old packet; a single towboat can handle the tonnage that used to fill 50 steamboats. There are more than 700 transportation lines on the Mississippi system, and in 1960 the Army Engineers reported to the Senate that within twenty years "the demands of industry will double the freight load now carried on the rivers."

But there will be no true river boats on these fine new waterways, except as nostalgic reminders of a past century. Several river towns on the Ohio and Mississippi have preserved and refurbished boats of the bygone days as museums—Marietta, Keokuk, and Winona, among others. The three-decker *River Queen* is now moored as a museum opposite Hannibal, Missouri, where visitors can gaze across the river at the home of Mark Twain. At the re-created Abraham Lincoln village in New Salem, Illinois, there is a replica of the stern-wheeler *Talisman*, which the Great Emancipator is said to have helped navigate up the Sangamon River.

There are a few operating river boats that cruise or carry excursions on the western rivers. The *Admiral* makes a daily excursion at St. Louis, the *President* at New Orleans. These are modern, diesel-powered craft that bear no resemblance to the old river boats. The *Admiral* is described by her owners as "the World's largest excursion steamer—five decks—block long—air conditioned—holds 4,000." The same line has two replicas of old-time boats, the *Huck Finn* at St. Louis and the *Mark Twain* at New Orleans. These little craft are, in a sense, fakes in that although the stern wheels revolve they are diesel-powered.

The *Belle of Louisville* and the *Delta Queen*, which cruises out of Cincinnati, are authentic old-time river boats in that they started as working boats and, although they have been modernized, they are still steam-powered and are essentially the same as the glamorous craft of the last century. The *Belle of Louisville* was built in 1914 and, as the *Idlewild*, operated as a packet carrying passengers and freight out of Memphis. In the early 1920s she became an excursion boat and during the war she went back to work as a towboat. Jefferson County, Kentucky, acquired her in 1962 and refurbishing her was a Louisville community project with amateur volunteer labor. When she was properly prettied up as an excursion boat, she made her bow in a race against the *Delta Queen* in 1963.

This steamboat race has now become an annual event, part of the celebration connected with the running of another race, the Kentucky Derby. The *Queen* won two of the first three races and her owners now smugly claim that they have to give the *Belle* a head start. The race is starting to become a tradition, arousing a public interest that even the owners of the *Queen*—Greene Line Steamers—do not understand. In the foreword of a history of their business they say:

It's hard to explain the enthusiasm for steamboat racing. It's not logical. If you think about it in a purely abstract way, two steamboats racing makes about as much sense as two army barracks lumbering along for the finish—and that's more or less how they look. Steamboats were designed as work boats, not racing boats, and the original design has not changed much. But Mark Twain claimed steamboat races were more exciting than horse races and we have our own races with the *Belle* and the interest of the press (indeed, the world) to shore up his word. Otherwise why would the Swedish Broadcasting Co. televise the race and The London Times show the *Queen* in a picture spread and call a cruise on her a "must" when visiting the U.S.?

The *Delta Queen* is the last of the floating palaces or, to be more exact, she compares to a plush floating motel. A four-deck stern-wheeler 285 feet long, she was built in Glasgow, Scotland, in 1926 and first saw service as a packet on the Sacramento River. Captain Thomas Greene—the fourth generation in an Ohio River steamboating family—bought her after World War II and made a river-boat voyage that harked back to gold-rush days: down the Pacific coast, through the Panama Canal, across the Gulf of Mexico, and up the Mississippi and Ohio rivers to Cincinnati. Here, after extensive refurbishing, she started a new career as a cruise boat carrying 186 passengers. In the spring and fall she makes five three-week cruises to New Orleans. In the summer, shorter voyages take her to St. Louis, Pittsburgh, Chattanooga, and St. Paul.

The *Queen* is the nearest one can get to the glamorous boats of yore, although there are some differences. None of the great boats of the past was air conditioned. The eight-foot wheel is gone from the *Queen*'s pilot house. She is steered by two little levers like a diesel towboat by a pilot who watchs radar and an electronic control panel and talks on a ship-to-ship phone. But the whistle is still there—a most melodious one, as is a calliope.

There are changes in the crew too. The clerk has become a purser and his helper has lost the fascinating appellation "mud clerk" to become an assistant purser. The wonderfully mustachioed bartender has become a mixologist and some of the personnel were unknown during the steamboat era—a hostess, an organist, a vocalist, and a manager for a souvenir shop. The eighty-man crew includes stewards, maids, porters, waiters, and galley help—but no roustabouts. For those willing to accept these minor deviations, the *Delta Queen* recaptures the glamour of the steamboat era with, it must be admitted, more comfort and safety.

Long after steamboating as a going business had virtually died on the midwestern rivers the river boats held on at a few points in the East, principally as passenger carriers. Until well into the twentieth century the approved way to go from New York to Albany or Providence and from Baltimore to Norfolk was by boat, although by the end of the nineteenth century the Chesapeake Bay craft were no longer river boats. By the 1880s the towns on the banks of the many rivers that flow into the bay were served by rail, and the boats were confined to the bay itself. All the vessels built after that time were propeller-driven steamships that would have been at home on the briny deep.

The biggest and best boats on the Hudson were all built in the twentieth century, the last, the *Alexander Hamilton*, a Hudson River Day Line boat, in 1924. The night liner *Berkshire*, at 440 feet, was the longest and largest boat to ever run on a river, exceeded only by the *Commonwealth*

GREENE LINE STEAMERS

Spectators line the bank of the Ohio to watch the Delta Queen *(left) vie for speed against the* Belle of Louisville. *Since 1962 this steamboat race has become an annual event as part of the celebration connected with the Kentucky Derby.*

on Long Island Sound. The *Washington Irving*, another Day Line boat built in 1913, had the greatest pasenger carrying capacity of any steamboat in the world—6,000. If a full load of the *Washington Irving*'s passengers were seated in the world's largest theater, Radio City Music Hall, there would be only 200 empty seats in the house. Another of the later giants was the *Robert Fulton*, which was built in 1909 and linked to the past by a bell. The original *North River* did not have a whistle; its arrivals and departures were signaled with a cast-iron bell. The bell survived the boat and passed through several hands during the nineteenth century,

GREENE LINE STEAMERS

The Delta Queen, *a cruise boat based at Cincinnati, is the last passenger-carrying river boat, except for a few offering daily excursions. In the spring and fall she makes three-week cruises to New Orleans and in the summer to St. Louis, Pittsburgh, Chattanooga, and St. Paul.*

ending up in Troy, New York, where it was mounted on the counter of a hotel to call bellboys until the Hudson River Day Line acquired it to grace the pilothouse of the *Robert Fulton.*

All these vessels were described at the time as floating palaces. Although the Hudson River mammoths were not as plush as their counterparts of the Fall River Line, a contemporary account of the *Hendrick Hudson,* which was launched in 1906, comments on the "private drawing rooms furnished in Louis XVI, French-Empire, Dutch and Colonial styles and a large writing room in polished teakwood" and the suspended bandstand in the forward saloon from which concerts "could be heard by three thousand seated passengers."

The Hudson River boats held their own against the railroads; enough people were willing to sacrifice the greater speed of the train for the greater comfort and luxury of the boat. But the steamers could not compete with the automobile and the new turnpikes that snaked along the river bank starting in the 1930s. In 1939 the last night-boat service was suspended, and in 1948 the Hudson River Day Line stopped running the last point-to-point passenger service on the river. It was surely appropriate

THE MARINERS MUSEUM, NEWPORT NEWS, VA.

The biggest and best boats on the Hudson were built in the twentieth century. The biggest passenger-carrying river boat of all time was the Washington Irving, *which was licensed to carry 6,000 people.*

that the last trip of a river boat in regular service on the Hudson was made by a steamer named for the man who had made the first trip—the *Robert Fulton*. Today there is but one river boat churning up and down the Hudson; from May to September the paddle wheels of the *Alexander Hamilton* take her on a daily excursion cruise to Poughkeepsie, with stops at Bear Mountain State Park and West Point.

Some of the eastern boats had interesting careers after they left the river. The most widely traveled was the *De Witt Clinton*, of the Day Line. In World War I the *Clinton* was requisitioned by the U.S. Navy and became the tender *Nopatin*. After her discharge she again ran on the river during the between-war years, ending this phase of her career by taking visitors from the North River pier around the Battery to the New York World's Fair in 1939. In 1942 she was drafted for her second tour of war duty, this time by the army, which used her as a transport, the *Frederick C. Johnson*. After the war she was sold to a private owner and laid for a year at Norfolk, closely watched by the Coast Guard because the British government was convinced that she was going to be used to run the Palestine blockade. There was probably some basis for this belief, for although she left the United States as the *Derecktor* flying the Panamanian flag, she ended up as the *Galilah* of the Israeli Line hauling former inmates of British detention camps to Haifa. She was apparently broken up in an Italian yard in 1953.

Another Day Line boat, the *Chauncey M. Depew*, had an almost equally checkered, and somewhat more pleasant, old age. She worked for the army in World War II as the *FS-89*, was then bought by a private owner and used briefly for excursion service between Boston and Providence on the Cape Cod canal, and finally was purchased by the government of Bermuda to serve as a tender to passenger ships too large to come into the harbor. In 1963 she was refurbished and is still leading an active life making excursions and moonlight sails in Bermuda waters.

The *Robert Fulton* had the most unusual end. In 1956 she was sold to a division of Owens-Illinois that processes pulpwood for paper boxes in the Bahamas. She was towed to Jacksonville where, after her machinery was removed, she was converted into a combination office, apartment house, supermarket, infirmary, school, and community center complete with movie theater, television rooms, and snack bar. She was then towed out to a timber-harvesting area on Great Abasco Island in the Bahamas where she now sits landlocked on Snake Cay, entirely surrounded by fill.

The famed Fall River Line did not last quite as long as the Hudson River Day lines, although many who consider themselves in the prime of life can remember traveling on the *Commonwealth* or the *Priscilla*. And it was a memorable experience, far more colorful and exciting, more luxurious and comfortable than a quick, rather cramped trip on a Boeing 707,

The bustle at the gangplank, with the gleaming white boat towering overhead; the gold-trimmed officers welcoming one aboard; the band blaring popular tunes of the day; the ringing of bells and moaning of the whistle as the vessel churned away from the pier made a sailing as thrilling as a departure for an Atlantic crossing, although one knew that the next morning would bring the end of the voyage. There are few modern travel experiences that equal breakfasting at a well-appointed table by a window far above the river as the boat coasted into New York early in the morning. And this was a breakfast. Melon at Hell Gate; cod-fish cakes in the East River as midtown Manhattan slid by; perhaps a waffle and honey as the Battery was rounded; and a second coffee and a cigarette as the vessel glided gracefully into Pier 14, North River.

This writer remembers a first trip on the *Priscilla* as a very, very young man. I had heard that some of the ladies who traveled on the boats were not exactly ladies, and as gay, laughing, smartly dressed females came up the gangplank on the arms of their male companions I stood back—puffing on a pipe to prove my sophistication—and wondered with titillating excitement: "Could *she* be one of *those*?"

On June 30, 1937, the *Commonwealth* was about to leave New York

The Hudson River boats held their own against the railroad, but they were unable to compete with the turnpikes of the 1930s. The C. W. Morse was one of the last of the Albany night boats. She was the last to fly the People's Line flag, which went back to the earliest days of river boating.

on a voyage on which there were few, if any, of "those" aboard. The majority of its 900 passengers were kids on their way to New England summer camps. The turmoil and bustle of departure was greater than usual, with shouting youngsters, mothers screaming last-minute instructions and blue-uniformed, white-gloved porters lined up at the purser's window to get the huge brass stateroom keys. The cry "All ashore that's going ashore" had sounded, and an army of mothers and fathers, uncles and aunts was trooping down the gangplank when the crew of the *Commonwealth* sat down. The sit-down strike, born in Detroit as part of the labor unrest of the era, had spread to the coast, and the personnel of the vessel announced that the *Commonwealth* was not going anywhere, nor were they going to leave, until their demands were met. At the other end of the line the same thing was happening aboard the *Priscilla*.

The children and other passengers of the *Commonwealth* were transferred to hastily assembled special New York, New Haven and Hartford railroad trains. A truce was declared, and the *Priscilla* sailed a few hours late, the *Commonwealth* next day, and the line continued to operate for two weeks while negotiations went on. Then another sit-down strike was called on all the company's boats. The crews sat aboard for six days, eating everything in the larder until there was nothing left but cornflakes. Then company spokesmen stepped aboard, called the crews into the ornate saloons, and read a terse announcement. The Fall River steamers would sail no more; the line had suspended operations forever after 91 years. The four remaining floating palaces, which had cost $6,000,000, were towed to the ship breakers at Providence. They brought in $88,000 as scrap.

There are some river boats left on the Hudson that carry passengers from point to point every day—some 30,000,000 passengers every year, the equivalent of almost one sixth of the nation's population. Little has been said in this book about ferries, but they are river boats, and the Staten Island Ferry, which crosses from the Battery at the foot of Manhattan to St. George on Staten Island at the bottom of New York's upper bay, is very much alive. Until as late as the 1930s there were more than thirty ferry lines connecting the island boroughs of New York City with each other and with New Jersey. Bridges and tunnels have put most of them out of business, but the Staten Island Ferry goes on as it has for over two and a half centuries. It is probably the oldest transportation route in America. The post roads of colonial days have all been replaced by superhighways, but the Staten Island Ferry is still operating over the same route on which it was originally chartered in 1712.

There are other superlatives than can be applied to the Staten Island Ferry. A ride on it is the only worth-while thing in America that a nickel will still buy. Some thirty years ago many commuters from Staten Island used to spend 15¢ to get to work: 5¢ for the ferry, 5¢ for a cup of coffee, and 5¢ for a shoeshine—roving bootblacks were symbols of the New York ferries. Today, the coffee costs 15¢, the shoeshine 25¢—but the ferry ride is still 5¢. The City of New York does not begin to break even, operating the boats at this price, but the 5¢ ride across the upper bay has become a tradition that no city administration would be wise to upset.

Cornelius Vanderbilt had no such eleemosynary ideas when he started to amass his fabulous fortune by operating a ferry to Staten Island in 1810 nor when he introduced steamboats to the route with the *Nautilus* in 1817. The *Nautilus* was a small single-ended river boat, as were all her successors until shortly before the Civil War. The double-ended ferries made their appearance here just in time to be drafted into the U.S. Navy, which commandeered anything that would float to aid in the blockade of Confederate ports. Three of the four Staten Island boats that went to war were casualties: the *Southfield* was rammed and sunk by a southern iron-clad in Pamlico Sound off North Carolina; the *Westfield* was burned to prevent capture at Galveston, Texas; and the *Clifton* met the same fate at Sabine Pass, Texas.

This was the only excitement the ferryboats saw until 1871, when the boilers of another *Westfield* burst as she was loading at the Battery with 400 passengers aboard, of whom 66 were killed. Things were then quiet until 1905, when two ferries crashed head-on with a loss of five lives, and again until 1918, when the *Bronx*, making a sharp turn, keeled over so badly that five feet of water coursed through the starboard cabin and three passengers were swept to their deaths. No cause for the freak accident could be discovered in repeated attempts to duplicate it. This is the total record of accidents involving fatalities for over a century of round-the-clock seven-day-a-week operation, a record that is truly in-credible when it is considered that fog sometimes reduces visibility to zero and that the vessels operate in one of the world's busiest harbors.

Six of the nine boats that comprise the Staten Island fleet are steam-powered, the three newest are diesels. All are screw-driven with propel-lers, rudders, and duplicate pilothouses at each end; the last side-wheelers were retired in 1905. The three newest boats are 273 foot-long three-deckers, with a capacity of slightly over 3,000 passengers plus three ranks of automobiles between the cabins on the lower deck. They make the 5 $\frac{1}{10}$-mile trip in from 18 to 22 minutes, depending on the tide, at a speed in still water of 18 miles an hour.

Most of the ferry riders are residents of Staten Island who commute to work in downtown Manhattan. There has been talk of connecting the two boroughs with a bridge or a tunnel since late in the nineteenth century, but it is still talk and such a replacement for the ferries may never become a reality. The island is now connected with Brooklyn by the new Verazzano Bridge for vehicular traffic, but this does not affect the ferry riders who work in Manhattan. Between the morning and evening rush hours the boats are one of New York's best tourist attractions.

It is safe to say that nowhere else in America can one see so many sights of varied interest as from the deck of a Staten Island Ferry. The tourist who stands at the bow and looks over his shoulder while the boat is in the Manhattan slip is dwarfed by the skyscrapers of the city's financial district that have made the New York skyline world-famous, and on the trip back he will get fine distant and near views of this skyline. If the traveler glances to his left before the boat leaves he will see, about 1,000 feet away, the famed Brooklyn Bridge. As the boat pulls out, the Verazzano Bridge over the Narrows comes into view—the longest suspension bridge in the world. Two minutes later, to the right in the distance, he beholds the world's longest arched span, Goethals' Bridge across Kill Van Kull, connecting Staten Island and New Jersey.

There are three famed islands to view. Directly ahead of the ferry slip is Governor's Island, so named because it was the official preserve of New Amsterdam's Dutch governors before the English took over. It later became the city's principal defensive barrier against a seaborne invasion. Circular Fort Wood, which was Vanderbilt's first stop when he was carrying supplies to the harbor defenses during the War of 1812, still stands unchanged on the point of Governor's Island; the ferry passes directly under the embrasures from which its guns used to frown.

A few thousand feet to the right, near the New Jersey shore, is Ellis Island with the red-brick, green-turreted French Renaissance buildings through which passed tens of millions of immigrants in the early years of the twentieth century. The imposing buildings are still there, although the island is no longer used as a reception center for immigrants since restrictive laws have reduced the flow to a trickle. For the last few years the Federal Government has been wondering what to do with it.

By the time the tourist has finished inspecting Ellis Island he finds himself abreast of a dot of land that was called Bedloe's Island until, with the modern passion for change, it became Liberty Island. This is the home of the tall, green lady whose proper name is "Liberty Enlightening the World," although that world knows her, perhaps better than any other landmark, as the Statue of Liberty. The Staten Island Ferry sweeps by about 500 feet in front of her.

Ahead and to the left is the Narrows, connecting the upper and lower bays as the main gateway to America. If the tourist plans his trip at the right time, between 7 and 9 A.M., he will probably pass within a few feet of one of the world's crack ocean liners inbound from her Atlantic voyage. The ferries plow the same channel as the passenger lines and provide the best spot for photographing one's family with a famed ocean queen in the background. Fifteen minutes after he arrives in Staten Island the tourist may take another boat back—for another nickel. The whole voyage takes about fifty-five minutes, and it is safe to say that nowhere else in the world can a traveler see so much of varied interest in less than an hour.

The running roads still flow to the coasts and through the heartland of America, and with their man-made improvements they are far better roads than of yore. For some purposes they are the cheapest roads and will always carry the lion's share of that commerce for which speed is

There are few worth-while things that can still be bought for a nickel, but a ride on New York's Staten Island Ferry is one of them. On their short cruises between Manhattan's Battery and Staten Island these river boats carry some 30,000,000 people a year—equivalent to a sixth of the U.S. population.

not of the essence. But in this age of speed worship they are shunned by those to whom a saved hour seems to be more precious than relaxed living. There are a few left who might prefer to go from New York to Boston, Pittsburgh to St. Louis, Baltimore to Norfolk or San Francisco to Sacramento aboard a river boat rather than more precipitantly on an expressway or through the sky, or who would rather travel leisurely between the ever-changing banks of the rivers to almost any point than be whisked to a destination unmindful of the passing scene. But those who look back with longing to the more interesting, if slower, river travel are so few that their whims cannot be gratified with profit.

The river boats lasted a century, give or take a few years. It was a great century, but it is a past century. The bells, the haunting whistles, the glamour and excitement of the river boats are preserved only in a few attempts to re-create the past in excursions and cruises, and in the memories of those who are getting old. In another generation, or perhaps two, there will be no one left with a personal memory of the river boats.

Suggestions
for Further Reading

BALDWIN, LELAND D. *Keelboat Age on Western Waters.* Pittsburgh: University of Pittsburgh Press, 1941.

BLAIR, WALTER, AND MEINE, FRANKLIN J., eds. *Half Horse, Half Alligator: The Growth of the Mike Fink Legend.* University of Chicago Press, 1956.

BOYD, THOMAS. *Poor John Fitch, Inventor of the Steamboat.* New York: G. P. Putnam's Sons, 1935.

FLEXNER, JAMES THOMAS. *Steamboats Come True; American Inventors in Action.* New York: The Viking Press, 1944.

GRAHAM, PHILIP. *Showboats; the History of an American Institution.* Austin: University of Texas Press, 1951.

HAVIGHURST, WALTER. *Voices on the River: The Story of the Mississippi Waterways.* New York: The Macmillan Company, 1964.

MINNIGERODE, MEADE. *Certain Rich Men.* New York: G. P. Putnam's Sons, 1927.

PRATT, FLETCHER. *Civil War on Western Waters.* New York: Henry Holt and Co., Inc., 1956.

RIVERS OF AMERICA SERIES: *Allegheny; Brandywine; Chagres; Charles; Chicago; Colorado; Columbia; Everglades; Connecticut; Genesee; Housatonic; Hudson; Humboldt; Illinois; Kaw; Lower Mississippi; Merrimack; Minnesota; Monongahela; Ohio; Potomac; Sacramento; St. Croix; St. Johns; St. Lawrence; Salt Rivers of the Massachusetts Shore; Sangamon; Savannah; Shenandoah; Susquehanna; Tennessee: The Old River; Tennessee: The New River; Upper Mississippi; Wabash; Winooski; Wisconsin;* and *Yazoo.* New York: Holt, Rinehart and Winston, Inc.

SUTCLIFFE, ALICE. *Robert Fulton and the "Clermont."* New York: The Century Co., 1909.

TWAIN, MARK. *Life on the Mississippi.*

Index